BEYOND OBEDIENCE AND ABANDONMENT

Beyond Obedience and Abandonment

Toward a Theory of Dissent in Catholic Education

GRAHAM P. McDONOUGH

McGill-Queen's University Press

Montreal & Kingston • London • Ithaca

© McGill-Queen's University Press 2012

ISBN 978-0-7735-4053-8 (cloth)
ISBN 978-0-7735-4054-5 (paper)

Legal deposit third quarter 2012
Bibliothèque nationale du Québec

Printed in Canada on acid-free paper that is 100% ancient forest free
(100% post-consumer recycled), processed chlorine free

This book has been published with the help of a grant from the University
of Victoria.

McGill-Queen's University Press acknowledges the support of the Canada
Council for the Arts for our publishing program. We also acknowledge the
financial support of the Government of Canada through the Canada Book
Fund for our publishing activities.

Library and Archives Canada Cataloguing in Publication

McDonough, Graham Patrick, 1975–
Beyond obedience and abandonment: toward a theory of dissent
in Catholic education / Graham P. McDonough.

Includes bibliographical references and index.
ISBN 978-0-7735-4053-8 (bound). – ISBN 978-0-7735-4054-5 (pbk.)

1. Catholic Church–Education–Canada. 2. Catholic schools –
Ontario–History. 3. Intellectual freedom–Religious aspects –
Christianity. 4. Catholics – Canada – Intellectual life. 5. Academic
freedom–Canada. I. Title.

LC504.M33 2012   371.071'271   C2012-904387-7

This book was typeset by Interscript in 10.5/13 Sabon.

Contents

Acknowledgments   vii

Introduction   3

1   Problems of Writing on Catholic Education   19

2   Education, Authority, Dissent, and Conscience   37

3   The Context, Challenge, and Changing Face of Canadian Catholic Education   83

4   Foundational Aims and Concerns in the Theory of Catholic Education-Schooling   124

5   A Theory of Dissent   145

6   The Limitations of Current Practice   173

7   Pedagogy of Dissent   223

Notes   259

Works Cited   281

Index   295

Acknowledgments

My research for this book was made possible by the financial support of the Ontario Ministry of Education, the University of Toronto, the Gift of Time Foundation, and the Association for Moral Education. The University of Victoria's Provost and Dean of Education assisted greatly in funding its publication.

The ideas in this book are my own, but many people contributed care and support as I worked to express them. This book developed out of my doctoral dissertation in the Philosophy of Education program at the University of Toronto. It was there that I received immeasurable care and support from my supervisor, Dwight Boyd, and committee members John Portelli and Mark McGowan (St Michael's College, University of Toronto). I also thank Brent Kilbourn, Noel McFerran, Margaret O'Gara, Gordon Rixon, sj (Regis College), and George Smith, csb, for their consultations at various stages of this work. During my doctoral study I was also fortunate to have colleagues who were both first-class scholars and friends. My thanks go to Trevor Norris, Ann Yeong, Jim Lang, Laura Page, and Kristin Main for their questions, insights, and support along the way. Thanks also to Kyla Madden at McGill-Queen's University Press for her patience and assistance as I worked through transforming a dissertation into a book manuscript. Likewise, the reviewers of this manuscript were very helpful and provided much inspiration along this journey.

Some of the material in this volume has been previously published. Chapter 5 was previously published as: McDonough, G.P. 2010. "Why Dissent is a Vital Concept in Moral Education." *Journal of Moral Education* 39 (4): 421–36. It is published here with the permission of Taylor and Francis. A portion of chapter 6 was previously published as: McDonough, G.P. 2010. "The Problem of Catholic School Teachers Deferring to the Home on Controversial Religious Issues." *Catholic Education: A Journal of Inquiry and Practice* 13 (3): 287–305. It is published here with the permission of that journal.

I am grateful to my parents, Ken and Edie McDonough, for their ongoing support, and to my late mother, Angela McDonough, who with Dad did not discourage me from facing questions of incongruity between authority and justice. My in-laws have also provided much care and support.

Finally, I am most grateful to my wife. She stood with me through proposing, writing, and defending the dissertation; and then again through the heavy work of transforming it into this book. I am grateful for her academic and professional insights as I shaped my ideas, and no less for her hope for me, which has remained when I needed it most.

BEYOND OBEDIENCE AND ABANDONMENT

Introduction

It is easy to slip into binary views about Catholicism. For example, if a person presents themselves as Catholic, others sometimes assume that they align strictly with the pope or an encyclopaedia definition. If that alignment is off, then they are assumed to be either non- or imperfectly Catholic. Those assumptions are not helpful to the degree that they distort the intellectual, devotional, and cultural breadth within Catholicism; but at the same time, they also raise important questions about how one might describe relationships within a tradition that are not exclusively defined by complete adherence to or rejection of its prevailing views. Not all Catholics agree perfectly with the pope, sometimes for very good reason, but still consider themselves to be faithful. It is not only adults who disagree, either, since many adolescents also present reasonable disagreements with certain teachings. As adolescent disagreement often takes place within Catholic schools, questions emerge as to what educational theory is available to describe an intellectual engagement with those who call themselves Catholic and wish to maintain an attachment to the Church, but disagree with certain Catholic teachings. How can Catholic students who disagree with these teachings be taught to express their dissent in a pedagogically and religiously meaningful way?

The following three cases are examples of problems that students have with controversial Catholic teachings. Each case reveals the tensions within the prevailing view and practice, and is important because it connects curricular issues to the institutional relationships within the Catholic school. Each case also challenges one to think past strict or superficial binary assumptions about Catholic orthodoxy and the aims of Catholic Education. The first case shows some of the prevailing view's limitations when responding to the presence of non-heterosexual[1] students:

> CASE ONE   A Catholic high school principal forbids a non-heterosexual male student from bringing his boyfriend as a date to the graduation banquet because, although the Catholic Church loves homosexual[2] people, it abhors homosexual acts and cannot condone a dating situation that may potentially lead to immoral sexual acts. The implied message is that the student can "be gay, but not act gay."[3]

The second case exemplifies a major point of difficulty with respect to gender and sex role differences. Here, the teacher is put into a position where he or she has to acknowledge and respect competing realities within the school, and so provide a student with a respectful response within the context of remaining loyal to the Church:

> CASE TWO   A female student in a Catholic school wonders why it promotes sex/gender equity in the secular world – her principal is female, for instance – but does not transpose that stance into a critique of the fact that the Catholic priesthood does not admit women.[4]

These two cases show that there are concerns about justice for non-heterosexual persons and women within the Church. These concerns may be rooted in a desire that the Church ought to adapt to the equity norms that modern secular institutions have. At the same time, to diminish the reasons for such intra-ecclesial tension to merely a sacred-secular tension is to overlook the diversity within Catholicism. The complainants in the above cases might also present reasons for their views that originate within their reading of Catholic history or theology. Since the above two cases are characteristic of issues which have gained greater prominence since the Second Vatican Council (1962–65), and views which support greater ecclesial rights for non-heterosexuals and women are rooted in a particular interpretation of that Council's meaning, they are here called the "post-conciliar" perspective.

By contrast, the "pre-conciliar" perspective believes that the most authentic Catholicism existed before Vatican II, and concludes that the Council is responsible for Catholicism's recent decline. When applied to education, pre-conciliar views suggest that many Catholic institutions have lost their rigour and so require a return to the discipline of strict obedience to the pope, doctrinal norms, and traditional observances. Otherwise, Catholic identity and the salvation of souls are jeopardized.[5] The third case is based upon the tensions this segment of Catholic society experiences with the prevailing view in the school:

CASE THREE   At home a student's parents emphasize the example of the Blessed Virgin Mary's obedience to God, uphold motherhood as the ultimate vocation for women, and maintain that people must be "good Catholics" to avoid damnation. At school the message is that Mary's virginity is a narrative symbol of the miracle of Jesus' birth, parenthood is but one of many choices available to people, and Jesus is your friend, not your judge. However, the student's questions about the difference between messages receive nothing more than a polite hearing before the teacher moves on with the rest of the lesson.

The establishment of pre- and post-conciliar categories of thought comes with recognizing that Catholic thought and practice is complex and diverse; nonetheless, considering them as general rubrics under which a continuum of Catholic thought passes is a helpful means of describing Catholicism's intellectual range.

All three cases represent one family of problems that Catholic educators might encounter in their experiences with learners. Currently, the typical responses to cases like these amplify dissidents' moral frustration with the Church and/or School, because educators and institutions lack a theoretically rigorous approach to the issues that govern the clash of internal ideologies. This problem reflects the fact that there is a general lack of theoretical vocabulary with which to (1) begin a less frustrating and more intellectually rewarding examination of controversial issues within Catholicism, and (2) consider how those issues sit within the larger pan-Catholic problem of understanding, expressing, and receiving dissent. It also reveals that (3) the current theoretical grounding for Catholic Education is inadequate to the task of accommodating dissent and reforming its treatment of dissenters, ostensibly for fear of undermining the Church's or School's Catholic identity and organizational stability. The lack of a theoretical vocabulary and framework with which to understand salient internal differences thus finally points to the fact that there is a paucity of research in support of Catholic Education.

The expansion of Catholic Educational theory of course requires relevant topics and questions. The first purpose of this book is to respond to the pedagogical problems of student dissent on controversial Catholic teachings. The frustration students experience in the above cases is the result of being presented with an apparent false choice between complete adherence to the prevailing Catholicism, complete abandonment of it, or, as in Case Three, existence uneasily at odds with prevailing norms. While it is oftentimes very helpful to make distinctions and observe binary tensions for descriptive purposes, this volume is ultimately concerned with overcoming restrictive dichotomies by exploring and mapping the theoretical territory between polarized views. The second governing purpose of this book is therefore to direct that development into a pedagogical theory which would inform and reform current practice, including: the development of curricular objectives, content, teaching methods, and assessment; administrative decisions at all levels; and the ways in which students and parents respond to the teaching and learning experiences that the school presents.

How widespread is dissent throughout Catholicism? Sociological data shows that, since the late 1960s, significant numbers of Canadian and American Catholics disagree with several Church teachings. In Canada, Reginald Bibby provides data for adolescents in Catholic schools specifically and then again for adolescent Catholics generally, which recognizes that not all Catholics attend Catholic schools, nor do Catholic schools exclusively serve Catholics. For students in Catholic schools he finds that the "accept and approve" ratings for premarital sex, homosexual relations, and same-sex marriage are 69%, 45%, and 45% respectively. This set mirrors nearly perfectly the national data, including students of all (or no) religions in all schools, which are 72%, 44%, and 47%.[6] None of these approvals accord with Catholic teachings; the Church disapproves of homosexual acts and considers homosexual desire disordered, but does not disapprove of persons with homosexual desires.

Bibby observes that these figures are lower for Canadian Catholic adolescents outside Quebec who attend Mass monthly or more often. A majority generally approves of premarital sex if the two partners love each other (59%), while a significant minority of respondents approve of homosexual relations (33%) and same-sex marriage (36%). Quebec's Catholic adolescents show nearly the same profile at 61%, 32%, and 31% respectively. The approval figures are almost all higher for those who attend Mass less than monthly (83%, 46%, and 48% outside Quebec, and 92%, 28%, and 51% within).[7] The rates of participation also fall after adolescence. Data on Mass attendance for the year 2000 on eighteen- to thirty-four-year-olds shows a drop from 21% in adolescence to 12% nationally: from 31% to 18% outside Quebec, and from 7% to 5% within.[8] Overall, Bibby finds that weekly attendance for Catholics outside Quebec is 32%, and 20% inside. The majority attend yearly: 41% of non-Quebecers and 66% within Quebec.[9] Overall these figures suggest a trough-shaped pattern of decline that begins during adolescence and reaches its nadir in early to mid-adulthood. A resurgence of attendance in later adulthood[10] and the attendance of families with pre-adolescent children possibly account for the difference between the adolescent and early adulthood figures and the overall attendance rate.

American sociologist Andrew Greeley reports a similar pattern. He refers to 1998 data from the International Social Survey Program, which surveyed the attitudes of Catholics in twenty-two countries on premarital sex, homosexual sex, and abortion. The data was mainly drawn from Europe but includes also Australia, Brazil, Canada, Chile, the Philippines, and the United States. A short extraction shows similar patterns across these countries, with the Philippines being a notable outlier on all three questions, and Brazil and Chile on the last two (see Table 1). While the results vary by country, it is immediately apparent that in many places, those who disagree with the Church on these questions are either the majority or part of significant dissenting minorities. Dissent is not limited to these areas either. Greeley's own research from 1998 finds, generally speaking, that there is widespread support for a pope who would allow priests to marry (ostensibly for the Latin rite), ordain women to the priesthood, and be more open to change (see Table 2).

American data from the past decade shows continued disagreements with Catholic teachings. The Pew Forum's 2008 "Religious Landscape Survey" finds that only 45% of American Catholics believed that "abortion should be illegal in all or most cases," and 30% that "homosexuality is a way of life [that] should be discouraged by society."[11] Pew data from 2010 show that 46% of American Catholics were in favour of same-sex marriage, and 42% were opposed.[12] Similarly, the Public Religion Research Institute finds that

Table 1
Sexual attitudes of Catholics (adapted from ISSP, 1998)[1] showing percentages
answering in the affirmative

	Premarital sex always wrong	Homosexual sex always wrong	Abortion always wrong, even for the poor
Australia	23	54	38
Brazil	42	83	88
Canada	9	36	40
Chile	30	88	76
Ireland	21	62	41
Italy	19	59	46
Philippines	63	84	71
Poland	19	76	46
United States	20	55	54

[1] Printed in Greeley 2004, 92.

Table 2
Attitudes toward role of next pope[1] showing percentages answering
in the affirmative

	Allow married priests	Ordain women to priesthood	Be more open to change
Germany	83	71	76
Spain	79	71	74
Ireland	82	67	79
United States	69	65	65
Italy	67	58	51
Poland	50	24	56
Philippines	21	18	48

[1] Adapted and condensed from Greeley 2004, 96. This survey was taken during John
Paul II's reign, before the ascent of Benedict XVI in 2005.

in 2011 "[n]early three-quarters of Catholics favor either allowing
gay and lesbian people to marry (43%) or allowing them to form civil
unions (31%). Only 22% of Catholics say there should be no legal
recognition of a gay couple's relationship."[13] Concurrently, over half
of respondents stated that they did not consider sexual relations
between two adults of the same sex to be sinful.[14] On the question

of contraception, Jones and Dreweke find that 98% of American Catholic women who have had sex use(d) contraceptive methods other than natural family planning.[15]

Dissent in the Catholic Church is not limited to these questions, however. In addition to calls that teachings on sexuality and ordination change, there are also Catholics requesting a return to pre-conciliar traditions. Some groups, like Catholics United for the Faith, recognize the Second Vatican Council and the current Church hierarchy, but call for a return to more traditional practices. These groups' views on subjects such as salvation inform their disapproval of the orthodox religious education programs in Catholic schools.[16] Other pre-conciliar groups, such as the Society for St Pius X (SSPX), maintain strained relations with the pope and the Church hierarchy. The SSPX website states: "Founded as a refuge from the torrent of errors propagated by liberals at the Second Vatican Council, the Society is one of the few havens left for those seeking the Catholic Faith in all its integrity."[17] Its history with the Vatican has included the 1988 excommunication and 2009 rehabilitation of its bishops. There are also *sedevacantist* (the pope's "chair is vacant") groups, such as the Society of St Pius V (SSPV), who do not recognize the legitimacy of any pope after Pius XII (r. 1939–58),[18] nor the 1983 *Code of Canon Law*,[19] and evaluate some of the sacraments in the post-conciliar era as "doubtful and invalid.[20] Some groups even go further than sedevacantism and recognize their own candidate as pope. (Michael Cuneo's book *The Smoke of Satan* provides a well-detailed synopsis of the "conservative and traditionalist" phenomenon in the Church.)

Dissent of many kinds is widespread.[21] Since this short survey reveals (and upcoming chapters demonstrate) that dissent is a feature of adult Catholicism, it cannot be attributed to being merely a phase of adolescence. So if dissent on certain teachings is such a prominent feature of Catholic life, what are the consequences of not treating it explicitly and in depth in Catholic Education-Schooling?

The Catholic Church is currently suffering from a credibility problem which causes disenchantment, disengagement, and even the complete withdrawal of some of its members. If its poor response to the sexual abuse scandals of recent decades has been the primary contributor to this problem, disagreements with its teachings on reproductive ethics, sexuality, and ordination have only made matters worse for many people. At the same time, the Church is also troubled by the polarization of its members who adhere to pre-conciliar ideologies. How do Catholics respond to a Church that they love but cannot change? And how do they respond to those who disagree with them? If dissidents of all sorts perceive that the Church cannot receive disagreement, and that the institutions of Catholic Education are unable to assist them academically in working out their disagreements, then further frustration, polarization, or abandonment of the Church is inevitable.

If the decline in participation that Bibby observes from adolescence to early adulthood can be attributed to this credibility crisis and perceived lack of receptivity, then it signals the need for a more rigorous means *from within Catholicism* by which lay persons can respond to controversial and divisive religious issues. I hypothesize that when the current system of receiving dissent, which either de-emphasizes, marginalizes, or restricts its expression away from a public audience, does not satisfy their needs, then many people, not knowing where to go next, simply resign themselves to abandoning Catholicism before they have an opportunity to work out their disagreements in greater depth. Catholic Education-Schooling cannot singlehandedly improve the Church's credibility, but it can, given the theory I propose here, provide currently disaffected, alienated, and disenchanted Catholics with a means of staying in their Church. If they do leave it, and some still may, they should at least have done so having been given the greatest intellectual resources with which to make a choice for staying. The result should be a more adult faith.

INVESTIGATING A MULTI-DIMENSIONAL QUESTION

The method of moving toward a prescriptive educational treatment of intellectual diversity within Catholicism is complex. Catholic Education and Catholic Schools are worldwide phenomena that in each incarnation achieve some balance between the norms of the whole Church and their particular local contexts. Because of this dynamic tension, there emerges the problem in method of what to focus upon. To what degree are the dictates of the global Church valid descriptors of and applicable to the teaching-learning experiences in any one school, and, conversely, to what degree are local phenomena representative of and generalizable to the global norms? The risks are therefore alienating context by speaking too globally, or losing global validity and theoretical transferability by speaking exclusively within a particular context. Nonetheless, in a volume that proposes a general theory for intellectual religious disagreement, it is difficult to speak of relevant tensions in Catholic Education without reference to how particular schools interpret their existence within a larger theoretical framework. Catholic schools are not merely documentary phenomena; they exist as concrete institutions. The dilemmas in Cases One, Two, and Three above could conceivably appear in any Catholic school. The problem is to choose a set of schools that provides a strongly plausible instance in which they might appear.

This book's investigative method balances the local-global tension by offering a picture of publicly funded Canadian Catholic schools in the province of Ontario[22] next to the general theological, pedagogical, and philosophical norms for Catholic Education. The selection of Ontario's Catholic schools as they understand themselves to be an authentic representation of the global Church's norms accomplishes two tasks. First, it provides the context of a regional history where Catholics have been shown to be loyal dissenters from mainstream society. An interpretation of their history shows that dissent is a normal and authentically Catholic behaviour, thus establishing it as an ironic instance where civil society offers a Catholic minority external protection, but the minorities within Catholicism are restricted by the faith's own prevailing hegemony. Second, while all Catholic schools offer the general public a service by educating its citizens,[23] Ontario's publicly funded Catholic schools present this service in high relief because government money, over and above the state's passive sanction, enables their existence. The problems that teachers in these public schools face regarding controversial issues are similar in theory to those in private schools, because private schools also negotiate with varying student intentions and parental interests; but the fact of the state's direct investment in Ontario's schools makes them a particularly relevant context for proposing reforms. Ontario offers a special picture of publicly funded Catholic Schooling, but the implications of its schools' examination has greater than regional import because they follow the same ecclesial, philosophical, and pedagogical norms as other Catholic institutions. If they did not look to the global Church in this way, they would arguably not be normatively Catholic.

While there are possibly some limitations to using the experiences of one province to inform a more general prescriptive proposal, it remains true that the issues in educational theory which Ontario teachers experience are concurrent with, and inherently generalizable to, the worldwide enterprise of Catholic Education-Schooling. In this way, context is understood to be a valid reflection of the worldwide Church, and not an aberration. The fact that these issues exist in one place provides enough illustration of a theoretical problem to inform its discussion elsewhere. In spite of their particularity, these schools still integrate the interests of Church, state, student, and the norms of the teaching profession; it is that property and its problems which make these schools interesting globally.

It would be prejudicial to assume that dissent occurs in Ontario's Catholic schools simply because they are publicly funded. That view presumes that in places where there is no public funding, all students and parents choose Catholic schools for the same reason, and there is no difference of opinion among them. Dissent can occur in any Catholic school at any degree of intensity, and this proposal is applicable to any case, large or small. As the issue of dissent is interesting within, but most certainly not dependent upon, a context of publicly funded schools, there is therefore no necessary limitation of the final prescriptions to publicly funded Canadian Catholic Education.

Having raised these foundational problems with Catholic Education as a "beginning" and then promising to make a proposal toward resolving them as an "end," the next logical task is to outline the joining path. In a volume such as this, there are some considerations about method that must be expressed at the outset because they concern an attempt to make as comprehensive an argument as possible and to avoid over-generalizing from a single discipline's perspective. One could look at any of the above cases through only one of the historical, theological, philosophical, or pedagogical lenses, and each could provide many ways of creating a valid picture of the problem. However, to make generalizations about Catholic Education from a single discipline would be to arrogate prescriptive power to it at the expense of other perspectives. If one were to develop a philosophical concept of dissent or a secular model of critical thinking and then immediately prescribe its application to Catholic Education without providing any other context, its contribution would be diminished because it would have gaps in the historical, theological, and pedagogical dimensions which concurrently ground teaching-learning relationships in Catholicism and Catholic schools. Its high level of abstraction would also be inappropriate to the social science of pedagogy and the professional contingencies inherent in this relationship, and it would therefore have limited practical validity and applicability for practitioners, administrators, and parents. In its defence, however, abstract theory is absolutely essential for providing an analytical interpretation of practice; additionally, consulting teachers for their views of practice helpfully enriches theory. The best approach to proposing a reform of Catholic Education is therefore an interdisciplinary study.

THE CASE FOR A PEDAGOGY OF DISSENT

Each of the first six chapters in this volume contributes a unique disciplinary piece to the proposal in chapter 7 for a pedagogy of dissent. Chapters on the history of Canadian Catholic schools as a dissenting political entity, the theological understanding of dissent and authority within Catholicism, curricular issues in Catholic religious education, and the creation of dissent as a philosophical concept carry its foundational weight. As these chapters take turns explicating a unique disciplinary perspective on Catholic Education, they also oscillate in scope. Global topics such as how the worldwide Church understands authority, dissent, and education contrast with the localized incarnations of relevant dissent, such as the historical precedent in Canadian Catholic schools. A philosophical analysis of the epistemic, moral, and political value of dissent in the abstract stands next to an examination of how teachers typically respond to students' dissent. This oscillation between global and local, theory and practice, is a deliberately constructed means of acknowledging the complexities in Catholicism and Catholic Education. These chapters ultimately all prepare for and inform the final chapter.

Chapter 1 defines the foundational terms for this volume and articulates some of the fundamental problems one encounters when discussing Catholic Education-Schooling. To this end it proposes that distinguishing between Catholic Education and Catholic Schooling is a helpful way of interpreting the various aims and intentions which surface in those (often combined) enterprises. It also names some of the theoretical tensions which are features of Catholic Education-Schooling, anticipates potential criticisms, and concludes with a message of hope.

Chapter 2 brings the theoretical discussion to the highest ecclesial and theological level of abstraction by introducing the normative Catholic Church understandings and relevant theological debate on the concepts of education, Magisterium, conscience, and dissent as they are relevant within the context of this discussion. These concepts might be viewed as mutually consistent within some comprehensive views of the Church, but this chapter demonstrates that they can also be interpreted as problematic topics that are in mutual tension. The purpose of exposing these tensions is not to undermine the Church, but rather to point to relevant places where further work is required in order to improve Catholic Educational theory and from which appropriately creative innovations might descend. These concepts are all theoretical requisites for the proposed pedagogy of dissent's grounding within a framework of Catholic thought.

What takes place in particular educational relationships necessarily reflects global theoretical concerns, and so chapter 3 speaks about issues within the particulars of Canadian Catholic Education. An historical account of Ontario's regional context shows how the growth of a separate, publicly funded system of religious education since the early nineteenth century represents a strong example of how many Canadian Catholics dissent from the mainstream of secular public schooling, understand themselves as a dissenting minority, and still simultaneously are good citizens of secular society.[24] This observation stands in ironic contrast to the apparent difficulties with recognizing diversity of thought and a fluid conception of loyalty within Catholicism. Catholic Education is certainly a much larger and older phenomenon than a brief account of it in Ontario can reveal, and certainly other regions and minorities have important histories as well, but this particular story has been chosen because it exemplifies a theoretical context for dissent in practice to which the general proposal can refer. The sheer size of separate Catholic Education in Ontario dictates its importance relative to other jurisdictions, and it remains that one example is sufficient in theory with which to demonstrate how dissent is not a concept alien to Catholicism or Catholic Education. The chapter then proceeds into a discussion of the ways in which Catholic Schools understand their role and the prominent issues which dominate their politics in this current day.

Chapter 4 moves away from the foundational understandings of institutional Catholic Education, and its incarnation in context, and explores in greater depth the theoretical issues of concern to the classroom pedagogy of religious education in Catholic schools. It relates the general hopes which institutions have for students and discusses them in the classroom context, where religion teachers have to negotiate between their competing responsibilities of maintaining the norms of an authoritarian institution while also attending to the students' individual pedagogical needs. The chapter then critiques any affective or formative aims that these hopes might convey. In response to student frustration, chapter 4 argues for a greater academic breadth and honesty in response to the concerns which students bring to educative relationships.

An understanding of the historical, political-ecclesial, and pedagogical issues in Catholic Education is necessary, but nonetheless insufficient for grounding a pedagogical theory. For a pedagogy of dissent to have theoretical validity, it also requires a philosophically sound concept of dissent that bears scrutiny for moral-political education generally. Chapter 5 returns to a higher level of abstraction and presents a conceptual analysis of dissent. It proposes that good dissent is not subversive; in fact, good dissent reflects a strong loyalty to the group or institution, and in its ideal form aims for and promotes the group's improvement. The chapter makes this case according to a comprehensive set of evaluative criteria. Dissent stands as this book's central philosophical hinge.

One might reason legitimately that a book on dissent would exhibit its conceptual grounding much earlier than the fifth of seven chapters. However, by its nature this grounding cannot be introduced suddenly. Prior understanding of the pedagogical and ecclesial context in which Catholic schools sit is required in order that one can imagine where and how this concept is helpful; otherwise, too early a presentation would clumsily reduce away the complexity of Catholic Education. Moreover, although my conceptual analysis of dissent relies on Catholic thinkers such as Pope John Paul II and Margaret O'Gara, the concept itself remains a piece of secular thought that I transpose into Catholic application; thus, the first four chapters are required to appropriately foreshadow this transposition. Care for the context of Catholic Education requires this sort of beginning.

Chapter 6 makes a significant turn away from engagement with texts and toward engagement with people. It elucidates typical methods religion teachers use in response to students' dissent. While these methods reflect teachers' general dispositions to do everything within their professional power to accommodate intellectual differences and develop student thinking, they are ultimately limited by a combination of the school's social-professional ethos and the inherent restrictions of the methods themselves. While these techniques are helpful toward achieving the current prevailing aims, they are shown to be limited insofar as they do not respond fully to legitimate dissent.

The data which illustrates these techniques is taken from interviews with fourteen religion teachers, from five of Ontario's Catholic Separate School Divisions, on the question of how they respond to student dissent with Catholic teachings. All participating teachers were practicing lay Catholics who taught religion in either an urban or a suburban secondary school (grades 9 to 12), and represented a range of career stages from beginning (<10 years experience) to middle (10–20) and later (>20). Participants were interviewed individually in sixty- to ninety-minute sessions which were recorded, transcribed, and analyzed for themes. These participants were professionally trained experts in Catholic religious education and pedagogy for adolescent youth. Their responses thus provide their own reflective integration of theory and practice, and so they reflect a wide range, although not necessarily the complete spectrum, of practitioners' observations on their own work. They reveal the challenges that teachers in Catholic schools face today, and so have the paramount function of placing the contingencies of professional context next to all the abstract theoretical observations, claims, and conclusions in prior chapters. The use of practitioners' language to contribute to pedagogical theory in this case provides a means of shrinking any gap between theory and practice in Catholic Education.

It is important to note that all participating teachers had religion as a primary subject area, and several in fact lamented that some of their colleagues who primarily taught other subjects had been pressed into teaching religion simply because they were practicing Catholics, but had little other training. Seven participants hold graduate degrees in religious education, theology, or divinity; two were subject area department heads in religion; two were formerly lay chaplains in the school before switching to teaching religion as a credit subject; two had worked at their board offices on religious education staff development; and one was concurrently a catechist at a local parish. As it is also customary for school divisions to submit to the local bishop a list of teachers who will be teaching religious education courses,[25] it is safe to say that beyond their secular professional qualifications, these persons represent the kind of teacher the Magisterial Church approves to undertake this assignment. The practices the teachers describe are useful illustrations of reasonably held beliefs about good professional practice.

At the same time, however, the small sample size does not permit any kind of quantitative generalization: it is impossible to say that a certain percentage of teachers most commonly appeal to conscience, while another fraction would instead encourage dissident students to ask their parents for help. The generalizability of these teachers' statements is limited to their value for illustrating typical tensions in theory and practice; they show specific instances of the more relevant theoretical challenges that a pedagogy of dissent will face and of the overall theoretical and practical problems it intends to overcome. The significance of the interviews lies in their application of practitioners' language to theory. By presenting specific data that points to larger theoretical topics, these participants "provide evidence that supports (but does not definitively prove) a theory."[26]

Finally, chapter 7 brings together the work on abstract concepts and interview data to propose a pedagogy of dissent. This chapter provides the volume's ultimate contribution to the theory and practice of Catholic education by presenting a seven-part pedagogical theory that will justify later reform to curriculum, administrative practice, and the establishment of schools. These seven parts are its (1) grounding in a concept of dissent, (2) recognition of student interests as an integral beginning point, (3) placing of students in the imaginative place of the theologian, (4) adaptation of dissent to Catholic critical thinking, (5) resolve to critique ideology, (6) dissolving of dichotomies, and (7) insistence on maintaining a conceptual and practical breadth of interpretation for what counts as legitimate Catholic Educational Service. The argumentative basis for this chapter is based upon its unique constellation of these components, none of which is foreign to Catholicism. It will also address possible criticisms that dissent may be too advanced a topic or approach for adolescents. *Pedagogy of Dissent* is theory *for* the development and justification of the reform of the formal and informal curriculum in Catholic Education, but it is not a curriculum itself. The practical question of realizing this pedagogy in practice is the problem for another, future book.

So why this approach, and why not define the problem simply as "how critical thinking is taught in religion courses"? While this volume is at least contingently concerned with the curricular content and methods in religion classes, the proposed reform is much larger than the subject matter, experiences, and techniques in the formal curriculum because it concerns the heart of the institution's identity and purpose. In this way, dissent in Catholicism has much broader implications than its appearance in religion classes and its role as a lesson on critical thinking for citizenship; because whereas Canadian society is predicated upon some tolerance for questioning authority, the ordinary Church is not. So to propose a reform that cuts to the heart of an institution's identity and authority structure, one must use a method that can validly represent the various influences upon the institution, and that method needs to be as inclusive as possible. In this way the institutional organization is the curriculum. Catholic Education is comprised of multiple informants and stakeholders, and so the professionals who work within it have a responsibility to coordinate them. The theoretical validity of any prescriptive reforms will therefore depend upon a multi-dimensional integration of information, arguments, and conclusions that can satisfy each of Catholic Education's concerns.

Having finished this book, a reader will have the theoretical means with which to accomplish many tasks. He or she will have an expanded depth and breadth of theoretical vocabulary with which to identify cases of dissent. He or she will also know multiple angles by which to approach a resolution of a case of dissent. Finally, he or she will be able to justify his or her response along one or many disciplinary lines of thought. The possibilities for applying *Pedagogy of Dissent* to practice do not simply end at responses to incidental events or crises, either. The reader may be a professional teacher interested in designing experiences so that the learners in his or her charge will learn to think religiously about dissent. This work may contribute to that aim. Instructional leaders in that teacher's school may also require some background with which they may permit dissent to be engaged more directly than it is at present, and whereby they may support that teacher in the event of challenges from colleagues, the parish, or the greater community. Finally, the same use may be made by parents who, as the primary educators of their children, are often the last resort when lines of communication stall or fail at school. This work is written with a spirit of generosity to the whole Church and the good work that all Catholic educators and schools do. Many great things happen because the partners in Catholic Education and Catholic Schools agree on common aims. I hope that these partners will be able to accomplish more if they are able to disagree better.

I

Problems of Writing on Catholic Education

While preparing this book I frequently fielded questions from people interested in its topic and purpose. Before answering, I would often respond with a short question of my own, asking my interlocutor if he or she had ever been admonished to avoid speaking of politics or religion in polite company. The answer was always "yes," with a smile that uncovered the anticipation of a well-planned rejoinder. My reply was that not only do I blend politics and religion, but I do so within the field of education. This fact presents a third dimension of sensitivity, for if politics and religion are difficult to discuss reasonably in certain settings, no doubt adding the question of how we as a society ought to think about the way in which we teach and learn about politics, religion, and especially the politics of religion is similarly troublesome and even, if the admonishers are correct, "impolite."

That reply may be glib, but it accurately identifies the territory in which this book sits. Catholic Education-Schooling is the subject of much debate and controversy, but also much interest and hope. It can arouse passionate well- and ill-informed opinions that range from support to disparagement. All discussions of Catholic Education-Schooling also take place before the backdrop of the Catholic Church, itself an old organization that has influenced many people throughout the world, and upon which these schools rely for their nominal, curricular, communal, and sometimes even material existence. To speak to the question of what shape and direction it ought to take is a very important and complex task, and so before making any proposals an argumentative treatment is required of the major foundational issues in Catholicism that are raised by talk of dissent and education.

This chapter lays out a theoretical basis upon which arguments for a dissent-founded reform of Catholic Educational theory can be made. First, it distinguishes between the aims of Catholic Education and Catholic Schooling in order to demonstrate theoretical breadth in the kinds of service which are possible. An analysis of the terms reveals first that there are many kinds of both Catholic Education and Catholic Schooling. When the possibilities of both terms are combined, it becomes apparent that there are several distinct kinds of aims, expectations, and experiences that may be had within the same institution, depending on its orientation and the orientations of those it serves. So where it may be argued that dissent is incompatible with any stated or perceived aims of Catholic Education or Catholic Schools to form students as faithful Catholics, it can be countered that these aims, while worthy, represent only one side of a relationship and one particular kind of experience in the school. Dissent may arguably be incompatible with certain conceptions of Catholic Education, Catholic Schooling, and what it means to be Catholic; but not with all. The distinction demonstrates that the official aims many schools advertise may not reflect the expectations of all students, and that there might be several other kinds of services occurring concurrently in the same place. This expansion of the territory in which aims may be written thus opens the theoretical space in which a legitimately Catholic pedagogy based on the concept of dissent might be proposed alongside the more traditionally understood aims (or hopes) that ostensibly do not comprehend or cannot admit dissent.

Second, this chapter articulates a theoretical framework that describes the institutions of Catholic Education and Schooling in terms of a confluence of aims. It argues that the normative descriptions the Church or school gives about the nature and purposes of Catholic Education-Schooling are only a limited constitutive part of what these institutions are. Students and parents bring their own intentions to the relationship, and so each institution's character is shaped by this mixture of formal aims and informal expectations.

Third, this chapter undertakes a brief description of critical thinking in "pure" terms and then in comparison with the aims of Catholic Education-Schooling. This term is often contested, misunderstood, and misused in the academy and in professional practice, so for the sake of providing a theoretical handhold there is an explanation of what it does and does not mean in this volume.

Finally, there is a consideration of some potential criticisms that this volume might receive, and a conclusion which places it within a spirit of hope.

REGARDING THE TERM "CATHOLIC EDUCATION"

What does the term "Catholic Education" mean, how is it different from "Catholic Schooling," and why does the distinction matter? Confronting that problem begins with considering the definition of what counts as "education," and how it overlaps with "schooling." Here it is sufficient to say that *education* is the broad phenomenon of learning, experienced throughout one's whole life, and *schooling* is the experience of an institution that is dedicated toward promoting learning in those it serves. One might assert that all schooling is educative, but not all education is schooling: and of course one might offer qualified statements like "all schooling *should be* educative." At one extreme of "schooling," therefore, it is possible to describe an experience akin to the bare formal institutionalization of persons, which may or may not offer an experience congruent with the institution's own stated aims or seemingly ostensible purpose "to educate." The field of teaching and learning, whether religious or secular, contains many competing ideas about both these terms, even if only implicit.

To this point I have used the term "Catholic Education" in its most inclusive sense of learning across the entire life experience: including, but not limited to, the roles of the family and parish Church as participating institutions, and the more specialized formal and informal curriculum of an institutional Catholic school. This benefit of inclusiveness, however, is achieved at the risk of over-writing the differences between it and Catholic Schooling. Both terms imply many different things that sometimes may overlap, but just as easily may not. The breadth of both terms, and the wide variety of experiences and offerings implied in each, thus requires that definitive precision be obtained not through a narrowing of their scope but instead through an enumeration of their possibilities.

The observations of Gabriel Moran, a Catholic theorist of religious education, are very helpful in the efforts of definition. He observes that "'Catholic Education' is a very ambiguous phrase. It can be and is used to refer to: (1) the Catholic church's involvement in education, (2) the education of people who are Catholics, [or]

(3) the education in what it means to be Catholic."[1] One, some, or all of these conditions may obtain in a given context and it can still be called "Catholic Education." Catholic Schools may be admitted to this picture, but notice that none of Moran's possibilities *necessitate* schools or schooling.

So what might Catholic Schooling be in relation to Catholic Education? Following Moran's pattern of analysis, the theoretical construction of "Catholic Schooling" is at least as ambiguous. It could refer to (a) the operation of schools that are nominally Catholic, (b) the establishment of institutions that deliver some version of Catholic content and experiences across the whole formal and informal curriculum, or (c) the simple provision of schooling in the name of Catholic social service – possibly even without catechesis. The latter kind could be offered to persons in need, to persons who are non-Catholic or non-Christian but who choose to attend Catholic schools, or in the thin demographic sense of formally schooling a cohort of Catholic persons as Moran describes in (2) above. Again, one, some, or all of these conditions may apply for a given person or institution. When multiplied together, both terms could describe a mass of orientations, intentions, and phenomena coexisting within the same institution. One student may be present to receive (1c) and his or her neighbour to receive (3b).

For those whose commitment to Catholic Schooling is heavily invested in displaying the institution's "Catholic identity" through the formal and informal curriculum, via an emphasis on evangelization, catechesis, the formation of Catholic persons, and possibly even the monitoring of the beliefs and extracurricular behaviours of its staff and students, that latter part of the definition might seem quite impossible or "un-Catholic," even if interpreted as a spiritual work of mercy such as "to instruct the ignorant." Still, it is worth noticing that other Catholic agencies such as hospitals, homeless shelters, and soup kitchens do quite well to work *from* a religious orientation of providing service to all in society, but without an expectation that the objects of their care are or will become Catholic persons, and without that fact being a threat to the institution's Catholic identity.[2] That the provision of educative experiences in a Catholic school could be so thin in its formal religious curricular content but yet so thick in its Catholic orientation to a desired charitable outcome illustrates well one end of the range of possibility for what counts as Catholic Schooling. Presumably, another end of that spectrum could be a school which has a very thick religious content that is well-integrated across the entire curriculum and openly oriented toward evangelization, catechesis, and the formation of students: some variation of my second (b) sense of Catholic schooling, and strongly overlapping with Moran's sense (3) of Catholic Education. The exposition of this range illustrates very well the distinction Catholic educator Neil McCluskey makes "between Catholic formal education or *schooling* and Catholic education in the larger sense of formation."[3] So in spite of the school's formally explicit aims, students may very well attend with different expectations. If used as the end rather than the beginning of a discussion, the ambiguity of these terms can contribute to obscuring the interpretation of aims and events in the school. When analyzed as above, that same ambiguity is quite helpful for describing and interpreting the range of educative offerings as they vary from place to place, and, depending on who is being served, even within the same school or classroom. The distinction between these terms is also helpful for challenging any narrowly prescriptive ideas about Catholic schools; hence allowing that where one conception of Catholic Education would unfortunately find dissent incompatible with formation in the prevailing view, another may easily accommodate it as an almost "prophetic" kind of formation within the same intellectual and spiritual tradition. This discussion, of course, takes place without first investigating the normative theological and philosophical arguments about dissent's worth. Those disciplinary discussions will be taken up in chapters 2 and 5 respectively.

The breadth of possibility in these terms exposes the breadth of scope in this volume. The hyphenated term "Catholic Education-Schooling" is most precise when referring to an inclusive picture of a life-long and life-wide educative experience including, but not limited to, the institutions of Catholic schools. The argument in this volume applies across this entire spectrum. Integrating dissent within the context of the Catholic Education one receives at home, through one's interactions with the parish, or in any other place besides the school can be justified using this volume because the normative ecclesial and pedagogical theory it provides does not depend upon schooling for its applicability. At the same time, I focus mainly on Catholic schools to make the argument for a publicly available pedagogy because these institutions represent the largest public organization of educative offerings from a Catholic perspective. This volume articulates a pedagogy which is argued to be valid within the public forum that is any Catholic school, government-funded or not, because as a publicly articulated theory this proposal departs from the current iterations of dissent which remain confined to personal expressions of disagreement or marginalized within the private sphere of individual homes. The full, hyphenated term is a useful reminder of the argumentative scope in this volume. At the same time, to repeat it continuously would be a cumbersome ritual; hence, a shorter form is required.

To accomplish this, an enumeration of this volume's aims is necessary. The primary focus of this volume is on the whole public enterprise of Catholic Education. Even though much of that public aspect is situated in Catholic schools, and the design of this volume speaks to the institutional realities of Catholic schools as public places (both in terms of the State's involvement and as gathering places for Catholic persons), for this volume to be applicable to Catholic schools it must first be applicable to Catholic Education generally. Parents and families, especially, should find it speaks to the religious education of all in their charge, as should lay catechists, parish priests, bishops, and curial officials. Hence, to avoid repeating "Catholic Education-Schooling" any further, I will set the above distinction as a standing caution and henceforth carefully use the shorter term "Catholic Education." In moments where the heuristic value of distinguishing between Education and Schooling is of interpretive value for analyzing how professionals understand their role, I will refer specifically to Catholic Education, Catholic Schooling, or Catholic Education-Schooling in order to avoid ambiguity.

An explication of the distinction between Catholic Education and Catholic Schooling is no mere trivial matter, for its itemization of potential meanings enumerates the breadth of political-ecclesial views within the Church. Education and Schooling in the more "secular" sense are, of course, not politically innocent, and some of the several specific general demands within the field are pressures for reforms that are intended to resolve current social problems. If there are problems in society it is hoped, sometimes naïvely, that schools can fix them completely. "More and better education" seems to be the usual response to perceived problems with maintaining a reasonable level of employment, physical and sexual health, good manners and morality, scientific innovation, public safety, political participation, and so forth. Reform movements in education have attempted to meet and coordinate various socio-political demands over the years, with results being mixed due to competing political, professional, and personal interests which mitigate the effects of any sweeping large-scale changes.[4] All education is political, whether it takes place in "public," "private," "church," or "family" institutions, because the decisions as to where, for whom, and for what purpose it takes place are at any scale inherently questions of what is best for society and its individuals.

So in this context of complex socio-political systems, one observes that the addition of Catholicism to this conversation enriches the relationship. Surprising as it may be to some, a Catholic school is not somehow excluded from the world of competing views (1) on "secular" topics like those above, and (2) *within* Catholicism itself. There are many competing ideas about what Catholic Education should be, and likewise there are many kinds of Catholic schools reflecting at least some of the stronger movements behind these ideas. Philosopher of education Walter Feinberg (2006, 47–50), for instance, enumerates four distinct types of Catholic high schools which he calls "traditional," "modern," "liberation," and "feminist" based upon their position *vis-à-vis* the Magisterium, social outlook, critique of ideology, and the relative emphasis they give to either doctrinal legalism or care for persons. So while it might be attractive for polemicists to posit that Catholic schools are simply an institutional organ of the Magisterium which pass along its teaching to an audience of students who are eager to receive it, one need only remember that the Catholic school is actually a meeting place at the intersection of the Church, State, teaching profession, parents, and students. Sometimes these constituencies agree, but sometimes they do not.[5] It would be naïve to think that Catholic schools can be reformed all at once, because for every view that would imagine the school should be re-aligned to broadcast doctrine clearly, another view would call for a more student-centred approach that instead emphasizes liberation theology.

FOUNDATIONAL TENSIONS

The question of how and why controversy exists within a Catholic school requires one to consider the school's philosophical character as an institution like any other. *Character* here refers to its constitution as the confluence of partners, which is separate from the narrower theological question of "What makes a school Catholic?"; answers to that question tend only to reflect the Magisterial aspect of this partnership. If the larger political confluence is ignored, the theoretical construction and constitution of a Catholic school can sometimes be caricatured as an instrument of the Magisterium and its apologists designed only to indoctrinate students in a faith, piety, and moral discipline that is quite intellectually narrow and socially sheltered.[6]

Catholic schools do not exist apart from this world and they are not merely the enforcers of conformity. As a Church does not exist without its parishioners, so a school does not exist without its students, parents, and surrounding community. These persons bring their own intentions, characters, and culture to the school, and so they approach the Catholic school with varying ideas of what the Church and school are, might be, and should be. The school certainly depends on the bureaucratic Church for its spiritual, social, and curricular foundation, but this normative referent can be no greater than a *constitutive part* of the school. True, some may wish the school to mirror precisely the official Church in a one-to-one relationship, but, as will be shown below, these are not the views of all persons in the school. As partners who must work with the Magisterium for a Catholic school to exist, students, parents, and the teaching profession represent other equally constitutive parts of the institution. Finally, as with any school, there is the State's desire to have its citizens educated well so that they become productive, contributing members of society.

In short, it can be agreed that if Catholic Education were grossly incongruent with the educative aims of its host society, then there would be an inundation of media attention calling for its immediate disbandment on those grounds. In Catholic schools, where the formal and informal curricula extend past the bounds of secular schools and into a generally spiritualized and particularly Catholic setting, these foundational questions also inevitably extend into controversial Catholic Church issues and arguments over the establishment of appropriate aims for Catholic Education. This book concerns that very topic.

Controversy exists primarily as the result of several social and political features that are inherent in the Church, Education, and Schooling as *human* institutions. The observation of these tensions in no way suggests that Catholic Education is flawed. In fact, it suggests Catholic Education is quite normal; but it should disabuse any notion that Catholic Education exists in a state of sacred institutional grace, somehow immune from the mundane squabbling which is characteristic of other institutions. That view is naïve and elitist. Rather, this observation simply reveals an intrinsic property of the fact that one is in the business of education, and as Catholicism's various ordained, religious, and lay ecclesial bodies have entered this enterprise, they have discovered or inherited particularly religious and Catholic versions of these problems. This book proposes a new way for Catholic Education to approach the religious tensions which inhere in the socio-foundational structure of its institutions.

Given the complex institutional nature of Catholic Education, the observations, proposals, and arguments throughout this book are presented in a spirit that is generous to each partner and to what arguably should be reasonable for each to accept. In an age where the Catholic Church may feel threatened by what it perceives as "anti-Catholic" elements or "religious relativism"[7] in the world, it is perhaps most prudent to acknowledge now that this theory is proposed to support and encourage Catholic Education, even though it will do so in a way that emphasizes the pedagogical importance of intellectually developing religious differences more than the current pedagogy emphasizes doctrinal unity as the basis for institutional cohesion. Most certainly this theory is not intended to be wielded as a rhetorical weapon which would undermine Catholic Education; still, this generosity is also not blinkered by unquestioning deference to the Magisterium or a disposition to overlook the flaws in Catholic Education for fear its opponents might capitalize upon them for its destruction. Those whose biases preclude agreement with the methods, proposals, and conclusions in this volume – and there will be many such disagreements – are asked to read it with an eye to its value as an exploration of territory that contributes to the further development of Catholic Education. They are also asked to consider its potential as a way of reaching out to persons who are disaffected with the Church and for whom traditional invitations and presentations have proven ineffective.

ON CRITICAL THINKING IN CATHOLIC EDUCATION

The place of dissent at the foundations of and within the formal and informal curricula of Catholic Education inevitably implies the question of what role critical thinking has in that domain. The debate on critical thinking is too large to be taken up in its entirety here, but there are two general issues within it which have immediate importance.

First, there is the issue of its definition and relation to the disciplines. The "critical" adjective should be framed in terms of higher-order reasoning that is fundamental to problem-solving and the appraisal of evidence and arguments. It should also be considered a fundamental part of creative thinking within a discipline, and not as simply a set of discrete or generic skills that exist independently of any established mode of inquiry.[8] Nor is thinking critically about religion limited to its analytical fragmentation or the reinforcement of negative portrayals. It is instead learning to "think religiously" about a problem in the theology, philosophy, institution, or culture of religion[9] – analogous to "thinking mathematically" or "historically" about problems in those disciplines.

Second, there is the issue of the aims of critical thinking: (a) *how* and (b) *for what* are curricula designed so students learn to think critically? This question of aims is inherently a political-ecclesial one, for if the answers are limited to (a) a critical appreciation of what the Magisterium has already proposed as its critical thinking so that (b) one can defend the prevailing doctrinal views on contraception, ordination, homosexuality, and salvation (for example) in lockstep with the Magisterium, then one must immediately question what assumptions about ecclesial membership and authority ground this view. The three cases in the introduction are controversial because they uncover the question of who and what is authoritative in Catholicism (and when and why). If critical thinking is anything beyond a trivial exercise limited to a scholastic world divorced from reality, then at its heart the Catholic religion class should include critical thinking about authority in the Church on the topics of (1) Church-wide socio-ecclesial problems and (2) in-school curricular problems within theological-ecclesial-social education. What sort of "ecclesial citizenship" do the Church and School envision will result after education for critical thinking,[10] and what relationship between a critically thinking student and the Magisterium is imagined?

To place dissent within the rubric of critical thinking about the Catholic Church is not to undermine my affirmation that to be critical includes positive evaluations of its object just as much as negative ones. It is quite possible that one could arrive at a negative critical appraisal about certain parts of the Church and nonetheless still love it, and certainly Case Three above provides one very strong example of such a disposition, even if that love is motivated by the longing for a Church which may not exist anymore (in many places, anyway). As the burden of this volume is to propose a pedagogical response that opens paths within Catholicism which are irreducible to the

binaries of complete adherence and complete rejection, so by implication "to dissent" means to explore, justify, and live a theoretically
rigorous Catholicism along uniquely developed and legitimated lines
of ecclesial thought, "citizenship," and authority. In particular, the
problems of diversity and ecclesial membership which are inherent
in the cases above are educational in and of themselves, and so they
should be part of the foundation for how one conceives of religious
education. If these problems are ignored, then it is at the peril of good
teaching and learning, and of the Church itself.[11] Within this volume,
dissent carries the conceptual weight of describing and justifying a
pedagogically responsible approach to encouraging and developing
a "disagreeing ecclesial membership."

POTENTIAL INITIAL CRITICISMS

Having read all the foregoing, a reader might still retain some questions as to the meaning of "pedagogy" extant in *Pedagogy of Dissent*,
and these questions might lead to some problems with understanding
how the final chapter is titled "Pedagogy of Dissent." These questions
and problems arise from the multiple meanings that "pedagogy" has
within the field of education: to some it implies the methods of teaching and learning, and to others it denotes a theoretical approach to
the aims of education and their justification. *Pedagogy of Dissent*
expresses the latter sense. Now methods and theory are not mutually
exclusive domains, and so neither are these meanings of "pedagogy"
completely separable. A teaching method will always have some
theoretical basis, and so will foundational theorizing make prescriptions for the organization of educational institutions and the many
practices and places of teaching and learning. There cannot be practical action without theoretical justification. Similar use of the term
is found in Paulo Freire's famous *Pedagogy of the Oppressed*. More
recently, religious educator Andrew Wright argues in his chapter
"Pedagogy of Learning" that "the pedagogy of religious education
cannot be reduced to the pragmatic task of bridging theory and practice"[12] and warns that there are "dangers [in] moving too quickly
from the task of theorizing the subject to that of addressing practical
questions of teaching methodology."[13] Aims come prior to methods.

   This "pedagogy" is thus a foundational "pedagogical theory" or
approach to curriculum that teachers might use when interpreting
curriculum objectives, content, methods, and assessment in their

classroom to their students. It also obtains for the arguments and decisions that administrators, parents, and other partners make in justifying the aims of Catholic Education. Since all current curricula conform to the prevailing view, and since schooling is also irreducible to its subject matter, no review of any formal curriculum is done here because any review would be a distraction from the larger institutional and curricular (formal-explicit and informal-hidden) realities that they negotiate. All curricula are extensions of the Church to the degree that all are founded on the same conception of authority, and it is this notion of authority and the political-ecclesial spaces it affords with which I am concerned. Therefore this proposed pedagogy is less concerned with *what content is taught* than with how teachers have a theoretical means to (1) interpret curricula; (2) "be" the curricula (which they are already insofar as they filter curricula and present themselves as apologists, defenders of the faith, neutral facilitators, catechists, and so forth); (3) respond to student needs (insofar as any prescribed curriculum is only half the relationship); and (4) define and negotiate goals for their class and with their students and local community, and decide what counts as a "good pedagogy," and so forth. This "pedagogy" is about redefining the professional approach to determining what is authoritative for curriculum design and curricular content/experiences, hence opening the way to create many different "thick" approaches to being Catholic, besides the official view.

It is important here to note that the "pedagogy of dissent" does not presume that the foundation of Catholic school curriculum is corrupt and that the whole system requires immediate overthrow. That conclusion would misrepresent this argument. There is, however, an observation that besides the many very good qualities within Catholic Education, the current construction of political, social, and moral relationships at the foundation of the curriculum is inadequate to meeting fully the pedagogical needs contained within certain kinds of cases that go to the heart of the institution's sense of self. Catholic Education is good, but it could be better.

If one agrees with this assessment, then the temptations at this point to skip theoretical contemplation and leap immediately into a new method that "would work" are numerous and possibly quite attractive. If a student is facing a problem, after all, the inclination should possibly be toward the most prudent remedial action that puts a resolution within that student's grasp. It would seem counterintuitive to anyone, practitioner or not, to recognize a problem in theory and practice but then limit one's response to discussions in the staffroom, principal's office, or in-service or graduate seminar without actually translating ideas into practice. But before any practical reforms of this kind can be tried, the questions which arise from the following observations must be cleared.

Recall that the first two cases are of a "post-conciliar" kind and the third is of a "pre-conciliar" kind. It is highly conceivable that both these generalized perspectives, along with representatives of the prevailing view, are present within the same school, and even within the same classroom. As such, they reflect the diversity of views within the community's families and parishes. Without meaning to draw upon any unfair and prejudicial stereotypes, it stands to reason that if a teacher were to take it upon him- or herself to move immediately to actions that would favour dissent from only a "post-conciliar" bias, there would be resistance from the prevailing and "pre-conciliar" camps. Likewise, immediately acting in favour of the "pre-conciliar" point of view would draw resistance from "post-conciliar" and prevailing quarters. To anticipate later arguments in this volume, one might wish to dispense with actions that favour only particular kinds of dissent and instead take action that would favour *dissenters in general* with the intent of accommodating all persons within the school. As all the current curricula are based upon an orientation to the prevailing view which renders them unable to explore fully the educative possibilities that all kinds of dissent provides, this "pedagogy of dissent" must therefore include them all. *How* dissent is handled has more educative value than what content is considered or what outcome is reached.

A potentially more serious question might arise regarding disagreements with certain articles of Canon Law. Specifically, to announce one's disagreement with the Church's position on female clergy or homosexuality is one thing, but the penalty in Canon Law for procuring an abortion amounts to an instant self-excommunication.[14] Would this pedagogy be openly contravening Canon Law if it were used to justify the procurement, promotion, or rationalizing of abortions? The response to this question requires some foreshadowing of arguments I make in later chapters. The importance of this question lies less in whether the response to it is a bare "yes" or "no," but primarily in how one uses it as an educational opportunity to track back to (1) the pedagogy's assumptions about the role of the teacher or school in relationship with the student and the Church, (2) the scholarly debate within Catholicism on abortion and its relationship to sociological trends among lay Catholics that make this a controversial issue, and (3) the question of the role of Canon Law in Church life.

In response to (1), it can be said that while this theory recognizes that Catholic schools are dependent upon the Magisterial Church for their nominal designation[15] and are theorized to exist in partnership with the Church and the Home to provide for the complete educational experience of Catholic persons,[16] once one looks past the naming of that triad their educative roles within this relationship are much more ambiguously defined. For example, in addition to providing what might be considered a basic informative overview of Church doctrine on matters such as abortion, schools and the profession of teaching also have a responsibility to provide students with opportunities to think critically about such matters. The Church has its responsibility to produce and disseminate doctrine, but the role of the school is much larger than to promote doctrine on behalf of the Church, because the school has a primary educative responsibility to get students *to think religiously* rather than *to be religious generally* or *to be religious in a certain way.*[17]

This leads to point (2). In cases where students do not agree with the Magisterium, there is an educational opportunity to examine the language of Canon Law and its supporting documents, the reasons within these documents, and the claims which provide the warrants for those arguments (including all the way down to claims that the pope and bishops, as successors of the apostles, are authentic teachers in the Church). Is it proper to view the Church as composed of the two distinct societies of "those who teach" (*ekklesia docens*) and "those who obey" (*ekklesia discens*)? What role should the laity have in today's Church? Additionally there is an opportunity to examine what debate on abortion there is within Catholic theology and the popular press and among the laity, to examine how enforceable this law is, and to inquire into the rationale behind excommunication as the consequence.

In response to (3), the question of the role of Canon Law in the Church concerns whether being Catholic is simply a matter of conforming to a written code (and to what degree); and if so, what place does the lived, cultural experience of Catholicism, Catholic service, conscience, and devotion have in relation to it? Is Catholic life reducible to Canon Law, and is Canon Law being over- or under-emphasized in the Church today? What is the proper place of pastoral care for persons in Church doctrine? From responding to questions like these, students could arrive at conclusions – even if only tentative – on the question of who and what is authoritative on moral questions in the Church. These are all legitimately posed topics that are relevant to the public life of the Church, and if the public institution of the school is not prepared to engage with them, then it is difficult to name any other Catholic institution with the same publicly available resources and organized spaces where lay persons might engage them. Congruent with the aim of exploring other relevant Catholic options in a way that dissolves binary constructions of the relationship between religion and secular society, students require a reasonable educative means of developing their own views. As it is not the task of the school to indoctrinate students or impede their participation in the faith, if students come to school with questions like this one, it is the school's task to provide the most rigorous academic means of developing responses.

CONCLUSION, REGARDING AUDIENCE AND PURPOSE

It is obvious that all practicing and aspiring teachers in Catholic schools are an important audience for this book, but it is also aimed at a much wider group than teachers because, no matter how important their work is, religious education also occurs outside classrooms. This volume is also aimed at those who supervise and support the daily affairs in schools and school systems, including principals, in-school and out-of-school administrators, policy-makers, and trustees. It is hoped that parish priests, National Bishops' Conferences, and the Vatican Congregations for the Clergy and Education will see promise here for reaching out to persons who are disaffected, leaving, or who have left the Church. It is also hoped that academics, including lay and religious Catholic educators and academics of other religions or no religion, will have an interest in this book as it is relevant or transferable to other pedagogical and social areas and the promotion of "religious literacy" in society at large.

Not least of all, however, even though it has a heavy emphasis on what concerns the public life in Catholic schools, this work is also directed at parents and families. They are the first educators of their children and are witness to the joys and frustrations of their children as they attain intellectual, social, spiritual, and ecclesial maturity. In the midst of any hope that this work will have an influence upon the institution of Catholic Schools in Canada and worldwide, it must not be forgotten that such schooling is only a part of the total Catholic experience, and that parents and families form another very important part. Parents and families establish religious environments and dialogues for their children, have an increasing influence over the school environment, and often host a final forum for the expression of the problems that students feel are left unresolved in the school. The scope and measure of success for this *pedagogy of dissent* is therefore not limited to its possible influence as a catalyst or underwriter of major reforms to Catholic Schools in Canada and elsewhere in the immediate or far future. It is equally applicable to those situations where a family is struggling to find meaningful intellectual solutions when one of its (adolescent) members returns home and presents a frustration with the outcome of a religious discussion that day. This volume thus speaks to the parental and familial role in Catholic Education writ large. If parents are worried about how to explain (without glibly "explaining away") incongruities between Church or school teaching and their particular, lived family experience of Catholicism, then this book provides the theoretical framework for where to look, how to look, why to look that way, and how to justify such looking.

So far as introducing a book on dissent in Catholic Education goes, there may be some initial concern about what precisely dissent is and whether it is being promoted wantonly, or for its own sake. If there are lingering doubts about this term, I hope that here I have set enough of an argumentative and methodological framework with which to lend enough currency to my promise that in later chapters I can argue that good-quality dissent is a faithful act. The justification which opens up the freedom to dissent should not be mistaken for unqualified license. The freedom to dissent is thus established with a concordant responsibility not only to abide by the appropriate moral, political, and epistemic criteria which ground the most desirable sense of the concept, but also to dissent when dissent is required to promote justice (see chapter 5). The use of this concept to describe some kinds of critical thinking and to think critically *with and within* the Church as one of its members on important educative cases thus grounds its use as a heuristic concept in mapping out the territory between the contingently held binary conceptions of religious and non-religious.

As a final word, it is worth describing the disposition that this book takes toward Catholicism and Catholic Education-Schooling when it uses the word *dissent*. Dissent is a difficult word to use in discussions about religion because much of religion implies assent to faith.[18] To promote dissent as an approach to the formal and informal religious curriculum might be interpreted as the disruption of religious learning (especially where Catholic Education is embedded in a culture which is perceived to be irreligious and even hostile to religion), thus doing intellectual damage to students and undermining the Church and school. For the present purpose of describing a disposition, however, I wish to suspend temporarily the assent-dissent question because the forthcoming chapters will propose a much more nuanced presentation of dissent as a kind of loyalty to the group or organization, and use that presentation to sustain the argument in this book. Instead, I would like to focus on the emphasis that hope receives in the treatment of religion and religious education.

The Catholic concept of hope and its relationship to faith speaks directly to the spirit of this work. Moran provides some instructive commentary on the over-exposure "faith" receives at the expense of "hope." He remarks that while faith, hope, and charity are Catholicism's three core theological virtues, the body of truths that constitute faith and the right treatment of our neighbour are often over-emphasized, and hope relegated to status as the "forgotten virtue." Saints Augustine and Thomas Aquinas afford extensive space to the discussion of faith in their major theological works, while by comparison they scarcely explore hope.[19] The de-emphasis on hope, Moran finds, is the result of splitting a single New Testament term (Greek Septuagint: *pisteuein*) which meant simultaneously "belief" and "trust," and privileging "belief" to the degree that, over the course of centuries, hope was reduced out and the remnant theology of faith meant little more than "assent to propositions." Moran thus prescribes an end to this theology of faith as "revealed truths" and a return to a theology that views revelation as the process of uncovering and coming into relationship with a person, and not an abstract idea.[20] Hope is therefore not a naïve optimism that "everything will turn out all right,"[21] but a way of looking upon oneself in relation with God and others in order to see humanity "in all the unrealized potentiality of being."[22]

So long as the word *dissent* sets in motion a series of intellectual events that conjures questions of assent and loyalty to Catholicism styled as "the faith," and the inevitable sympathetic, sceptical, or dismissive responses that will accompany any pedagogical or ecclesial models grounded in dissent, I submit that this entire work is under-written by a hope for what Catholicism and Catholic Education might potentially become for the good of all. To dissent from Church teaching or from the prevailing view within a Catholic institution (the two are not always congruent) implies one's existential desire to maintain spiritual ties with the group while being true to the self. Further, where maintaining these ties also implies the anticipation that the group will benefit from encountering dissenters and dissent-ing views, a pedagogical framework which argues that such academic encounters can fruitfully engage students in the intellectual potential of what Catholicism has to offer is also congruent with a disposition to preserve relationships for the sake of finding the divine in the other. These encounters between "selves and others" are the foundation of hope; for since it is these "selves and others" who constitute the Church, to overlook dissent simply on the grounds that it may offend the propositional faith is to drift into a problematic pattern of disre-gard for the ongoing divine revelation through the personal Body of Christ simply for the sake of protecting and preserving the encoded Church. "In this view every child is a world of infinite worth. No effort is useless or futile that may advance the child one step in the direction of God's designs."[23]

A pedagogical model based upon dissent and hope thus comes between the poles of complete adherence to faith propositions and complete rejection of the Church. From an educational perspective it presents an opportunity for students to grapple with the important foundational questions which are at the root of their concerns, and to do so in an intellectually honest fashion. From a point of view that wishes to maintain a generous attitude toward Catholicism and the institutions of Catholic Education, this model displays, if only softly and sometimes even silently and subtly, a hope that students, who constitute part of the Church, will discover for themselves their own selves in it.

2

Education, Authority, Dissent,
and Conscience

Catholic Education depends upon the presence of the global body of
the Catholic Church for its normative sense of purpose, its curriculum, and, not least of all, its self-understanding as an institution. This
fact presents an interesting methodological challenge for how one
might examine institutional responses to and make proposals about
student-presented dissent in these institutions. Since Catholic Education is a worldwide phenomenon which looks to the Magisterial and
administrative aspect of the Church for guidance, one cannot speak
of dissent in Catholic Education without exposing the Church's normative understanding of education and authority. Similarly, as individuals respond with varying degrees of assent or dissent to certain
teachings, a normative description of dissent and the ways in which
an individual makes judgments in conscience is also required, because
the tension between individual and group brings the constitutive institutional reality of schooling to bear on the three dilemmas presented
in the introduction. This treatment necessarily speaks to the universal
theory that informs the whole Church.

This chapter therefore begins with a brief look at how the Church
understands education, broadly speaking. Second, as there cannot be
dissent in education or in the Church unless a prevailing view exists,
this chapter describes how the Church considers its Magisterium. As
questions of authority within institutions inevitably raise further
questions about how to treat challenges to it, the third section intro-
duces a discussion on how the official Church understands dissent
and how theologians have critiqued that understanding. Finally, a
discussion of the promises of and the difficulties with the Catholic
concept of conscience is offered, as this is one commonly known

means of responding to conflict between official teaching and the moral law one learns through his or her personal relationship with God. The burden here is not to make a comprehensive theoretical synthesis of education, Magisterium, conscience, and dissent, but rather to demonstrate how these concepts in Catholic thought are thrust into a socio-political union that both expresses their hope and uncovers and magnifies their imperfections.

FOUNDATIONS OF CATHOLIC EDUCATION

On Catechesis and Religious Instruction

Responsibility for all aspects of Catholic Education sits within the pope's ministry as successor of Peter the Apostle.[1] Today, the Vatican Congregations for Catholic Education and the Clergy aid the pope in the task of providing normative reference to the Church concerning Catholic Education.[2] The Congregation for Catholic Education (CCE) "sets the norms by which Catholic schools are governed. It is available to diocesan bishops so that, wherever possible, Catholic schools are established and fostered with the utmost care, and that in every school appropriate undertakings bring catechetical instruction and pastoral care to the Christian pupils."[3] For its part, the Congregation for the Clergy (CC) "has the function of promoting the religious education of the Christian faithful of all ages and conditions," and ensuring that that catechetical service is "correctly conducted" and "properly given" using catechisms and other materials that have received "the prescribed approval of the Holy See."[4] The CC is concerned with the application of the *Catechism's* authoritative teaching. Its *General Directory for Catechesis* (GDC) thereby complements the *Catechism* with "the basic principles of pastoral theology taken from the Magisterium of the Church, and in a special way from the Second Vatican Council by which pastoral action in the ministry of the word can be more fittingly directed and governed."[5] The CCE oversees the institutional organization and mission of Catholic schools, while the CC is responsible for ensuring "competency" in "religious instruction of the faithful" both in and beyond schools.[6]

The relationship between catechesis and religious instruction in a Catholic school is not always well understood, and the emphasis on each certainly varies from school to school depending on the social context in which they are situated. Generally speaking, all catechesis is religious instruction, but not all religious instruction is catechesis. The CCE makes the distinction that "catechesis aims at fostering personal adherence to Christ and the development of Christian life in its different aspects ... whereas religious education in schools gives the pupils knowledge about Christianity's identity and Christian life."[7] Catechesis is the subset of religious instruction that aims to educate for belief. It instructs for the purpose of inducting the learner into the committed community of believers through information, invitation, and persuasion.[8] It is imagined as "a comprehensive and systematic formation in the faith," conceived of as "an apprenticeship of the entire human life."[9] Religious instruction in the broader sense aims to provide cognitive growth, but is not (necessarily) partial to an affective outcome or induction in a group. The CC frames religious instruction in schools as providing the cognitive character of "a scholastic discipline with the same systematic demands and the same rigour as other disciplines."[10] The twin aims of catechesis and religious instruction are nonetheless complementary.[11]

From this distinction one can recognize that catechesis and religious instruction might at any one time consider the same content, cognition, and skill, but for catechesis the learner's intended outcome is "I know and believe," and for the instructed person it is simply "I know." With catechesis, the Catholic school aims to give witness to the truth of the Catholic faith, build a Catholic community, and reinforce and enhance the faith of the faithful. A confessional theme thus permeates the Catholic school's formal academic curriculum and informal socialization, including proclaiming the Gospel, contemplating the reasons for belief, living in Christian community, and celebrating the sacraments. The whole institution catechizes in this respect. The Catholic school does not proselytize or attempt to convert non-Catholic students, but at the same time does attempt to display an attractive model of Catholic morality, culture, and spirituality to them.

According to religious educator Thomas Groome, the catechetical formation of persons must emphasize the learner's[12] religious freedom, and likewise should not regress to indoctrination or some form of education that merely aims at uncritical socialization. In his estimation, a desirable Catholic education is one that "brings people to know the data of the tradition, to understand it, to personally and critically appropriate it, and to come to life decisions in response to it. Precisely because the intent is to move beyond knowledge to wisdom, beyond information to the 'being' of participants, such pedagogy must personally engage students, all of their capacities and dispositions."[13] The most significant aspect in Groome's formulation is its inductive structure from the specifics of data to the guiding purpose that organizes and gives it meaning. Possessing a distinct body of Catholic knowledge for its own sake is worth less than critically responding to and forming a life through engagement with it. An affective response may be hoped for, but is not necessarily required. By bringing the attitude toward knowledge into place as a means of informing the person's critical capacities, Groome has underlined personal and religious freedom as two major goals of Catholic education.

Further on in Groome's analysis, however, the description of a morally thicker Christian community starts to pull away from any precise overlap with secular notions of community. "A Catholic school is not a parish," he writes. "Yet its very nature and purpose calls it to be a community of Christian faith."[14] Groome specifically refers to love as the basis for Christian community, and speaks of the challenge to integrate both secular and Catholic values within the school: "The love commitment to the school should be realized as a profound care and 'right relationship' among and between teachers, administrators, and students, and toward the school's extended community of parents, former students and the parish(es) of its local context. For analysis, we can think of this communal characteristic of Catholicism requiring a school to be both a public community and an ecclesial community."[15] This characterization underscores the multiple and simultaneous aims of formation and social service that are present in the school.

The aim of promoting education as a religious and civil service to the world, and the very fact that Catholic schools serve practicing and non-practicing Catholics and non-Catholics alike, establishes a situation where any image of the school as a doctrinally pure Catholic society is subordinated to its constitution as a more cosmopolitan Catholic atmosphere. The Catholic school as an institution sits at the intersection of religious and secular cultures, and as it mixes these two influences it takes up the task of balancing sometimes-competing aims: "On the one hand, a Catholic school is a 'civic institution'; its aims, methods, and characteristics are the same as those of every other school. On the other hand, a Catholic school is a 'Christian community' whose educational goals are rooted in Christ and his Gospel. It is not always easy to bring these two aspects into harmony; the task requires constant attention, so that the tension between a serious effort to transmit culture and a forceful witness to the Gospel does not turn into a conflict harmful to both."[16] Such statements are sufficiently open-ended so as to be congruent with most, if not all, of the various permutations of Catholic Education and Catholic Schooling.

The concept that Catholic schools aim to catechize all their students, or that they *should* aim to catechize all those they serve, needs some important qualifications. While some religious instruction in schools serves the initiation of new Christians,[17] the theoretical and practical problems with too strong an emphasis on catechesis follow from two main points. First, while it might seem intrinsically obvious to some that a Catholic school would teach only Catholic students and would aim to preach a Catholic message to them, such is not the case. Not all students in the Catholic school are Catholic.

Second, any effort at formation is misspent if the student is unreceptive. The student might desire to be religious in a particular way that is explicitly tied to the program the instructor leads, but may also be intent on learning cognitive content without any affective commitment, or on being religious in some sense that is encouraged by the instructor but governed by the student's own ideas of application.[18] In this vein the Congregation for the Clergy aptly recognizes the "diversity of the religious situation" possible among those a Catholic school serves, including those who are unbaptized, incompletely initiated, "in grave crises of faith," or "moving towards making a decision with regard to faith," among the many possibly resistant or unreceptive students. Additionally, those who the CC recognizes "have already made such a decision and call for assistance"[19] should not be excluded from this group, since their intentions regarding all aspects of the faith might not completely match the school's or Church's.

Catechesis may be a well-intentioned aim for all, but it is not necessarily a *de facto* core outcome within the broad array of educational and pastoral services the Catholic school provides. The purpose of teaching religion therefore necessarily remains an open question in policy that can only be resolved more precisely once the student's intentions are known. Another open question, that of whether a Catholic program of education can be viable without an emphasis on catechesis, has also recently attracted some attention,[20] but generally the lack of any strong contemporary philosophy of Catholic education in the post-conciliar era exacerbates this problem.[21]

On a Personal and Communal Anthropology

Catholicism regards the human person as a being who is created in the image of God, free, and formed in political community with others. This assumption is backed by a universal claim that God purposefully created humans to be simultaneously corporal and spiritual beings in God's own image.[22] The soul, or innermost part of every person, is regarded as that which most closely resembles God,[23] and as such becomes a place in which the Spirit of God resides. Each person is to be loved as the reflection and presence of God's spirit, and not because of their worldly status, behaviour, or accomplishment. Finally, each person is assumed to possess a freedom that is experienced in relationships with other persons.[24]

Notice that there is no reference to a "Catholic" or "Christian" person: Catholicism sees this image of God in all persons, regardless of their belief or affiliation. The spiritual duty of care in the Catholic school is thus to promote and maintain this conception of the person against offence and corruption. Catholic Education's offer and example of the Catholic faith and emphasis on forming the person is thus not characterized by any formal attempts to coerce reception or indoctrinate the learner. Saskatoon Catholic Schools, for example, qualifies its evangelizing commission by stating that its purpose is not to convert non-Catholic students to Catholicism, but to inspire "a conversion of the heart where Christians, Muslims, Buddhists, Hindus, and sisters and brothers of other faith traditions become better Christians, Muslims, Buddhists, Hindus, and sisters and brothers of other faith traditions."[25] The ideal of the human person is thus maintained as a means of describing and interpreting a person's corporeal and spiritual dignity, no matter what their religious belief.

Catholicism does not conceive of persons existing in isolation. It posits that a person is only fully formed when in relationship with others, and that formation obtains through the experience of learning how to negotiate freedom and responsibility, given the challenge of working and living together to promote the needs and the good of all. It is through this kind of interaction that the true nature and identity of the Christian self is found. Groome states that the communal nature of Catholic existence is a combined expression of its anthropology and cosmology, the former suggesting that persons "have a natural affinity for relationship and are capable of 'right relationship' with others," and the latter that worldly culture and institutions are not necessarily doomed to sin and "can be an instrument of God's saving grace."[26] The social nature of Christian participation in the institutional Church is thus the primary aspect of contributing to the common good.

The application of the Catholic understanding of community to Catholic Education suggests two things. First, Catholic Education's goals are not reducible to the individual and individualized learning; nor is highly abstracted learning emphasized at the expense of sacrificing its relevance to the real world and persons. The goal of Catholic schooling is not therefore "to produce" learned atomistic individuals, nor a learned community that requires conformity at the expense of individual freedom. The goal, rather, is to achieve a balance between the individual and the community. Academic subject matter in Catholic education should therefore serve this end. Second, the application of the Catholic understanding of community says something about the way in which a Catholic school is organized and the atmosphere in which a Catholic education takes place. Catholic schools, in one way or another, are rightly thought of as places that should promote a socio-moral atmosphere for encouraging the growth of persons-in-relationship: a religiously "thick" moral description congruent with a secular expression of individuals-in-relation.[27] Any school, Catholic or not, is a community of persons-in-relation to some degree. Groome emphasizes that in the Catholic school, a sense of community should promote a "spirit of freedom" that is "reflected in an atmosphere of openness, intellectual and social, where students and faculty feel free to become their own best selves and to pursue knowledge and truth wherever they can be found, where the school strives to be a community of welcome and hospitality for all."[28] A second glance at that statement finds that it is sufficiently "thin" to apply equally to secular or non-Catholic religious schools, if the reader did not have any prior expectation that it *should* be descriptive of a Catholic institution. Any secular school in a liberal society might at least quote intellectual and social openness as aims.

Catholic schools fashion themselves as institutions that promote an atmosphere where interpersonal relations constitute the root of community and full personhood. These schools are normatively

Catholic in their approach to the student, the curriculum they offer, and the institutional values they espouse, but they very importantly also display an ecumenical offering of service for all, regardless of their religious beliefs. The CCE emphasizes that the distinctiveness of the Catholic school subsists in "its attempt to generate a community climate in the school that is permeated by the Gospel spirit of freedom and love"[29] and that upon entry into a Catholic school the student "ought to have the impression of entering a new environment, one illumined by the light of faith, and having its own unique characteristics."[30]

Although it has a distinctively Catholic character, such a school is not meant to be an exclusively Catholic enclave, but is rather intended "to be a school for all" regardless of race, class, religion, ability, or sex.[31] As the CCE emphasizes, although the Catholic school is "clearly and decidedly configured in the perspective of the Catholic faith, [it] is not reserved to Catholics only but to all those who appreciate and share its qualified educational project."[32] The Catholic school as such is ecumenical in scope and hopes to serve and promote the general good of all society by providing education as a public service. Catholic Education thus promotes the growth of persons and communities in society, whoever they are.

As Catholic Education, broadly understood, promotes a synthesis of the spiritual, intellectual, physical, social, and moral dimensions of one's personhood, in theory its institutions aim to integrate all these dimensions of an educated human person's development throughout its programs. That mission "is based on an educational philosophy in which faith, culture, and life are brought into harmony,"[33] through development of the whole human person in relation to the community and the world at large.[34] As Archbishop Daniel Pilarczyk notes, the school, like the Church itself, "teaches about the whole spectrum of human reality for the simple reason that since the incarnation of the second Person of the Holy Trinity,[35] there is no aspect of human reality which is alien to God and to God's people."[36] Seeing education through the lens of faith gives its experiences meaning in the totality of life, which is an aspect of Christian Education that the CCE asserts is especially important in tempering the overemphasis on science and technical skill as reductive ends of education in today's world.[37] The Christian concept of personhood and the promotion of a spiritualized environment for a person's development are therefore set against a social backdrop of fragmentation and malaise that is perceived to impoverish human life in the extra-ecclesial civil society.

The integrative, synthetic nature of Catholic schools is demonstrated not only in their attention to the whole person, but also in their opposition to all that might threaten the unified integrity of personhood. This quality most explicitly and importantly presents itself in contrast to a perceived social trend that filters out spirituality and reduces the purpose of human life to a singular or limited range of aims. The CCE is especially mindful of the dangers of reducing a person's value to his or her economic utility. Moreover, the Congregation posits that the social environment in civil society is so affected by this restrictive trend that it "produces" people who are spiritually destabilized and confused by "a crisis of values which, in highly developed societies in particular, assumes the form, often exalted by the media, of subjectivism, moral relativism and nihilism"; this crisis of values, along with the pluralism of contemporary society, "undermine[s] any idea of community identity."[38]

The results of such instrumental social "production" affect the populations that Catholic schools serve, and thus social trends in civil society spawn moral issues that threaten the integrity of the complete person. "Many young people," the CCE asserts, "find themselves in a condition of radical instability" when secular society's reductive educational aims toward economic and technological progress come into conflict with these students' own emerging and broadening psychological awareness of a world beyond such a "narrow universe."[39] In response to the de-spiritualization of society, Catholic Education's purpose is to counter these negative social trends and to embrace "the huge challenge of helping these young people discover something of value in their lives."[40] The difficulty of achieving a fully spiritualized sense of personhood and social relationship is thus a primary concern that Catholic Education addresses in serving the public good.

While the Catholic school is charged with promoting a spiritualized experience according to Catholic views on the dignity of personhood, it is also charged with promoting "respect for the State and its representatives, the observance of just laws, and a search for the common good."[41] The Catholic school thus assumes the task of maintaining "traditional civic values such as freedom, justice, the nobility of work and the need to pursue social progress" in coordination with its own uniquely Catholic Christian aims.[42] However, as the depressing aspects of life and values in civil society influence students and their families to such a degree that large parts of their lives are almost alien to Catholic thought, the Congregation recognizes that the Catholic "school is undoubtedly a sensitive meeting point" that confronts "children and young people who experience the difficulties of the present time."[43] In this way the CCE also recognizes the awesome socio-moral task that is inherent to Catholic educational institutions: "The responsibility of a Catholic school is enormous and complex. It must respect and obey the laws that define methods, programs, structure, etc., and at the same time it must fulfill its own educational goals by blending human culture with the message of salvation into a coordinated program."[44]

The Catholic school community, then, exists on two levels. On the first level it realizes that the interdependence of individuals represents the institutional integration of individual and group needs for self-fulfillment. On the second level it realizes the place of the Christian Catholic community within the world at large, which in the Canadian context is a multicultural society that encourages democracy and pluralism. The Ontario Conference of Catholic Bishops places the Catholic communitarian value within the Canadian context by emphasizing Catholic integrity and its foundational place within the political warp and woof of Canadian society: "Canadian society continues to define itself as one in which communitarian values (linguistic, cultural, religious) are respected rather than denied. We have staked our hope as a nation on the possibility of strengthening our common social fabric by safeguarding the distinctive quality of each thread within it. Our ongoing commitment to the development of Catholic education represents one such contribution to the common fabric."[45] That solidarity and the presence of the Catholic Church in the Canadian political landscape are of course significant,[46] but the ways in which solidarity is conceived of are unclear, and so for all that is gained collectively, there may also be problematic outcomes for the individual.

Catholic Church detractors might argue on the one hand that by standing in solidarity with the Church, the individual signs over his or her thinking agency to the Church and allows the Magisterium to think for him or her. The individual in that case would have little agency or autonomy in religious matters beyond the bounds of what the Church directs. On the other hand, it might be argued that the individual loses no freedom by standing in solidarity because he or she is completely free to make that choice and does so without coercion. The key questions of how this relationship between the individual and the community is theorized, what the political-ecclesial nature of community is, and how Catholic community and individual are intertwined with the Magisterium are major theoretical pieces in this discussion. As of yet, they tend to receive only superficial and procedural discussion in the public sphere, rather than comprehensive intellectual debate. In addition, beyond how this issue emerges or flounders in theory is also the important issue of how it is applied in practice. The lack of learned investigation on that question is one of many important places where the theory of Catholic Education-Schooling requires improvement.

On Social Justice

Archbishop Michael Miller writes that "[t]he purpose of Catholic education is the formation of boys and girls who will be good citizens of the world, and also citizens of the world to come."[47] At the heart of this good citizenship are "social charity"[48] and "ordered service to the community" that are based on love.[49] Understandings of the Catholic school as a community fluctuate between the "thicker" descriptions that tend toward the language of ecclesial membership on the one hand, and the morally "thinner" understandings that can overlap with notions of persons-in-relation in secular philosophy, on the other. With all appearances being equal – that is, if the existence of religious curriculum, atmosphere, and paraphernalia were assumed away – the major difference between highly functional secular and Catholic communities would be found in the expressions of their respective communal understandings and aims, with the Catholic community having a distinctively spiritual basis for these. The Catholic expression of finding the presence of God in self and other would be matched – although not equalled – by a liberal secular emphasis on intersubjective moral growth. "Thick" notions of Catholic community in this sense are generally not controversial ideals; however, like their secular counterparts, they are also often not compatible with the structures of traditional schooling.

Emerging from the conception of the Catholic community, however, is an aspect of Catholic education that is much more politically controversial than debates over the primacy of the individual versus community, or over whether the Catholic ideal is practical. The political direction of the Catholic community is directed by distinctively idealized and "thick" Catholic notions of the common good and social responsibility that form the content of a curriculum and institutional atmosphere directed at promoting social justice. In so promoting social justice, the Catholic School follows the Church's position of standing in distinct difference from the rest of the world, because efforts at substantially improving the economic conditions of justice throughout the world conflict with prevailing secular neo-liberal and neo-conservative views. "Strong convictions about social justice," writes Dennis Murphy, are "a counter-cultural trademark of Catholic schools." Beyond a mere secular challenge to the perceived dominance of neo-liberalism and neo-conservatism, Murphy bases his view in a theistic relationship, asserting that in addition to direct political action, "an equally counter-cultural activity and trademark of Catholic education must be the school's commitment to introducing students to a life of prayer as the power to sustain the desire that justice and peace be done in our world."[50]

The idea of being "counter-cultural" has many forms, and may even be learned in disinterested cognitive terms as a concept that sits in relation to "prevailing culture," without the expectation that any affective response such as "appreciating" or "valuing" would develop. Murphy goes further than the cognitive domain, however, to take the bold step of suggesting that Catholic schools should challenge the very ground upon which many Catholic students are raised: "Our students will be encouraged to listen to the church leader in Robert Bellah's book, *The Good Society*, who says that 'the Church's greatest challenge ... is to enable middle-class folks to recognize that their nice consumerist existence is killing them, plus killing the Third World.'"[51] As the prevailing economic values in North American society are based upon achieving some kind of material prosperity, Murphy's application of Bellah's critique to the program of the Catholic Church might be taken as scandalous by those who have both some degree of attachment to the Catholic Church and a strong commitment to their own prosperity, and feel expected to learn to feel in some undesired way. The Catholic school is thus put into a position where its counter-cultural stance against secular schooling in Canadian society is defined by the mixture of the values present in the (Catholic) population that it serves and the institutional values that the Magisterium promotes. The school finds itself in a precarious spot when the population and the hierarchy have conflicting values, and any aims toward encouraging social justice are thus contingent upon the way in which the school and students can negotiate a common intent. This area is also under-examined in the theory of Catholic Education.

On a Critique of the Modern Secular World

Examples of Church dissent from the secular world can be found throughout Vatican documents. Pope Pius IX's 1864 "Syllabus of Errors in the Modern World" is a reactionary attempt to repel the perceived threats that science, democracy, and secularism posed to papal power in a time when the Vatican was losing its Papal States and other temporal influence to Italian unification and liberal revolutions in Europe. Papal critiques adopted a different character following Pius IX's death and the succession of Leo XIII in 1878. With Leo's 1891 encyclical letter "*Rerum Novarum,*" the theme of Catholic social justice begins to emerge in terms of a critique of the damage that modern secular society was doing to people through inhumane working and living conditions caused by industrialization, capitalism, and communism. "*Rerum Novarum*" thus initiated a new course in the papal critique of current political ideologies. During his long reign (1978–2005), John Paul II was especially critical of both capitalist and communist countries for restricting the development of people and communities.[52] Modern societies, according to John Paul, lose their grasp on the saving nature of divine truth when they reduce the spiritual into the political: "This is the risk of an alliance between democracy and ethical relativism, which would remove any sure moral reference point from political and social life, and on a deeper level make the acknowledgment of truth impossible. Indeed, if there is no ultimate truth to guide and direct political activity, then ideas and convictions can easily be manipulated for reasons of power. As history demonstrates, a democracy without values easily turns into open or thinly disguised totalitarianism."[53] While the Catholic Church participates in the world, and its members form and sometimes lead the world's political structures,[54] the Church hierarchy maintains that as the world loses touch with its spirituality it finds itself increasingly susceptible to the problems of embracing ethical relativism.

For the Catholic Church hierarchy, at least, truth is singular and found in God, and the moral law emerges from it. Any disregard of this truth – especially in the advances of secularism and relativism – thus threatens Christianity's Good News, which means it threatens the development of persons and communities. In "*Veritatis Splendor*," John Paul II describes ethical relativism in Christian-centric terms of secular departures from the one truth that God gives and that is God. He does not specifically use the word "sin," but he uses the descriptive language of sin when he describes ethical relativism as the product of humankind's proud conviction that it can find truth in multiple places, not just in God or in the Church. Sin – the breaking of healthy and loving relationships with God, others, and one's self – eventually leads to spiritual death. Relativism is therefore defined in terms of baseless subjectivity. For relativists, "[t]he saving power of the truth is contested, and freedom alone, uprooted from any objectivity, is left to decide by itself what is good and what is evil. This relativism becomes, in the field of theology, a lack of trust in the wisdom of God, who guides man [sic] with the moral law."[55] With the effects of globalization, cultural plurality, and postmodernism currently acting upon the world, the Catholic Church fears that the message of God's salvation is being lost, and that the Church itself is at risk of succumbing to those forces unless it takes action to prevent their spread throughout Catholic institutions:

> Dechristianization, which weighs heavily upon entire peoples and communities once rich in faith and Christian life, involves not only the loss of faith or in any event its becoming irrelevant for everyday life, but also, and of necessity, a decline or obscuring of the moral sense. This comes about both as a result of a loss of awareness of the originality of Gospel morality and as a result of an eclipse of fundamental principles and ethical values themselves. Today's widespread tendencies towards subjectivism, utilitarianism and relativism appear not merely as pragmatic attitudes or patterns of behaviour, but rather as approaches having a basis in theory and claiming full cultural and social legitimacy.[56]

The Church, therefore, dissents against secularizing forces that threaten the relevance and authenticity of the Christian message and Christian institutions.

Summary

Archbishop Michael Miller, formerly Secretary to the CCE, bases his "Challenges Facing Catholic Schools" on the outline of eight major features of Catholic Schools which have concerned the Magisterium in recent years. This outline provides a helpful summary of contemporary Catholic School aims:

1 *Subsidiarity*: Sharing responsibility for education between family, community, and Church in service of the common good, while opposing a state monopoly over education;
2 *Accessibility*: Providing educational service to the socially disadvantaged and in the service that the school promote social justice among all persons;
3 Ensuring a *Catholic Identity* by integrating spirituality throughout the entire curriculum and attending to the needs of the whole child; opposing technocratic or other reductive instrumental ends in education; emphasizing a communal anthropology; and promoting a visible sacramental environment;
4 *Catholic Vision Across the Curriculum,* which means an orientation to God's truth; and integrating faith, culture, and life. The whole institution is responsible for this; it is not the exclusive purview of religious education classes;
5 *Service to Charity and Justice*: The transformation of society in order to promote the well-being of all according to principles of life, fraternity, solidarity, and peace;
6 Promoting and building a *Spirit of Community and Communion* through which all partners cooperate in dialogue to develop educational aims, including school, family, bishop, students, and teachers;
7 The *Vocation and Witness of Teachers* both as professionals and as practicing Catholics (with limited exceptions) who understand the spiritual dimension of their role in service to society; and
8 *Cooperation between Religious and Laity,* which is concerned to blend the witness of Religious persons with the special competence of the laity in the education of students.[57]

The Catholic school sits at the confluence of Church, student, and State aims. While catechesis and religious instruction are important for some in the school, there is no requirement that the religious instruction in Catholic schools should aim to catechize or initiate the students. The school might simultaneously offer a range of services from a very "thick" act of preaching the Gospel to a "thinner" act of simply being a presence that stands as a spiritualized alternative to mainstream, secular schools. The specific kind and quality of Catholic school, and the specific characteristics of a student who attends and graduates from it, arguably cannot be reduced to a singular image.

MAGISTERIUM AND AUTHORITY IN THE CHURCH

If the concern of this volume is dissent as it is expressed from within Catholic Education, then a normative exposition of the prevailing view is required because dissent is always relative to what rules. Views can prevail for many reasons, including majority agreement, minority rule by coercion or force, a contract among interested parties, a socialized ideology that keeps them in place, or an epistemic tradition tied to institutionalized authority. The final option in that list is not the most elegant description of the Catholic Magisterium, but it is what constitutes Catholicism's administrative-juridical teaching authority. Beyond being simply helpful, an understanding of what this prevailing authority is, how it came to be, and what its purposes and limitations are within the Church is required before one can understand where a differing point of view might situate itself.

The Latin word *magister* corresponds to the English word *master* in its broadest range of meaning, from administrative mastery of an organization to the mastery of a machine or a skill. In its most simple meaning, the Magisterium is the Church's teaching authority.

The simplest application of "teaching authority" to formal structures in the Church finds that the Magisterium is composed of the pope and bishops, but this is not its complete definition, nor has the Magisterium as it is understood today existed in that form since the beginning of the Church. The meaning of "Magisterium" in the Church has changed over time, and it also works (and has worked) in diverse ways throughout the Church. Theologian Francis Sullivan remarks that the breadth of meaning *magister* carried in antiquity and the early Middle Ages eventually narrowed into a degree of specificity through common usage, and in the later medieval period was used with increasing frequency to describe a function of authority.[58] If one transposes that simple understanding of Magisterium-as-authority to the hierarchical administrative structures of the Church it becomes intuitively obvious that teaching authority lies with the pope, the Congregations and curial bodies acting under the pope's authority, and the bishops acting in ecumenical councils, in national or regional synods, in universal coordination, or individually within their own dioceses. These appointments and organs compose the Catholic Church's Magisterium.

The kind of authority each of these offices and bodies may exercise is best explained through an outline of the three levels of teaching that constitute the Church's Magisterial function. The first is the level of "formally defined, infallible truths" that the Church expresses with absolute certainty as accurately representing God's revelation. Such definitions may be proclaimed either through the solemn decree of an ecumenical council, or by the pope speaking *ex cathedra* as head of the universal church outside a council. The First Council of Nicaea's dogma that Jesus Christ is both fully human and fully divine is an example of the former, and Pope Pius XII's teaching that the Blessed Virgin Mary was assumed directly to heaven upon her death is an example of the latter.[59]

The second level is "those truths about faith and morals which have been proposed as certainly true, even though they have not been the object of a specific and formally infallible definition." Although they are not expressed with the certitude of infallibility, they retain an "absolute and obligatory" nature as official pronouncements of the pope and bishops speaking "consistently, consciously, and deliberately" in solidarity. These teachings may come through the ordinary universal teaching[60] that comes via papal encyclical,[61] synodal teaching,[62] the decree of a Vatican congregation with approval of the pope, or an ecumenical council.[63] Pilarczyk offers that "the responsibility of the bishops to proclaim the Gospel and the prohibition of deliberately taking human life" are two examples of such teaching.[64]

Notice that while bodies like the papacy and ecumenical councils might define infallible truths, they do not always or necessarily speak in that register. They might also pronounce ordinary universal teaching or teach at the third level, which is ordinary, non-infallible teaching. Ordinary, non-infallible teaching includes teachings that "the church proposes as true, though not defined as infallible and not necessarily unchangeable." Pilarczyk points to Church teachings about labour and politics as examples of those that, while "not infallible, [are] the fruit of mature consideration and reflection on the part of theologians and church authority, and enjoy the regular guidance from the Holy Spirit which Christ promised to his church."[65]

The levels of Magisterial teaching therefore follow a regression of epistemic stability that begins with the inerrant and definitive truths at the confessional core of faith and belief, and then moves toward

less definitive propositional statements about socio-moral and
political life, as such constituting more "official positions" than
"required beliefs."[66]

In the popular press, and even in some academic writing, Magisterial teachings at all three levels are referred to as doctrine and dogma
without notice of any difference between the two terms. Doctrine and
dogma are Magisterial teachings, and the relative meaning of these
terms is tied to the level of teaching that they represent. *Doctrine*
refers simply to a teaching. Some doctrines are defined through Magisterial pronouncements, but others, like that of the cross, have not
been formally defined although they are quite important within
Catholicism. *Dogma* is doctrine that has been taught solemnly as a
fundamentally irrefutable and infallible definition on an aspect of the
Catholic faith.[67] Rejection of dogma constitutes heresy and thus
places the holder of such a view outside the believing Church. While
McBrien suggests that the Church has used normative statements
since the apostolic age,[68] "it was not until the eighteenth century that
the term *dogma* acquired its present meaning." The First Vatican
Council (1869–70) codified the notion of dogma under the following
conditions: "(1) It must be contained in Sacred Scripture or in the
post-biblical Tradition of the Church, and as such considered part of
God's revelation; (2) It must be explicitly proposed by the Church as
a divinely revealed object of belief; and (3) This must be done either
in a solemn decree or in the Church's ordinary, universal teaching.
Such teachings are 'irreformable' and are not subject to review by
a higher authority in the Church."[69] Dogmas may be revised and
expressed with greater clarity throughout the living history of the
Church, although the kernel of truth within them and the meaning
that these dogmas have to the faith of the Church remains constant.
Revisions to dogmas are therefore only clarifications and greater
developments of their meanings. The Catholic notion of dogma is
therefore that it is "a true word, but it is never the last word that can
be said about a mystery of faith."[70]

While the papacy and membership of an ecumenical council or
synod obviously represent an exclusive Magisterium, McBrien
observes that the broadest understanding of Magisterial authority in
fact "belongs to the whole Church as the People of God,"[71] since the
Catholic laity, through the sacrament of Baptism, "participates in the
threefold mission of Christ as Priest, Prophet, and King" in their
ecclesial membership. A lay Magisterium is rarely, if ever, seriously

considered in the modern Church, but this situation does not mean *today's* Magisterium did not descend through an historical process of change and development. In the Church's history there is evidence of a plural Magisterium that "is not linked exclusively with the office of the bishop or superior in the New Testament."[72] McBrien writes that during the apostolic period there were "many different charisms and ministries involved in the teaching process," among which were included "apostles, prophets, evangelists, teachers (*didaskaloi* = theologians), and administrators."[73] The diversity of Magisterial roles and functions within the Church during this period was not conducive to a conflict-free environment, however, and McBrien notes that such diversity was the source of "many tensions among prophets, teachers, and pastors."[74] McBrien writes that the role of the prophets slowly declined and eventually vanished from official recognition as the third century progressed, and that the bishops gradually assumed superiority over the teachers. These developments were no doubt due to the desire for the unity of belief and community among the Christian churches during a period where many prominent heresies threatened to divide and possibly destroy the Church.[75] The teachers did not submit quietly, although political expediency and solidarity in response to diverse heresies solidified the role of the bishop as a unifying figure by the end of the fourth century.[76]

The idea and practice of a plural Magisterium did not end there, however. The lay Magisterium re-emerged during the medieval period when prominent lay persons emerged as academics and temporal political rulers who were able to regain some of the influence that earlier had been assumed by the episcopacy. *Magisterium* here was understood as a dual partnership between those who possessed authority by virtue of its attachment to their offices, and those who were authoritative on Church matters by virtue of their intellectual competence. St Thomas Aquinas writes of distinctly parallel *Magisteria* that bear referential synecdoche to the chairs (Latin: *cathedrae*) in which authority was vested: the bishop's Cathedral chair (*Magisterium cathedrae pastoralis*) and the theologian's professional-academic chair (*Magisterium cathedrae magistralis*).[77] The bishop's authority rested on his consecrated office as head of a diocese, while the theologian's authority rested on scholarly expertise.[78]

"In the late Middle Ages and in early modern times," writes Avery (now Cardinal) Dulles, "university faculties of theology exercised a true Magisterium, rendering ecclesiastically recognized judgments as to the orthodoxy or heterodoxy of new opinions."[79] Religious orders shared some influence with an increasingly strengthening papacy, and theologians were even included in the Church's ecumenical (Constance, 1414–18) and general (Basle, 1431–49) councils. This influence was interrupted, however, by the Protestant Reformation. During this period of institutional upheaval and fracture in the Western Christian Church, "the juridical and clerical character of councils and of the *Magisterium* generally was underscored. Teaching became less a matter of insight and enlightenment and more a matter of the imposition of approved formulae. The Church divided according to those who taught [*ekklesia docens*] (and presumably no longer had to learn) and those who learned [*ekklesia discens*] (and presumably had nothing to do with teaching)."[80]

This rigid distinction between *ekklesia docens* and *ekklesia discens* as ecclesial sub-populations continued past the Reformation period and well into the twentieth century. Canon 107 of the 1917 *Code of Canon Law*, for example, asserts that "by divine institution clergy are distinct from laity in the Church."[81] Franchise in the Church was limited to elites in administrative positions, while the remainder of the Church was to exercise its role in subordination to them. Pope Pius X offers a famous formulation: "The Church is by essence an unequal society, that is, a society comprised of two classes of persons, the pastors and the flock, those who occupy a rank in the different degrees of the hierarchy and the multitude of the faithful ... The one duty of the multitude is to allow themselves to be led, and, like a docile flock, to follow the pastors."[82] In this model the laity was to pray, pay, and obey.

Over the course of the twentieth century, though, an expanded role for the laity was recognized within the Church, so much so that the Second Vatican Council eschewed a distinction between clergy and laity that mirrors "superiority/inferiority" and "active/passive" in favour of describing complementary roles:[83] "In the Church there is a diversity of ministry but a unity of mission."[84] Moreover, Nilson remarks, the Council declared that "while the ordained and the laity differ, each is necessary to the mission of the Church and so they must cooperate with one another, indeed, serve one another for the good of the Church and the world."[85] Most importantly, as Nilson continues, the Council recognized that "[t]he mission of the Church does not rest on the shoulders of the ordained alone."[86] While the Church's constitution has changed since Pius X's reign, though, the post-conciliar social norms and administrative structures have struggled to keep pace: "What is proper to the laity, however, excludes them from participation in the governance of the Church in their own right, since the code [of canon law] links governance to the sacrament of orders. According to canon 129 [of the 1983 *Code of Canon Law*], the ordained are able (*habiles*) to exercise power, while the laity may only cooperate in the exercise of power in the Church ('*cooperari possunt in exercito potestatis*'). As James Coriden notes, this restriction is not a matter of divine law but of mutable human law in the Church."[87]

The continued application of the *docens/discens* distinction to distinguish sub-populations within the Church is not helpful insofar as it continues to use the language of hierarchy and thus to confuse *who* teaches and learns within the Church with *how* it teaches and learns *as a whole*. In this respect, theologian Margaret O'Gara observes that Frederick Crowe makes a more helpful "contrast between the teaching Church and the learning Church" that is "not as between two groups, but as between two *processes* in which the whole Church must engage."[88] Within that paradigm, the question thus becomes one of discerning new descriptions of roles for the Magisterium and the laity as they have a part in developing the Church. In Crowe's words, the Catholic Church has "laid so much stress on the teaching Church – and this is not as a function related to and integrated with a learning function, but as an office belonging to certain people – that we have not attended to the learning function."[89]

O'Gara stresses that the learning Church is an important aspect of Catholicism's historical development, as the truths of revelation have developed "through a process of inquiry which takes time." She follows Richard McCormick's thesis that as part of the learning process inherent in Christian life, dissent is not a luxury or "personal right" exercised by contrarian or selfish individuals, but rather is "only the possible outcome of a respectful and docile personal reflection on noninfallible teaching. Such reflection is the very condition of progress in understanding in the Church. Dissent, therefore, must be viewed and respected as a part of that total approach through which we learn."[90] O'Gara continues along this developmental course, concluding that "dissent is the way that the Church learned earlier in its history that it needed to change its teachings about slavery, religious liberty, the matter and form of some sacraments, the use of historical-critical methods in biblical study, etc. If Roman Catholics had not raised questions about the teaching they heard from the Magisterium in earlier times, the learning finally achieved would not have occurred."[91]

Sullivan affirms that broader definitions of *Magisterium* exist in the Church's past, but he observes that through its historical development the term has arrived at a point where it is almost exclusively equated with the pope, curia, and bishops. Besides this fact, an "even more recent development, is that the term *Magisterium* has come to mean not only the teaching function of the hierarchy, but also the hierarchy itself as the bearer of this office."[92] Teaching authority is thus subsumed within the administrative and juridical office of the curia and episcopacy. While this relatively restricted understanding is true to a large degree, it is also incomplete because it fails to recognize the complexity of ecclesial authority.

McBrien writes that theologians in the modern day have the duty to refine and raise questions about the formulations of doctrines and dogmas: "Without the possibility of raising questions about the meaning and the suitability of certain dogmatic expressions theologians could never make their full contribution to the faith of the whole Church."[93] At the same time, though, he maintains that he is not suggesting there should be a dual Magisterium of bishops and theologians in the Church. Sullivan likewise discounts arguments for restoring a dual Magisterium on the basis that it might create the unwanted impression of "a rival pastoral authority" in the Church.[94] Theologian Ladislas Örsy, while agreeing with Sullivan's conclusion,[95] quite skilfully suggests that Magisterial bodies should be aware of their role within the Church and should not attempt to speak for "the whole Church," but rather should emphasize that their statements come from the office of the bishop of a particular diocese or from a specific Vatican Congregation; thus both the statements' authors and those who read them will recognize that although these clerical offices are important, "new insights into the mysteries require other qualifications than ordination."[96] The whole Church, after all, is its own Magisterium,[97] and "theologians, therefore, are not theologians on the basis of a *missio canonica*, but on the basis of their baptism: they are theologians as members of a believing and thinking 'people of God.'"[98]

The fact that there are reservations about resurrecting and transposing the medieval notion of a dual Magisterium into modern times does not mean, however, that the role of the theologian is limited to clarifying and affirming papal, curial, and episcopal announcements.

Rather, the theologian is in an ecclesial station where he or she might, from time to time, disagree with the clerical Magisterium as an inevitable result of his or her contribution to the Church:

> [If] theologians are to serve the Church not only by explaining and defending its official teachings but also by recommending better ways of expressing and of understanding some of those teachings then it is entirely possible that theologians will, on occasion, find themselves at odds with other theologians, ecclesiastical leaders, and laity who just as sincerely believe that the official teachings are perfectly acceptable as formulated and as traditionally interpreted. If the theologian's view happens to conflict with that of the pope or bishops, the theologian's view may take on the character of dissent. Such dissent is almost inevitable over the long run of the Church's history and particularly in periods of great change.[99]

As theologians are charged with the task of clarifying and evaluating the expression of revealed truth, certain aspects of their work will bring them to the boundaries of orthodoxy because they inevitably evaluate doctrine and dogma, argue over the very meaning of those terms, and also argue over whether certain pronouncements qualify as doctrine, dogma, or neither.[100] "Development of dogma," writes McBrien, "goes hand-in-hand with some measure of dissent."[101] Over the course of Church history, the works of certain dissenting theologians have even become exemplars of paradigmatic shifts in Church thought, including St Thomas Aquinas, Marie-Joseph Lagrange, Henri de Lubac, Karl Rahner, Yves Congar, and John Courtney Murray.[102]

Although the dissenters in that list are all individuals, there is no necessary cause to say that all dissent emerges primarily from within an individual, or that groups of dissenters are simply followers after the fact of an individual's dissent. Whether dissent is a primarily individual action or whether it emerges from the spirit within a group is an interesting question best left to another place; but for the purposes of this volume I focus on the individual because that is where many of the arguments, justifications, and disciplinary actions regarding dissent within the Church tend to focus. The point in Catholic teaching upon which many dissenters rely for their justification is that of conscience, which the Church expresses in terms of its origin in the individual person. Agreements or disagreements on what conscience is and can perform have great weight in arguments about dissent, and so for that reason a brief exposition of that concept within Catholic teaching is required before it is possible to speak directly about how the Church frames dissent itself.

CONSCIENCE

The subject of conflicting notions of authority and truth invariably leads to the question of how one is to adjudicate between officially authoritative teachings and other views that partially or completely disagree with the Magisterium. Catholicism understands conscience as the focal point where evaluative judgments are considered and made concerning the application of authoritative teaching to an individual's life. Contrary to some popular misconceptions, the Catholic idea of conscience is not *post facto* remorse for misdeeds. It instead primarily refers to the relationship between God and the moral agent, wherefrom moral responses are discerned and actions prescribed in accord with divine law. Church teaching is an important consideration in the conscience, but does not necessarily represent its entire range of information; hence exercising conscience cannot simply be defined as the act of mirroring Magisterial teaching. Rather, a moral agent experiences conscience by weighing the Magisterium's teaching authority against the moral authority of his or her relationship with God and divine law. In broad strokes this is the stuff of justifying, acting on, and evaluating one's decisions to assent to or dissent from Magisterial teaching.

The documents of the Second Vatican Council provide important insights into what conscience is, and into the challenges that a person faces when confronting moral decisions that require an informed conscience. The Church's "Pastoral Constitution / *Gaudium et Spes*" (GS) describes conscience as the aspect of a person which contains "a law which he has not laid upon himself but which he must obey."[103] This law is not the product of any religious or secular human institution, but is found deep within a person's spiritual being. The Christian moral subject therefore encounters the most profound relationship with the divine and an enhanced vision of self in his or her conscience: "For man [sic] has in his heart a law inscribed by God. His dignity lies in observing this law, and by it he will be judged. His conscience is man's most secret core, and his sanctuary. There he is alone with God whose voice echoes in his depths."[104]

In an important respect, the Christian conscience represents a spiritual norm that is prior to human society. The highest forms of Christian moral decision-making are thus found in a clearly informed conscience, which is philosophically superior to reasoning that appeals to ecclesial or secular norms for their own sake. The divine relationship in the informed conscience is the means through which the Christian subject "recognizes the demands of the divine law" and realizes a spiritual and moral obligation to direct all activity toward knowledge of and relationship with "God, who is his last end."[105] In order to respect and facilitate the development of that relationship, the Council recognizes that the moral subject "must not be forced to act contrary to his conscience. Nor must he be prevented from acting according to his conscience, especially in religious matters."[106] By virtue of both GS and DH (the "Declaration on Religious Liberty / *Dignitatis Humanae*"), every Catholic arguably has the agency with which to exercise some ecclesial franchise irrespective of his or her ordained or lay vocation.

While the directives of conscience might not always match Magisterial teaching, the fact of conflicting interests does not diminish the Magisterium's relevance. While a Christian moral subject might not always follow what the Church directs, he or she will have made the best decision if Magisterial teaching has been appropriately weighed in the process: "In the formation of their consciences the faithful must pay careful attention to the sacred and certain teaching of the Church."[107] Ignorance of the Magisterium and the role of the whole Church in its journey toward discovering divine truth certainly degrades the quality of one's decision and overlooks the communal and ecclesial aspects of encountering and understanding God. The Council writes: "[T]he Church is, by the will of Christ, the teacher of truth. It is her duty to proclaim and teach with authority the truth which is Christ and, at the same time, to declare and confirm by her authority the principles of the moral order which spring from human nature itself."[108] The Christian person must respect the Magisterium but not confuse its teachings for his or her own moral agency and responsibility. From a minimalist perspective, therefore, the moral subject must always at least look to Church teaching for guidance before undertaking the step of making a personal decision.

As Christianity inevitably synthesizes the sacred with the profane as the totality of God's creation, the Council recognizes that lay people, in "carrying out this mission of the Church, exercise their apostolate therefore in the world as well as in the Church, in the temporal order as well as in the spiritual." The sacred and profane are "distinct," yet "nevertheless so closely linked in God's plan" that the Christian conscience is singular. A person, according to the Council, though "at one and the same time a believer and a citizen of the world, has only a single conscience, a Christian conscience; it is by this that he must be guided continually in both domains."[109] The Council's "Dogmatic Constitution on the Church / *Lumen Gentium*" (LG) directs, however, that an awareness of the domain one is in is essential for making decisions: "The faithful should learn to distinguish carefully between the rights and the duties which they have as belonging to the Church and those which fall to them as members of human society. They will strive to unite the two harmoniously, remembering that in every temporal affair they are to be guided by a Christian conscience, since not even in temporal business may any human activity be withdrawn from God's dominion."[110] In addition to its meaning for ecclesial franchise, conscience also represents the place where sacred and secular influences are integrated.

At the heart of synthesizing the complex triad of a personal encounter with God, ecclesial norms, and other relevant situational data is the philosophical tension between integrating subjective and objective aspects of morality into conscience. Theologian Charles Curran states that the subjective aspect of conscience may be measured in terms of the moral subject's sincerity: "A sincere conscience is in accord with [the agent's] sincerely held convictions," whereas "an insincere conscience is not in accord with [the agent's] real self." Likewise, the objective aspect of conscience may be measured in terms of its accord with objective reality (i.e., truth or error).[111] As each of the subjective and objective aspects contains two broadly conceived possibilities, when these concepts are multiplied together in the course of making a decision, four logical possibilities emerge. The agent's conscience might be (1) sincere and correct, (2) sincere and incorrect, (3) insincere and correct, or (4) insincere and incorrect. The balance between sincerity and truth in each situation and the permutations of possible outcomes underscore the complexity of such decisions. Catholic tradition has favoured the subjective aspect of conscience since even before it gave the same prominence "to the dignity and role of the person" that it does today; however, decisions of conscience remain serious because the agent must follow his or her conscience even though it might be in error.[112] Thus, although sincerity has priority, sincerity alone does not always or necessarily purify culpability, nor does it diminish the consequences that result from error.

In addition to the difficulties inherent in decisions of conscience, there are also exegetical difficulties that arise from a reading of the Second Vatican Council documents themselves. As Linda Hogan notes, some of the concept's intrinsic problems, which existed before the Council convened, were further obscured in its documents:

> Many of these ambiguities existed in theology of conscience from the beginning. They go to the heart of the problem of the role of conscience in Christian life. Is conscience about following church law or about determining for oneself what is right and good? Is conscience about discernment or obedience? How can conscience err if it is the voice of God? What is the relationship between individual and institutional moral authority? These are questions that Catholics need help in answering. Unfortunately, the documents of Vatican II did little to remedy the confusions. In fact they further complicated the issue.[113]

For instance, divine law and institutional Church (Magisterial) law are present in the Council documents as competing accounts. DH suggests a legislative conscience because it "declares that 'the highest norm of human life is divine law'" and that the faithful person, including any member of the Magisterium, "sees and recognizes the demands of divine law through conscience."[114] Hogan observes, however, that GS points in a different direction, suggesting that married couples are to "conform their conscience to the law of God." They, the document continues, "must be ruled by their conscience – and conscience ought to be in accord with the law of God in the teaching authority of the Church, which is the authentic interpreter of divine law."[115] According to Hogan, "[h]ere the role of conscience is identified with (and reduced to?) implementing Church teaching. Its activity in ethical discernment is limited to obeying the teaching authority of the church."[116] The Council documents thus obscure the relationship between divine and Church law in conscience, because they present these concepts not as integrative aspects of decision-making, but rather as competing accounts.[117] The question of whether conscience is to be a conformist or legislative concept thus remains open.

Similarly ambiguous is the question of whether conscience is meant to describe *discernment* or *obedience*. Hogan notes that in GS it "is not at all clear how we understand the phrase 'objectively right.' We are given no guidance regarding whether the 'objective moral order' is composed of very specific, concrete universal norms or whether it consists of more general values. The latter would allow for a significant amount of moral pluralism ... The former would rule this out."[118] Hogan again follows Fuchs and suggests that an understanding of conscience as a set of principles with which to discern correct action in a situation is preferable to understanding it as obedience to a fixed and externally imposed institutional law. Such an understanding "is not a ready-made and only passively accepted 'law' but rather a law that is discovered actively by us men and women and in human (and ecclesiastical) society and is found in this way."[119] The universalistic understanding, because it does not distinguish "between objective law and concrete solutions,"[120] limits "moral discernment to informing oneself of the teaching of the Church on each and every moral matter and implementing it without question. The primary work of conscience would simply be to obey."[121] In this way as well, the Council documents obscure the question of whether conscience should be in accord with the Magisterium or if it is to be the authoritative interpreter of divine law. Conscience as such remains an imperfectly understood concept both in its propositional form and in the way the Church has applied it since the Second Vatican Council.

The question of whether conscience emphasizes discernment or obedience raises the further question of how much moral-political agency an individual person has with respect to Church teaching. What degree and kind of obedience, assent, respect, or deference, for instance, does a Catholic moral agent owe to ordinary teaching? And what legislative or adjudicative power do Magisterial offices have in institutions such as Catholic families, schools, or hospitals? The Church's social teaching on subsidiarity suggests a line of Catholic thought that prefers the maximum amount of individual freedom in matters where the individual is most competent, with the justification that such freedom from constraint stimulates the individual's initiative and promotes the dignity of the human person. The principle of subsidiarity is intended to prevent centralist, bureaucratic, monopolizing organizations and powers from usurping that which is rightly the responsibility of individuals or smaller social units. Pope Pius XI's encyclical "On Reconstruction of the Social Order / *Quadragesimo Anno*" is the Church's touchstone on this topic: "Just as it is gravely wrong to take from individuals what they can accomplish by their own initiative and industry and give it to the community," he writes, "so also it is an injustice and at the same time a grave evil and disturbance of right order to assign to a greater and higher association what lesser and subordinate organizations can do."[122] For instance, on the subject of Catholic Education the Second Vatican Council establishes the primacy of parents and families over the larger institutions of schools. The Council maintains that parents are free to organize the form of religious life in their own households and to raise their children in accord with their decisions,[123] and the family's primacy should not be supplanted nor should educational interventions take place without "due considerations ... for the wishes of parents."[124] This norm is congruent with subsidiarity.

The Pontifical Council for Justice and Peace proposes that in civil society there should be a reciprocal relationship based on service between those who govern and those who are governed. "Governing" and "being governed" in terms of subsidiarity can be thought of less as being based on rigidly hierarchical distinctions and more as being unique but interdependent duties of social contribution. Governing bodies, especially, are to have their missions reformed in terms of enabling individual initiatives rather than hoarding an excess of power to themselves: "The principle of subsidiarity protects people from abuses by higher-level social authority and calls on these same authorities to help individuals and intermediate groups to fulfill their duties. This principle is imperative because every person, family and intermediate group has something original to offer to the community."[125]

Interestingly, the Council does not raise the question of how the Christian person is to direct this attitude into civil channels without it spilling into his or her approach to ecclesial structures, thus possibly dividing the self. Moreover, the application of subsidiarity to Catholic educational institutions, and the conceptual connection between subsidiarity and conscience, are also left unaddressed. Subsidiarity is considered a "social teaching" and directed at what the Church terms "civil society" and is therefore not necessarily prescriptive for ecclesial society; however, as it prescribes the proper relations between state, communities, and individuals, its relevance to the ecclesial life of Christian persons remains a pertinent and open question. Distinguishing Christian moral responses that are unique to only religious or civil realms is a difficult if not impossible task, especially in light of Church teaching that calls for harmony between the religious and temporal orders.[126]

How the moral agent is to reconcile the conceptual chasm that separates these two contexts presents a confusing and potentially frustrating problem that (in theory at least) places the integrity of the complete Christian person as moral agent in flux. If a minimalist interpretation of subsidiarity were to be imagined in the ecclesial realm, however, it might suggest that, depending on the level of teaching from the Magisterium and the response required from the Christian moral agent to this teaching, it could be the imperative of the entire People of God to recognize appropriate levels of control over certain decisions. By subsidiarity, teaching authority would not always extend to applied authority.

Clearly, the ways in which Catholic theology describes individual moral judgment in the conscience and positions smaller groups in proper social relation to larger groups leave many questions and even possibilities open for reframing the theoretical *status quo* on how disagreement is situated within the Church at large. The relationship that dogma and doctrine have with the norms of conscience and the principle of subsidiarity suggests that within Catholic life, including Catholic Education, there are many possibilities for productive disagreement that would not necessarily cross the boundaries of what is required for the faith. So what would it mean to disagree within the bounds of such agreement?

DISSENT

Interestingly, a discussion of dissent in Catholic theology can begin with considering what it means "to assent," and to this end one finds that in Catholicism more than one kind of assent is possible. Philip Kaufman observes in the documents of the Second Vatican Council a "careful distinction between assent due to infallible teaching of pope or council and *obsequium*, due to other hierarchical teaching. Assent is an act of faith in a statement as true; *obsequium* involves only a response of submission or respect."[127] The act of assent is associated with infallible teaching because subscription to dogmas at the core of the faith is required for membership within the Church. The Nicene Creed requires assent, since without belief that Jesus is the Son of God and at once both fully human and fully divine, one cannot legitimately call oneself Catholic. "On the other hand," writes Kaufman, "*obsequium* is a vague word that can mean compliance, respect, or deference, something quite different from *assent*,"[128] and this is the response, as opposed to an explicit and outright act of faith, that is due to ordinary non-infallible teaching. In the act of assent a believer becomes or affirms that he or she is "one with the believing Church: holding firm to a doctrine," while in the act of *obsequium* one's mind becomes "one with the searching Church, working for clarification."[129]

The difference between *assent* and *obsequium* mirrors the requirement for one to recognize dogma as the solemnly defined core of faith and doctrine as the official and important yet subordinate remainder. The distinction is perhaps best demonstrated in the responses due to each. While doctrine requires respect and a position of prominence *qua* Church teaching, it does not require the same act of belief dogma requires. The Canon Law Society of America describes *obsequium* as "a basic attitude of religious assent based on a presumption of truth and good judgment on the part of the teaching authority ... However, since teachings are included which are not infallible and can be erroneous, the principles of pursuit of truth and the primacy of conscience still come into play. In other words, dissent is possible because the teachers mentioned in the canon can be and *de facto* have been mistaken."[130]

One might posit two kinds of relationship between *ekklesia docens* and *ekklesia discens* as a helpful means of understanding the kind of authoritative and faithful responses that are required by dogma and doctrine. In the case of dogma, a rigid distinction between the teaching and learning churches holds with greater ease, because in this case the Magisterium assumes its authority as teacher to communicate something to the rest of the Church. (However, this formula warrants the qualification that the Magisterium must be in the position to learn if it is to develop the dogma, which, furthermore, in some cases might be an expression of what the whole Church already believes anyway.) In the case of non-infallible teaching, however, the distinction between these two aspects of the Church becomes more problematic, because in this domain it is even more important to recall that the Magisterium is also part of the learning Church, that the non-Magisterial Church exercises franchise through conscience, and that Magisterial authority to teach does not supersede or even replace personal authority to decide.

How Dissent Is to Be Expressed

While the above discussion of dissent has exposed some of the difficulties within the Church and some potential benefits that the content of dissenting views can contribute, a common concern relates to the ways in which dissent is expressed. Dissent is by its nature a moral decision where one must weigh one's disagreement against the response to Church teaching that the Church requires. O'Gara observes that the theoretical distinction between faithful assent and *obsequium* in Roman Catholic theology is often overlooked in practice, meaning that the same response that is due to infallible dogma is often assumed to be required for non-infallible ordinary teaching.

The treatment of dissenting theologians during Pope John Paul II's reign resumed an historical pattern of juridical censure, and even influenced a theoretical movement that supports the administrative practice of protecting Christian unity by reprimanding and silencing those who challenge orthodoxy. The supporters of this movement, writes O'Gara, "emphasize that dissent, especially dissent by theologians who teach in a Roman Catholic institution, can cause scandal to believers." For example, she points to the writing of Joseph Cardinal Ratzinger (now Pope Benedict XVI) as an example of a curial official "who has drawn attention to his theoretical hesitations about dissent by a theologian."[131] In Ratzinger's view, the act of dissent represents a selfish display of arrogance that can only contaminate and fracture the Church: "A [dissenting] person who teaches in the name of the Church is taking what is basically a personal dissent and exaggerating its importance and its damage by propagating it." Furthermore, while dissent might be the inevitable outcome of certain personal encounters with Church dogma and doctrine, Ratzinger's writing draws a clear distinction between the institutional Church's public beliefs and the views of private dissenting individuals, and maintains that individual views should not be expressed publicly.[132]

In an important way, the epistemic and political value distinction between the public institution and the private views of individual Catholics also mirrors the distinction in ecclesial franchise between the teaching and the learning Church. Whether a teaching is considered the solemnly certain truth of dogma or simply the official truth of doctrine, the Magisterium expects that the rest of the Church will understand, affirm, and follow it as the official public view. The distinction between assent and *obsequium* is thus reduced to triviality here if *ecclesia discens* is constructed as the non-Magisterial group which is simply expected to respond with consistent affirmation of and conformity to the Magisterial *ecclesia docens*.[133]

The place of the theologian, or of theologically rigorous views that challenge the official views within this relationship, likewise faces confinement to private or restricted internal dialogues. Neither appeals to academic freedom nor concerns for free speech are considered sufficient reason to allow dissent within the Church. These appeals are, in fact, considered erroneous for attempting to translate norms from secular civil society into ecclesial life. By this logic, Catholicism's academic aspect is therefore subordinated to the Church's administrative and juridical offices. "The Church," according to Dulles, "cannot accommodate the same kind of ideological pluralism that is acceptable in a secular state or university" because it is a fundamentally different organization that, unlike those in secular civil society, "is committed to [a] substantive set of beliefs about the ultimate nature of reality." In contrast, Dulles characterizes the modern secular state as "a community of people willing to live together under the same laws even though they may disagree fundamentally in their philosophies and theologies" and the university as "a community of scholars committed to adhere to certain methods of investigation and communication, but not necessarily sharing any common convictions about the way things are."[134]

Where authority in civil society is invested in elected or appointed officials and authority at the university lies in bodies of knowledge that are open for debate, authority in the Church is primarily that which is invested in bishops as representatives of the Church's apostolic tradition. "The popes and bishops," according to Dulles, "... enjoy authority by virtue of their status or position in the church," and respect for the authority of their declarations is not necessarily due by virtue "of their personal wisdom and prudence" but rather "because of their sacramental ordination and the office they hold."[135] Theologians, by contrast, even with their academic credentials and professional competence, only exercise ecclesial authority within the limited prerogatives assigned them by the Magisterium. While the Magisterium can and often does attempt to exercise authority with the persuasive language of theology and many of its members are presumed to be theologically competent, the warrant for their authority is broader than the non-Magisterial theologian's because it also rests on the privilege of consecration. However, the act of "doing" or studying theology is not limited to those who have official sanction to teach it in the name of the Church, and so any "unlicensed" lay or clerical person can still do research in the discipline.

Likewise, free speech as it exists in some secular nation-states does not exist within the governing and Magisterial structures of the Catholic Church, because the two institutions are underwritten by different conceptions of freedom. The liberal state admits and promotes the "liberties of free citizens to argue in public for their own distinctive views," whereas "Catholics freely bind themselves to an authority over matters of faith and morals vested in the Bishop of Rome."[136] The difference in freedom of speech, therefore, is that the state permits its citizens the negative freedom from coercion, political conformity, and other types of interference in their own conceptions of the good life. The Catholic Church, on the other hand, asks that its members place themselves in relation to an authority under God that requires obedience to certain principles and teachings in order to achieve spiritual freedom in salvation. This is the positive freedom to achieve a Christian ideal.[137]

In addition to the difficulties that the Catholic Church has with transposing concepts of secular academic freedom and free speech into ecclesial structures, the CDF also refutes the appeal to individual conscience as a warrant for free speech and justification for dissent. While the Congregation recognizes that an individual's act of moral judgment is separable from the act of teaching Christian truth, it considers the former to be incompatible with accommodating the revealed Truth of the Word of God into the Church as a whole because it sidesteps apostolic tradition.[138] According to the CDF, the destructive excess of appeals to conscience as justification for dissent lies in its potential disregard for the Church's history, its community, and the norms of faith and morals it has invested much effort in developing. To appeal to the subjective conscience as the supreme moral arbiter without considering the objective norms of the Church and its life in the world thus signifies relativism. In this sense, the dismissal of appeals to conscience carries much force.

However, in cases where an informed conscience considers Church law, is at pains to be sensitive to its communal life, but nonetheless still arrives at a dissenting viewpoint, the Congregation's proscription seems to confuse the respectful disclosure of an epistemically rigorous persuasive argument with a baseless appeal to the self. The counter-argument referring to apostolic succession also does not explain the history of changed teachings in the Church – many of which were prefigured by dissenting theologians (see note 102, this chapter).

In fact, the Magisterium's consideration of the question of whether one might dissent from certain aspects of Catholic teaching is not closed. The National Conference of Bishops in the United States admits that theologians might publicly dissent from non-infallible Magisterial teaching if the dissenting act conforms to certain formal criteria: "Only if the reasons are serious and well-founded, if the manner of dissent does not question or impugn the teaching authority of the Church and is such as not to give scandal."[139] The questions of what constitutes scandal, who is in a position to judge what is scandalous, and whether on certain issues the Church ought to be scandalized remain open to interpretation in this formulation. Similarly, the German bishops provide their own set of criteria that "(1) One must have striven seriously to attach positive value to the teaching in question and to appropriate it personally; (2) One must seriously ponder whether one has the theological expertise to disagree responsibly with ecclesiastical authority; and (3) One must examine one's conscience, for possible conceit, presumptuousness, or selfishness."[140] The German bishops' criteria for dissent are more explicitly stringent than the Americans', especially given the challenge that their second criterion poses to someone with a legitimate reason to dissent but no relevant theological expertise. *Expertise* is a broad term, though, and so it remains possible that its condition might be satisfied if one were to perform a rigorous reading and exegesis of the Church's public documents or to consult with a recognized expert.

William Cardinal Levada also discusses a possible misuse of the word *dissent* to describe academic experimentation: "Sometimes the word dissent is used – improperly, in my view – to describe the work of theological research and of scholars who are exploring the frontiers of some issues with hypothetical, speculative, and hence tentative, conclusions. It seems to me that such explorations do not properly fall within the area of dissent when they are presented as hypothetical and not as pastoral norms which can be followed in practice (for example, in the moral order) or as substitutes for the accepted understanding of church dogmas."[141] Levada's view upholds a strict distinction between the abstracted world of academic theology and the real world of the Catholic ecclesial institution, and from this distinction he maintains that the norms for exploring possibilities beyond established conventions are necessarily different. Michael

Novak presents a similar view that upholds the rights of theologians to experiment within the abstract laboratory of academic thought, writing, and discussion, and to thus explore some paths that non-theologians would not be able to explore. Theologians are qualified to make such explorations, and whether they arrive at truthful or erroneous outcomes, their work provides an important service that evaluates possibilities for Christian life: "Theologians need room to err. That is why we do not base our lives on the teachings of theologians. Their errors, despite themselves, can nonetheless be fruitful for the body of the Catholic people."[142]

The instrumental service Novak describes, however, maintains the model by which the Church's pastors retain control of integrating theology into practice before most lay Catholics have access to it. Levada's and Novak's formulations prefer dissent in the abstract to dissent as a way of Christian practice. Some views sympathetic with Platonic epistemology might suggest that this model is an appropriate means of exercising caution in moving from theory to practice. A critique that is sceptical about Platonic epistemologies might, however, suggest that allowance in the abstract provides only the illusion that dissent is possible and meaningful without actually binding the institution to any public commitment. Moreover, there seems to be little, if any, allowance for dissenting ideas that might emerge from their prior conception in practice.

The distinction between what is appropriate public and private expression of belief is a major point of contention in the debate about dissent in the Church. The institutional Church prefers that persons hold dissent within their individual selves or express it in channels that presume it to be a personal matter between themselves and the larger Church. Ostensibly the Church is most comfortable with this practice because it poses a miniscule threat, or none at all, to a standing preference for doctrinal and communal integrity. One of the Church's primary concerns is its institutional credibility in proclaiming truth and not misleading the public body of Christ; and so it is naturally suspicious of anything that challenges this truth, because to reverse or revise an absolute statement might embarrass or fracture the institution. Still, in spite of the fact that academic debate about the proper role of dissent persists within the Church, the administrative treatment of dissenters who take their disagreements beyond the officially preferred channels suggests that public dissent is not allowed at all.

These comments on the Church's de-emphasis, privatization, and censure of dissent might encourage those who feel that dissenters threaten the Church, and arouse feelings of resignation in those who favour an increase in the quantity and quality of public dissent within the Church. However, the possibility that dissent might improve life in the Church mitigates such stances. As Dulles notes, "there may be occasions when the dissenter has the right, and even the conscientious obligation, to go public. If theologians such as Yves Congar and John Courtney Murray had not publicly manifested their disagreement with certain official teachings, it is far less likely that Vatican II, under their influence, would have adopted new positions on subjects such as ecumenism and religious freedom."[143] Moreover, as Richard McCormick points out, the dissenter might in fact be pointing the Church away from error and toward either truth or a richer expression of truth: "It is simply no response to object that dissent 'encourages dissent in others,'" because "if the teaching is inaccurate, that is what dissent should do."[144] The difficulty the Church experiences in coordinating conscience with the assent-*obsequium* and public-private distinctions therefore contributes to maintaining a problematic situation where the justifications for who might dissent become confused with the proper means of expressing it.

Changed Teachings

As troublesome as the Catholic Church's past and current dealings with dissenters have been, there is evidence that on many occasions throughout the course of its history the Church has been shaped by contributions from dissenters. Walter Principe lists several major examples of teachings that were "formerly taught as authoritative or authentic but later altered or changed, most often as the result of theological research and discussion."[145] Among the many changes Principe lists, a few famous examples are noteworthy.

The teaching that slavery was a normal element in the structure of society persisted from apostolic times until the nineteenth century, when Gregory XVI's 1839 bull "*In Supremo Apostolatus*" officially condemned the slave trade and Leo XIII's 1891 "*Rerum Novarum*," "while not speaking of slavery by name, should have made it clear that slavery was incompatible with universal and fundamental human rights."[146] Kaufman notes, however, that Leo's correction was so slow to gain ascendancy in the Church[147] "that the morality of slavery was still taught down to the middle of the [twentieth] century by some of the greatest names in Roman Catholic moral theology: Lehmkuhl, Prümmer, Merkelbach, Génicot, and Zalba."[148] It was only the Second Vatican Council which finally made a forceful condemnation of slavery,[149] although Kaufman states that in these documents "there was no hint that centuries of false teaching were being corrected."[150]

Among other teachings that changed during the Second Vatican Council was the acceptance of religious liberty for all persons. This change was a significant departure from earlier doctrine that there was no salvation outside the Catholic Church,[151] and Principe remarks that "[t]he magnitude of the change is clear from the strong opposition against acceptance during the Council." The Council was in fact, according to Principe, confirming Pius XII's earlier modification of that centuries-old teaching.[152]

The Church has also reversed its views on Thomas Aquinas. This reversal has great significance to modern Christian life because it "[recalls] that several times in the first half of the thirteenth century the Popes forbade lecturing on the works of Aristotle and his commentators at the University of Paris." Resistance to the ban was strong at the University, however, and as a result of Aristotle's widespread popularity in academia and the pope's inability to enforce the ban through repeated iterations, Aristotle was eventually accepted.[153] This event is of great significance in the history of Catholicism because Thomas was canonized as a Doctor of the Church and Thomism became the Church's leading intellectual paradigm up to the twentieth century.

The development of a reversal from the original Church teaching as a matter of popular or organized resistance was also significant, according to Kaufman, in the events that led to the Church's revision of its laws on usury. According to Kaufman, an organized constituency of bankers, trends of administrative centralization in the Church, and the revolutionary growth of commercialism during the sixteenth century were all influential human factors in reversing approximately fifteen hundred years of condemnation of interest-taking. This change in teaching seemingly was done to bring the official theological views of the Church up to date with its own evolving administrative practices: "Churchmen up to the highest level were deeply involved in financial transactions requiring [the] use of credit. Ecclesiastical organizations and individuals were involved in both borrowing and lending ... It became easy to justify financial methods so widely used by the church itself."[154]

Kaufman goes on to argue how the organized initiatives of bankers and an increasing realization within the curia of the advantages of banking to the modernization of the Church stand in sharp contrast to the position the present-day laity find themselves in *vis-à-vis* the Church on the non-reception of Paul VI's encyclical "On the Regulation of Birth / *Humanae Vitae*" (HV). As the married laity does not have the same corporate means of expressing its solidarity as the sixteenth-century banking lobby had, and the institution of the papacy sees no advantage in reversing the proclamation in that encyclical, the probability of that teaching being reversed in a similar way does not, on the surface at least, seem as likely. As Kaufman puts it: "So condemnation of usury, biblically based and supported for centuries by popes and councils, was reversed, while condemnation of contraception, with no basis in revelation, remained unchanged."[155]

The Church's history as a human institution, therefore, confirms Örsy's observation that "because all God's interventions have taken place in human history, they are embedded in human events, are perceived by human minds, and are communicated by human words and images. The human elements around divine things do change."[156] History shows that in the Catholic Church a desire for institutional continuity is given pride of place over morally imperative change,[157] and concern for maintaining the institutional *status quo* strongly minimizes the historical significance of dissent and doctrinal change. As far as institutional continuity is concerned, several questions remain open, according to Principe. For instance, by what authority and inspiration do curial officials change their views? If the answer lies in an appeal to the Holy Spirit, then Principe suggests that the question of how the Holy Spirit was involved in making the previous, erroneous judgment would "stand in need of proof," especially since a present-day correction might itself be found erroneous.[158] The problem that Catholics face is how to consider their moral decisions in a way that integrates personal intellectual rigour, an historically conditioned tradition of Church teachings, and the respect due to the Magisterium.

Justifications for Catholic Dissent

While the above list of doctrinal changes and reversals in the Catholic Church is by no means an exhaustive account of all the theological, ecclesiological, philosophical, and moral warrants for dissent in the Church, it provides a helpful foray into considering how dissent is possible. The criteria that the American and German bishops have given for dissent are helpful for considering what it is and how it is done, but do not describe in detail the epistemic warrants that are required for its justification. In this respect, Charles Curran provides a helpful syllabus of six general reasons that I will describe closely.

Curran's first reason follows the distinction between infallible and non-infallible teaching. He affirms that to be a Catholic one must subscribe to the infallible dogmas of the Church, but asserts that his sixfold rationale is legitimate and warranted in the case of non-infallible teachings of the ordinary Magisterium. Although non-infallible teaching requires "*obsequium religiosum* (religious submission or assent or respect) of intellect and will,"[159] and has an intrinsic "presumption in its favour," such teaching is nonetheless not immune from error and is, by definition, fallible.

Curran's second reason is "[h]istorical examples of erroneous teachings of the hierarchical Magisterium." These errors include those discussed above, and Curran also points to the fact that several influential theologians at the Second Vatican Council – "Congar, de Lubac, Murray and Rahner – had all experienced disciplinary action by church authorities. Thus history indicates that hierarchical teaching in the past has been erroneous."[160]

Curran's third reason is based upon epistemology. In complex situations such as moral judgments, "it is impossible to claim a certitude that excludes the possibility of error." Besides the formal criteria for certitude, Örsy raises questions about how universal a human truth can be given that social location has an influence upon morality.[161] For instance, although the Gregorian University in Rome does not represent the entirety of the Church and Catholic thought, Örsy notes that popes like Pius XII "relied very heavily on some professors" from that institution. Even though these scholars were undoubtedly very well accomplished, Örsy proposes that this reliance "represented a limited portion of Catholic thinking" and as such "raised again the question of how far a given papal pronouncement was the proclamation of Catholic doctrine universally held, and how far it represented the opinion of a theological school"[162] that was possibly more locally Roman than universally Catholic.[163]

Curran's fourth reason is theological. He notes that some aspects of the Catholic faith constitute its core, while "others are more removed from the centrality of faith,"[164] and points to the Canadian bishops' "Winnipeg Statement" as an example. On the question of married couples who decide to dissent from the Church's proscription of artificial contraception: "Since they are not denying any point of divine and Catholic faith nor rejecting the teaching authority of the Church, these Catholics should not be considered, or consider themselves, cut off from the body of the faithful."[165] Dissent is possible against the doctrinal teaching on artificial contraception because it is a non-dogmatic teaching.

The fifth reason is the ecclesiological reason, which puts into flux the question of authority invested in clerical offices versus the authority conferred upon the whole Church by the Holy Spirit. Although the Church is guided by the Holy Spirit, "[t]here will always be some tension in the Church because no one in the church – pope or theologian – has a monopoly on the Spirit, who is the primary teacher."[166]

The sixth and final reason for dissent is to have an authority that functions in the service of truth. Although "the church needs authority," and "Catholics believe in the authority given to pope and bishops," Curran says that the authority of office is kept in check because "authority in teaching matters is not ultimate, but must always conform itself to the truth." In this sense, Curran appeals to the Thomistic tradition within Catholicism that "something is commanded because it is good," and is not good merely because it is commanded.[167] In this sense the whole Church serves the truth.

While Curran's rationales are helpful, it is important to note that he acknowledges himself as a controversial figure within the Church.[168] His theological work to justify dissent sits in the context of supporting his sustained public disagreement with the Church's teaching on artificial contraception since the promulgation of HV in 1968. His memoir *Loyal Dissent* describes the various ways in which he was investigated for publishing his views in print and in speech, and in 1986 the CDF stripped him of his license to teach theology, following which the Catholic University of America removed him from his post as a tenured professor. He remains a priest and is now a professor at Southern Methodist University.

Teaching Humanae Vitae *with "The Winnipeg Statement"*

The controversy surrounding HV presents a particularly salient case study of dissent in the present age. Its salience begins with its close historical proximity, and includes the fact that the teaching remains controversial within the Church and central to the lives of many

Catholic adolescents and their families. According to sociologist of religion Reginald Bibby, 69% of students in Canadian Catholic school systems approve of premarital sex if the act is based upon love,[169] while sociologist Andrew Greeley has found that only 9% of Canadian and 20% of American Catholics believe that "premarital sex is always wrong."[170] These reports are suggestive, but by themselves do not provide the full reason for why the contraception question is of particular interest as an example of teaching about dissent. There is, after all, similar disagreement on other issues such as female ordination and same-sex marriage. The substantial feature that makes the contraception question especially interesting is the presence of additional published documentary evidence from the Pontifical Commission on Birth Control and the Canadian Conference of Catholic Bishops (CCCB) that places absolute adherence to HV on problematic footing. The Pontifical Commission's report, issued prior to HV, recommended allowing artificial contraceptives, and the CCCB's 1968 "Statement on the Encyclical *Humanae Vitae*," commonly called "The Winnipeg Statement," explicitly states that those who find that they must disobey HV may do so in good conscience and consider themselves in good standing with the Church. To this point, some Catholic religion teachers use the facts of the Commission's report, "The Winnipeg Statement," and the controversies surrounding them to show students an example of dissent on some teachings within the Church. A brief exposition of the events which surround the Pontifical Commission, HV, and "Winnipeg," presented below, will demonstrate the possibilities for religious instruction predicated upon examining dissenting content.

The Church has considered the question of contraception throughout its history, but to appreciate the nature of its controversy in the twentieth century, a look to Pope Pius XI's 1930 encyclical letter *Casti Connubii* is sufficient as a starting point. That document is the authoritative touchstone from which Paul VI did not wish to deviate when crafting HV. *Casti Connubii* follows closely St Augustine's view that the primary purpose of sex acts is procreation and that those not aimed at procreation are immoral,[171] although it does legitimize the "subordinated" "secondary ends" of marital bonding, should "natural reasons" prevent conception.[172] This Augustinian attitude began to crumble in the years following, though, and a significant moment of departure from it occurred with Pius XII's 1951 teaching that affirmed natural family planning.[173]

Questions on the morality of contraception became very prominent in the Church after the introduction of oral contraceptives in the very early 1960s. Pope John XXIII responded in 1963 by creating the Pontifical Commission on Birth Control to study this issue. The Commission continued its work after John's death the same year, and also despite Pope Paul VI's 1964 instruction to the Second Vatican Council that it cease its own parallel deliberations on the subject and simply reaffirm *Casti Connubii*.[174] It was apparent that the pope "had reserved the question of the birth control pill to himself."[175] Nevertheless, the Council fathers treat the subject in paragraphs 47 to 52 of the 1965 "Pastoral Constitution" in a way that sustains a nebulous, equivocal position. The apparent tension is between paragraph 50, which upholds the judgments of married couples "before God" and maintains that they are "ruled by conscience," and paragraph 51, which on the other hand states that "[in] questions of birth regulation, the daughters and sons of the church ... are forbidden to use methods disapproved of by the teaching authority of the church in its interpretation of the divine law."[176] These two passages *could* be compatible in some cases, but not necessary so.

The Commission released its final report "On Responsible Parenthood" in 1966. By a strong majority decision the Commission recommended permitting artificial contraception. The Commission's 65 members included 15 cardinals and bishops (9 voting in favour, 3 abstaining and 3 opposing), 19 theologians (15 in favour and 4 opposed), and 31 lay persons (all in favour). These conclusions had no influence on HV. In its opening paragraphs, Paul VI explains that he could not adopt the Commission's recommendations because they were not "definitive and absolutely certain"; because they did not emerge from "complete agreement concerning the moral norms to be proposed"; and finally because "certain approaches and criteria for a solution to this question had emerged which were at variance with the moral doctrine on marriage constantly taught by the Magisterium of the Church."[177] Kaufman and Wills contend that Paul was more concerned with protecting Magisterial authority by maintaining consistency with past popes than he was with reflecting the views of the faithful.[178] The unwelcome response HV received led Paul to not write another encyclical during his papacy.[179]

The CCCB issued its "Winnipeg Statement" two months following HV. Among the many affirming and dissenting responses to HV, this document provides a perspective on how one might confront the problem of coordinating one's faith and devotion to the Church with a considered judgment that cannot adhere to HV. The Canadian bishops structure their response in a way that acknowledges their own pastoral appreciation of this problem. After stating their solidarity with the pope and their intent to harmonize their pastoral teaching with HV,[180] they acknowledge that "[i]t is a fact that a certain number of Catholics, although admittedly subject to the teaching of the encyclical, find it either extremely difficult or even impossible to make their own all elements of this doctrine ... Since they are not denying any point of divine and Catholic faith nor rejecting the teaching authority of the Church, these Catholics should not be considered or consider themselves, shut off from the body of the faithful."[181] This acknowledgment gives primacy to paragraph 50 of the "Pastoral Constitution" concerning conscience, and so subordinates the imperative in paragraph 51's instruction that artificial contraceptives are "forbidden." The conscientious actor must still consider HV's prescriptions, but ultimately might not act according to them. The bishops continue: "In accord with the accepted principles of moral theology, if these persons have tried sincerely but without success to pursue a line of conduct in keeping with the given directives, they may be safely assured that, whoever honestly chooses that course which seems right to him does so in good conscience."[182]

"Winnipeg" has attracted much criticism, and one of its most prominent Canadian opponents is Monsignor Vincent Foy. His article "Tragedy at Winnipeg" maintains that "Winnipeg" is erroneous and that HV should receive full adherence as the Church's authoritative teaching on the regulation of birth. Foy refers to paragraph 26 of "Winnipeg," quoted above, as "The Worst" because it is "self contradictory," "embraces the error of proportionalism," refers to Church teachings as "directives" instead of "divine natural law," and "embraces the wrong concept of conscience."[183]

In recent years the CCCB has itself moved away from the position it took in "Winnipeg," and currently expresses its support for HV in unambiguous terms. Its 2008 pastoral message "Liberating Potential" states: "Pope Paul VI's encyclical Humanae Vitae and the subsequent 'theology of the body' developed by Pope John Paul II issue an immense challenge to a world that is too often occupied with protecting itself against the extraordinary life potential of sexuality. In the wake of these two prophetic Popes, the Church, 'expert in humanity,' issues an unexpected message: sexuality is a friend, a gift of God ...

We invite the faithful to be the first to experience its liberating potential."[184] Even though the CCCB has not retracted "Winnipeg," neither does it mention that document in its most current statements. The significance of "Winnipeg" as an authoritative touchstone in the Church's history of moral theology, and in the lives of Catholics in today's world, remains a subject of debate.

From this brief exposition, one can appreciate the many avenues of inquiry that are possible in analyzing the question of the Catholic Church's response to contraception. The pedagogical opportunities to explore moral questions no doubt present themselves, but so do opportunities to explore Church history, ecclesiology, sociology, and questions of authority and authoritativeness, among others. Notably, the Congregation for the Clergy also recommends that the methods of religious instruction be open to knowing and accommodating "new ways which are open to the sensibilities and problems of this age group. They should be of a theological, ethical, historical, and social nature."[185]

In theory it is thus possible to consider catechesis and religious instruction which begin from a disciplined program of critical thought centred upon the learner's concerns to know about objections to prevailing teachings, notwithstanding that the prevailing culture of practice currently does not imagine the *probability* of such a curricular orientation. Even for those who would maintain that adherence to HV is imperative and a hallmark of one's Catholicity, the documentary facts of change, consultation, and non-universal reception of Church teachings in this area stand as events that require acknowledgment and honest treatment.

CONCLUSION

Catholic Education depends upon a normative Magisterium, but that Magisterium and the institutions which flow from the Church also provide the intellectual fodder and institutional means that might be used to challenge Magisterial teaching. In fact, these institutions place Catholic learners in a position where they can frame their thinking from a point of view that has intellectual authority. Those means are supported by Catholic teachings on conscience and the debate on dissent, which ironically provides authoritative means to disagree with some authoritative teaching. In this way, each of Education, Magisterium, Conscience, and Dissent is of importance to the others insofar as they are interconnected in the mission of the Church and of Catholic Education.

The complexity of this mission, however, is also revealed in the fact that these concepts do not always function in perfect concert but are occasionally in dynamic tension with each other. Moreover, the tensile nature of their relationship is amplified since each of the constituent concepts has its own inherent theoretical fuzziness, which means that the combination of singularly problematic understandings multiplies into a complex theoretical knot. At the level of educational practice, the question emerges as to whether it is more important to take an approach that attempts to *untangle* the knot and clarify the concepts that constitute its fibres with the aim of weaving a unified and solid-ified tapestry of Catholic thought, or instead to adopt a pedagogical method aimed at *describing* the knot, its fibres, and the reasons why it exists in its present form. And perhaps the most important conclu-sion to be drawn is that in spite of the good work that Catholic Educational institutions do, they are bound to an ecclesial and theo-logical framework that does not provide firm support for pedagogical innovations or even current practice. A re-articulated concept of dis-sent that can support a revised pedagogical model that will acknowl-edge and build upon the problematic nature of Catholic Education is called for.

This chapter has examined Catholicism and its discontents at a high level of abstraction because the normative concepts contained within are essential to an understanding of Catholic schools in any context, and are required for a comparative evaluation of how the political and curricular promises and problems one finds in Catholic schools descend from the common, general framework for a global enterprise. Chapter 3 moves from this global perspective and opens the subject of publicly funded Catholic schools in the Canadian con-text, proposing that these schools are themselves dissenting schools and, in spite of the problems that some commentators in the present day find with them, provide a template as such for more productive dissent in Canadian society. Chapter 4 moves away from these abstrac-tions to consider the particulars of curricular challenges that teach-ers find within classrooms in these schools, and provides a practical contrast to the abstract aims revealed here.

3

The Context, Challenge, and Changing Face of Canadian Catholic Education

Catholic Education does not take place in a vacuum. In order to happen, it requires real persons, with their needs and problems, in some sort of relationship, whether in a school, family, or elsewhere. The Magisterium's theoretical account of Catholic Education at least acknowledges as much in its references to the contemporary concerns of youth today and the mission of schools and other educative relationships to respond to them. Catholic schools' institutional reality, however, is a struggle with the twin tasks of reflecting the cultures and needs of the persons and communities they serve, while at the same time standing apart from the mainstream ideology that prevails in the socio-political context in which they are embedded. Chapter 2's presentation of the general theory of education, though acknowledging this struggle's concrete existence, does not offer an example of it. The *how* of this endeavour is at least as important to the theory of Catholic Education as the *why*, because it is in acting upon the imperatives to educate that the salient theoretical tensions within Catholicism and Catholic Education emerge in their most relevant manifestations. This chapter, which describes and interprets a certain part of the political history and contemporary experiences of Catholic Education in Canada, and the following chapter, which discusses the theory of the curricular-pedagogical challenges teachers face in the post-conciliar age, provide relevant illustrations of the ways in which theoretical ideals come into being and the constitutive problems which these enterprises discover as a normal part of their work.

A PARTICULAR HISTORICAL CONTEXT

Histories and discussions of how they inform contemporary problems are always important for their independent interest, but this historical argument carries the additional burden of justifying a philosophical argument for dissent within the context of Catholic Education. Catholic Education itself represents a story about dissent that is at the core of Canada's political history. This chapter demonstrates that the story of dissent is a traditional Canadian Catholic behaviour and experience; it sets the context for Canadian Catholic Education and prescriptive meaning in terms of finding an epistemic grounding for dissent across all Catholic Education.

In pre-Confederation Upper Canada, the Catholic minority had to cope with a prevailing Anglo-Protestant political atmosphere. Faced with social and religious persecution in the common public schools, Catholics successfully lobbied to control their own publicly funded religious education. Those schools count as an instance of dissent because they represent the distinctiveness of Catholic citizens and Catholicism from the social and political mainstream, without suggesting that either the citizen or the religious expression is disloyal to the state. At the macro-political level, Canadian Catholic schools are exemplary institutions that have established a tradition of dissent for all minorities.

The history of publicly funded separate schooling for Canadian Catholics in Alberta, Ontario, Saskatchewan, and the three Northern Territories is tied to Canada's social contract from the time of Upper and Lower Canada's (later Ontario and Quebec's) union in 1841. At the time of that union, common public schools were not secular schools. In 1807, the Legislature of Upper Canada had passed "An Act to Establish Public Schools in Each and Every District of this Province," but because government funding for these schools was "scandalously insufficient," many Western Christian denominations assumed the burden of sponsoring schools. Upper Canada's public education system thus continued to feel strongly the influence of institutionalized churches.[1] "Public" in this era did not mean "religion-free"; it still meant "assignable to all" but within institutionalized settings that were not necessarily "representative of all."

Publicly funded Catholic Education in Upper Canada began in its Glengarry County in the 1820s and 1830s as the result of Reverend (later Bishop) Alexander Macdonell's persistent petitioning of the colonial and British governments to fund Catholic schools. The Catholic families in Glengarry were the remnant of a Highland Scottish regiment in the British army, and upon its disbandment, a tract of land in Upper Canada had been granted to them.[2] Macdonell had served as this regiment's chaplain, and maintained a fervent disposition to improve the lot of its people, whom he felt experienced political and economic subjugation in the colony due to a lack of education and social status, because these privileges were at the time connected to membership in the dominant Church of England.[3] Catholics were often poorly educated, were considered socially inferior, were comparatively politically powerless, and were immersed in a society dominated by Anglo-Protestants who had little tolerance for papal claims to religious authority.[4] Without the necessary resources to establish schools for his people, Macdonell used his influence in the colonial and British governments[5] to secure the funds that would provide them with Catholic educational service. The establishment of government-supported Catholic schools was important, among other reasons, "to check a spirit of discontent" that by 1821 Governor General Lord Dalhousie perceived to be spreading among the Scottish Catholics.[6] By the 1830s, several of these schools had been established in settlements across the colony.

The 1840s witnessed the surfacing of controversy over the existence of both separate schools and common public schools. Although several prominent people within the Protestant-dominated colony continued to press for a single common school system,[7] there were also perspectives opposing the stripping of religion from schools. For instance, Dr Charles Duncombe, a leading defender of the proposition that common schools could teach "truths" from the Bible without offending any Christians, nonetheless conceded that should such a proposition prove impractical, it would be preferable for the dissenting groups to be allowed their own separate schools.[8] On this contentious issue the leading political trend within Upper Canada thus continued to favour a model of public education based upon a continuance of the religious system already in place.

Legal provisions for the colony's Protestant and Roman Catholic schools did not exist prior to the Act of Union between Upper and Lower Canada in 1841, but were formally introduced in that same year with Solicitor General Charles Dewey Day's Common School Act.[9] This Act stated that in addition to the common school or schools in a district in which one religious denomination is in the majority, "'any number of inhabitants of a different faith from the majority in such township might choose their own trustees' and might 'establish and maintain one or more common schools' under the same conditions and receiving the same government support."[10] Under this

Act, Roman Catholic and individual Protestant denominations had the right to establish separate schools in places where a vaguely defined "suitable number" found themselves in a minority. The 1843 "Act for the Establishment of Common Schools in Upper Canada," sponsored by Sir Francis Hincks, maintained public funding for Roman Catholic and Protestant separate schools, although individual Protestant denominations lost the right to form their own separate schools. The Hincks Act "set the pattern for education in Upper Canada."[11] Separate public education for all denominations continued, however, in some form or another through to the 1850s.

Amid the prevailing political climate that admitted Catholic (and Protestant) separate schools into the concern for publicly funded education, a social climate that was unfriendly to Catholics also began to stir. The period from 1841 into the 1850s witnessed a revival of the religious spirit within Protestantism that Walker relates as being generally in agreement with the aims of liberal society at the time; however, this revival also re-invigorated anti-Catholic sentiment within the population.[12]

It is true that, while Catholics as a group continued to experience the effects of socio-economic subjugation and oppression, periods of open anti-Catholic hostility and bigotry were not a constant feature of the 1850s. Periods of tension did interrupt the calm, though, and the periodical publications of the day provide a documentary account of the unfavourable sentiment that occasionally surfaced. Those opposed to separate schools maintained that public support for Catholic Education would transplant Catholic backwardness into governmental affairs. Catholic education would corrupt the secular or Protestant-dominated climate that was apparently encouraging economic, social, and scholarly progress, and give over too large a share of political influence to a population that, it was feared, was controlled by its clergy. Walker's analysis continues with an explanation of how this religious sentiment was transposed into the political climate of the time:

> Endowment of Catholic clergy and schools had long been a sore point among many Protestants in Canada. Separate schools were seen as a continuation of this evil. Aware that Protestantism was divided into many sects, many Protestants feared that united Catholicism stood to gain in any division of public funds according to religion. Many felt also that if Catholic children were to

receive education in common with other children, the now
literate Catholics could not help but cast off the stupid delusions
foisted on them by a power-mad priesthood. And many
Protestants who did not share the prevalent "no popery" notions
feared that separate schools of any description would weaken
a plan for general education.[13]

According to some who supported common schooling, the continued
existence of publicly funded Catholic schools also threatened to provide a privileged position for the Roman hierarchy and allow for
clerical interference in education, a situation which was "out of harmony with nineteenth century liberalism" and threatened to break
up the common schools.[14] Such was the argument against continuing
the practice of publicly funded separate Catholic schooling.

Where Protestants were generally wary of papal sovereignty and
clerical interference in the establishment of Catholic schools, Catholics were generally suspicious of the imperialistic aroma extant within
an education system dominated by the Church of England.[15] The
concerns of Irish-Canadian Catholics, in particular, were imported
from their homeland, which had been colonized by the English. In
Ireland, according to Walker, "the state clergy was Protestant and the
government in alien, Protestant hands, while the majority of the
people were Catholic. The Catholic Church was all but proscribed,
and poor Catholic peasants obliged to pay for the support of a hated
Protestant Church. It was natural, then, for these Catholics to see a
continuation of somewhat the same thing under the old 'family com-
pact' pro–Church of England rule."[16] The Irish in particular resisted
the claims of Egerton Ryerson, Upper Canada's and Ontario's Chief
Superintendent of Education from 1844 to 1876, that Irish students
in common public schools would improve both morally and intellectually.[17] Irish parents were suspicious of the common schools as
state-controlled mechanisms of assimilation, and "having observed
the Bishop, the religious and Catholic children stoned and insulted
in the streets by Protestant youths, [Catholic parents] questioned the
bigotry that evidently was being taught in the public schools in the
city."[18] There was awareness among the Catholic minority in Upper
Canada that common schools, whether Protestant or secular, represented an insult to their ethnicity and religion, and that their children
were likely to suffer greatly under that regime. The question of
separate schools was therefore not limited to debates over Biblical

authority, clerical power, or whether schools could teach from a neutral standpoint. The Catholic school question had become one of politics: the majority's resistance against the feared dominance of a minority, and the minority's desire to crawl out from beneath a blanket of socio-religious oppression. Religious distinctiveness was the condition that functioned as that salient political and social marker in this situation.

In addition to social problems, there were also practical problems with pre-Confederation Catholic schools that persisted due to legislative inadequacies. From 1841 to Confederation, the question of how best to collect and fairly distribute separate school taxes was a point of irritation for Catholics.[19] The dominant issue was how to release Catholics from paying common school taxes so that they might collect and administer their own levies.[20] The 1855 Taché Act was the first attempt to resolve this problem, by allowing Catholics to establish and support their own schools. Notable in the debate on this bill was the support expressed by Postmaster General Robert Spence, who maintained that "[the] right to establish Separate Schools was a protection to the minority against the arbitrary will of the majority."[21] The Taché Act was helpful to Catholics in spirit, but contained some deficiencies which made it prove inadequate and unjust in practice.

An Act introduced in 1863 by Richard Scott, member of Parliament for Ottawa, endeavoured to rectify the situation for Catholics. Walker observes that the Scott Act "removed obstructions to the administration of the system"[22] by "[extending] the facilities for establishing separate schools in rural areas and [making] much simpler administrative tasks in the listing of separate school supporters and obtaining government grants."[23] The Act passed by a vote of 76 to 31, with the Upper Canada tally showing 22 yeas and all 31 nays, which included nearly all the governing Reform Party members. The Reform government had introduced the Scott Act, but it was passed by a coalition of Lower Canada Catholics and Upper Canada Conservatives. That coalition included John A. Macdonald's opposition Conservatives and members of the Protestant Orange Order; Scott himself was instrumental in securing its support. The Orange Order supported Scott for the politically instrumental purpose of ensuring their own rights, and, in addition, then–Postmaster General H.M. Foley defended Scott's bill in the Assembly because "the facilities offered to Lower Canada Protestants to have their own schools should influence Upper Canadian

Protestants to be as generous with Catholics."[24] To the casual observer the Scott Act stands as a boon to Catholics, but notably it also stands as an example of parties respecting and promoting dissent for the good of all and not of one group exclusively.

Four years later, the Scott Act became the foundation for education in the Canadian Confederation when the British North America Act codified the establishment of Catholic and Protestant separate schools within the new provinces of Ontario and Quebec. Catholic schools in Upper Canada were therefore established as a reflection of the educational context of the early nineteenth century. While these schools were not initially established in order to protect a religious minority, with the passage of time they eventually came to represent and symbolize that very purpose. The distinctiveness of today's Catholic schools in that respect thus represents the adaptation of an institution that descends from a more diverse political context of denominationally based education.

The current-day conflation of Catholic socio-political and religious distinctiveness under the umbrella term "Catholic Identity" is no facile logical leap, given the oppressive nineteenth-century conditions. While the socio-political culture can be separated from the religious belief as a means of interpreting a distinct Catholic identity, there certainly would have been no socio-political Catholic distinctiveness without the contingent religious belief existing underneath. Religious life was the foundation for socio-political life in nineteenth-century Canada, and the institutional Church was often the social centre for Catholic persons during that time period. In urban parishes the "church, rectory, convent and school" represented the Church.[25] In spite of their spiritual aims, however, these personal, ritual, and iconic identifiers of institutional Catholicism were not politically innocent. Catholic identity is not reducible to Mass attendance, wearing a crucifix, or abstaining from meat on Fridays; but the Catholic identity so central to the political arguments surrounding the separate school question was intimately tied to the fact that these *external* religious acts, habits, rituals, and dress (most especially in the case of the clergy and religious who staffed the parish and schools) were largely also the objects of anti-Catholic socio-political bigotry. As external political protections for Catholics were created and maintained on the basis of Catholic socio-ethnic distinctiveness from the majority, the warrant for political distinctiveness existed commensally with the outward display of religious identity. Notwithstanding the diverse political views among individual Catholics, the political distinctiveness of Catholics *as a recognized social group* in Upper Canada was thus bound to and drawn from the religious distinctiveness of its ritual and customs. While it is easy and sometimes practical to conflate the two kinds of distinctiveness – Protestant-Catholic tensions of this kind in Canada were, after all, a relatively mild carryover from centuries of religiously driven political conflict and oppression in Europe – with the passage of time, the question of whether Catholic identity and politics could be conflated became significantly more complex, as issues of Catholic relations with the modern non-Catholic world and intra-Catholic pluralism became more widely discussed.

Through the 1880s to the 1920s, a transformation began to take place in the Catholic schools. Until the 1880s, a curricular focus on Irish Tridentine Catholicism had insulated students from the vicissitudes of persecution in the Anglo-dominated outside world, but following 1880 this curriculum was replaced with one that emphasized Canadian patriotism and Canada's relationship with England. As Catholics became increasingly part of mainstream Canadian society, so did their education system begin to reflect the values of mainstream Canada and its role in the British Empire. Historian Mark McGowan writes that as a sense of Canadian identity emerged within the growing nation, Canadian Catholicism was slowly becoming more integrated into the Canadian social and political mainstream, and certain socio-political resemblances became evident between the separate and public schools: "Separate schools were still primarily concerned with preservation of the Catholic faith in a Protestant environment, but they varied little from their public school counterparts in terms of inculcating children with the principles of patriotism and good citizenship. The Catholic bishops and educators alike considered strong and intelligent Catholicism, by its very definition, as the stuff of which good citizens were moulded."[26]

McGowan gives a detailed account of the effect the introduction of the generic Canadian and English curriculum had upon Ontario's Catholics. The textual content of language arts, literature, and history courses carried a heavy emphasis on Canadian and British themes. The tales of "Catholic heroes like Jean de Brébeuf and Thomas More" were presented alongside the secular political and military stories of men like Generals Isaac Brock and James Wolfe and Admiral Horatio Nelson.[27] In literature courses, "[t]he Catholic readers clearly illustrated the double-edged intent of Catholic schools.

Numerous pieces on the Virgin Mary, saints, Church history, Bible stories, and Catholic heroes put children in touch with the current Catholic devotional ethos. Canadian- and British-flavoured poetry and prose, some of it stridently nationalist in tone, provided students with the raw materials from which civic pride and strong citizenship could be cultivated."[28] Far from representing merely an insular refuge from persecution, the curriculum and socio-moral atmosphere in Catholic schools was adopting an approach that maintained a Catholic perspective on Canadian patriotism in common with non-Catholics. This approach thus favoured a kind of Catholic distinctiveness that was nonetheless integrated into the larger social world of Canadian culture.

The split between secular and sacred curricula was not lost upon these pioneers of separate public education, however. As much as the clergy was convinced that Catholicism provided the foundation of good citizenship, so did the provincial government intend that good citizenship be a primary goal of the Catholic schools. As compatible as Catholicism and good citizenship were perceived to be, neither were they mutually reducible. "Clergy and leading lay educators," according to McGowan, "consistently reminded Catholic teachers of their onerous duties in upholding these two pillars of piety and patriotism."[29] The tensions of maintaining this apparent compatibility were strongly felt by Catholics, who resisted pressures to completely collapse their spiritual distinctiveness into the larger Anglo-Protestant-influenced secular culture. This model of balancing "piety and patriotism" was stubbornly maintained in matters where ecclesiastical and civil jurisdiction clashed, and most often such clashes were over control of religious and moral education.

The split between secular and religious education became apparent along jurisdictional lines. Notwithstanding their distinctive socio-moral atmosphere, from the perspective of curricular organization Catholic schools in this period were already beginning to resemble their secular counterparts in many curricular areas, with the obvious exception that Catholic schools taught religion in addition. The goal of the Catholic school was to provide a home for each person's spiritual formation, and McGowan observes that once that ontological footing was assumed, secular subject matter was easily integrated into the school: "Spiritual education provided the foundation for the education of the Catholic child in the secular disciplines. Catholic educators were less jealous of complete control in these matters, which meant that Catholic schools borrowed and adapted the resources and materials used in the public common schools. In spelling, arithmetic, history, geography, hygiene, and algebra the public school texts were used widely in the TSSB [Toronto Separate School Board]."[30] It is apparent from McGowan's list, however, that there was little of curricular substance to arouse religious controversy. These subjects were instrumental means to generic good citizenship and likewise, with some possible exceptions in history and hygiene, could be presented from an apparently neutral or politically dispassionate perspective without necessarily introducing or referring to religious content. A distinctively Catholic curriculum and method for a subject like mathematics is even today considered absurd.[31]

While the Catholic schools had apparently assimilated the above secular curricula into their program with ease, the same could not be said for curricula that touched upon Catholic teachings on faith and morals. The schools, and even the bureaucratic Church itself, consistently and unshakably turned aside the provincial government's attempts to influence or interfere with religious education or moral education, and in doing so maintained their jurisdiction over these matters.[32] These actions represent early examples of the tension between secular and sacred jurisdictions and their roles as models of authority for Catholic Education.

Three important outcomes are reflected thus far in the historical analysis of Catholic education. First, Catholic education as a separate but publicly funded institution was recognized as a legitimate dissenting voice in Upper Canada in the 1840s. Catholics institutionally established themselves as macro-political dissenters during these days and in the period immediately following. They did not exert influence over the doctrines of their church or exercise internal dissent from its teachings, but as a group they were able to stand in solidarity against the outside pressures of the larger non-Catholic society without compromising their national loyalty. Distinctive faith and faith-based schooling were found to be legitimately simultaneous with fidelity to the Canadian union, and later Confederation. This is the model which continues to the present day. Second, the character of that dissenting voice slowly began to change from one that desired protection as an oppressed group to one that desired to maintain the spiritual distinctiveness of an otherwise integrated culture. Finally, the institutional Catholic Church retained much influence over these schools, and limited the spread of secular content and provincial government control over the curriculum to areas that could not easily be adapted to Catholicism.

THE GLOBAL INFLUENCE OF VATICAN II

During the nineteenth century, the gradual creep of secular content and generic Canadian values into Catholic schools was checked and challenged by Church authorities in an ecclesial climate that, according to McGowan, had been moving away from the devotional and moral laxities of a frontier institution and becoming ultramontane[33] in its orientation by adopting a more rigorous application of the norms established by the Church's Council of Trent (1545–63).[34] During the reign of Pope Pius IX (1846–78), the stance of the world-wide Church became more sharply defined in terms of its opposition to liberalism and modernism[35] and its definition of papal infallibility in the First Vatican Council (1869–70),[36] but in the first half of the twentieth century, new intellectual and cultural movements shifted the Church in a new direction, away from Tridentine Catholicism. Scholasticism, which had dominated Catholic thought since Trent, gradually diminished as the leading Catholic intellectual paradigm, and historical-critical exegetical methods gradually replaced traditional literal interpretations of the Bible.[37] Reactionary positions against liberalism and modernism also became outmoded, if only slowly; Timothy McCarthy remarks that although "[m]odernists within the church were marginalized, and even excommunicated" in the years between the First and Second Vatican Councils,[38] "the new theologians [who] were silenced by Pius XII [r.1939–58] ... were all eventually rehabilitated."[39] These and many other aspects of a changing climate within Catholicism would eventually culminate in the reforms of the Second Vatican Council (1962–65). In their time, those reforms became an additional problematic part of the Canadian Catholic culture's tapestry that, prior to the council, already included a tradition of macro-political dissent and a climate of creeping secularization brought about by curricular integration with the common public schools.

It is difficult to express the importance of the Second Vatican Council to the Roman Catholic Church with a precision and economy that does not open various important but tangential discussions. Vatican II is regarded as a significant point in the history of the Roman Catholic Church, but the quality of that significance is a matter of much debate. The Council was called for the purpose of updating the Catholic Church in the context of the modern world, as Catholic ecclesial, political, and personal life since the Protestant Reformation had in large part been defined according to the norms of the Council of Trent from four centuries earlier. Since the First Vatican Council (1869–70) reaffirmed Trent, the interval between it and Vatican II saw little visible institutional change within the Church. The doctrines, customs, and culture of the Catholic Church in Upper Canada and Ontario during the nineteenth century and the first sixty-two years of the twentieth century, and the relations between Catholics and Protestants in these places and worldwide, were in large part specified or at least highly influenced by these two councils.

A very brief survey of some of the Second Vatican Council's documents can, despite the acknowledged risks that accompany glosses, still demonstrate its spirit and allow one to appreciate how the important changes which emerged from it influence the world in which Catholic Education operates.[40] I find an existential reading of the Council documents to be a helpful beginning in this respect for locating the place from which the Church makes the observations and prescriptions about itself and the world. The council documents characterize the Church as an outsider that is *in* the world but not *of* it. LG describes this position in paragraph six, proclaiming that "[while] on earth [the Church] journeys in a foreign land away from the Lord (see 2 Cor 5:6), the church sees itself as an exile. It seeks and is concerned about those things which are above, where Christ is seated at the right hand of God." In paragraph eight it similarly announces that "like a stranger in a foreign land, [the Church] presses forward amid the persecutions of the world and the consolations of God." Arguably, these passages go some way toward illustrating a concern for balancing heavenly revelation with sincerely meeting the concerns of persons on earth – acknowledging that it is (some of) these persons who constitute the Church anyway.

Congruent with this existential reading is DH's statement that human persons should be free from coercion in religious matters,[41] although the Church steers away from any individualistic extreme by placing this freedom within a vision of the common social good of society that balances individual and community.[42] GS takes a lengthier and more comprehensive view of the role of individual, community, and Church in contributing to the common political and social good, especially in light of current social and political concerns that have arisen in the modern Church and world.

Aside from (but concurrent with) this existential reading, the Council also broke new ground on its official attitude toward relations with non-Catholics and non-Christians. Generally speaking, care of persons and respect for their experiences gradually took on a stronger and more central role in Catholic teaching compared to earlier emphases on legalistic enforcement of rules regardless of contextual, human factors. This pastoral concern, which emphasizes duty of care towards the well-being of persons, was restored in its place alongside Church doctrine – observing that pastoral attitudes have a doctrinal basis. Although LG maintains that salvation is to be found within "the unique Church of Christ which in the Creed we profess to be one, holy, catholic and apostolic which our Saviour, after his resurrection, entrusted to Peter's pastoral care (Jn 21:17), commissioning him and the other apostles to rule it (see Mt 28:18, etc.)," and "which is governed by the successor of Peter and by the bishops in communion with him," it does not restrict the possibility of salvation to the institutional Church and affirms that it may be found throughout the world. Beyond the Church's obvious associations, "many elements of sanctification and of truth are found outside its visible confines."[43] This passage is revolutionary in Catholic history because it retains dogmatic continuity with past claims that salvation is found within the Church, while breaking with a dogmatic tradition and ecclesial culture which in addition had taught that such salvation was to be found *only* within the Catholic Church. Trent asserts that "[t]he Roman Catholic Church is the ... only true church"[44] and "the mother and mistress of all churches"[45] to which all others must return or convert: a view which was echoed throughout North America in the widely read "Baltimore Catechism."[46] Throughout global Catholicism, the barriers between an insular Tridentine era and the modern, secular world were bending and breaking. Consequentially Catholic social identity was becoming less officially influenced by insularity and more integrated with the modern, pluralistic world.

The Council also formalized other important changes that directly influenced the ways in which Catholic persons experienced their Church. The "Decree on the Apostolate of Lay People / *Apostolicam Actuositatem*" (AA) opened the way for non-ordained or non-religious persons to participate in a greater capacity in the Church, and notably described the mission of lay persons to be ambassadors of the Church in the secular world.[47] In the "Doctrinal Constitution on Divine Revelation / *Dei Verbum*" (DV) the Council directed that laity should have access to sacred scripture[48] while reminding the Church

that the authority of revelation is balanced between scriptural authority and the authority of an evolving tradition.[49] Importantly, it also
insisted that a contextual interpretation of scripture should be preferred to a literal reading.[50] A short "Declaration on Christian Education / *Gravissimum Educationis*" (GE) is limited to affirming the right
of all persons to an education and briefly states that the Church,
family, and society as a whole are responsible for ensuring that all
persons receive education. Its significance is discussed in greater
detail below.

Finally, one of the more well-known changes that the Council
initiated was to its liturgy. The Tridentine Mass, which had remained
unchanged since the sixteenth century, was the common ritual which
functioned as a major identifying symbol of Catholic community and
the culminating event in weekly and seasonal Catholic spiritual
rhythms. This Mass was sung in Latin with the priest leading the
congregation from the altar while facing away from them. The laity
participated by praying along with the priest, but had little other
role. By contrast, Vatican II introduced a much larger allowance for
lay participation in the Mass. The priest faced the congregation for
the celebration, and the liturgy was simplified and modernized,
including the use of the vernacular instead of Latin and the integration of national and local customs.[51] Changing the expression of the
Mass changed perhaps one of the most notably distinctive outward
expressions of Catholic identity, and thus there was a profound shift
within the "thick"[52] content which had been the mark of nineteenth-
century Catholic identity. Be they ecumenical, intra-ecclesial, or liturgical, the reforms brought about were not merely theological, for
they also had a social impact on how Catholic identity was imagined
and constructed.

The Council's meaning for and impact on the Church in the present
day are not without controversy.[53] Some views regard it as having
damaged the Church by turning away from established traditions,
while others feel that its reforms did not go far enough. Certain
Catholics view the Second Vatican Council as an event that corrupted
the Church by abandoning the traditional Scholasticism, biblical
interpretation, and eschatological place of prominence for death,
judgment, heaven, and hell. Instead of being the rebirth of the Church
in the modern world, accordingly, the Second Vatican Council caused
a monumental decline in vocations to the priesthood and religious
life, and among the laity it has initiated, rather than remedied, a widespread disregard and dismissal of many Catholic teachings. The

mystery of the Church and its role in attaining heavenly salvation were usurped by a profane attachment to humankind's worldly situation. Overall, the Council caused the Church's influence among some of its believers to decline or die. Other Catholics have been disappointed that the Church has not adopted a more democratic structure that allows lay governance; moreover, there are concerns about female ordination, the place of non-heterosexual persons in the Church, contraception, and a host of other similar "social justice" issues.

The most important conclusion to be drawn from enumerating these views is that as the whole Church struggled – and struggles – to adapt to the Council's changes, so too do the conditions under which Catholic Education operates and represents itself reflect this struggle. The Council and the views Catholics have of it are constitutive of the curriculum and socio-political climate in the school; moreover, they are also foundational influences on the ways in which all partners in Catholic Education-Schooling *approach* the Catholic schools.

The changes brought about during Vatican II are authoritative in modern Catholicism, but what can explain the reasons for these changes and the significance of the processes that enabled them? Theologian Gregory Baum's book *Amazing Church* is instructive here. Baum illustrates several Church teachings that have changed across the nineteenth and twentieth centuries, and expresses his "amazement" regarding these developments. Beyond offering a mere descriptive account of doctrinal change, Baum provides an historical and theological explanation for how and why these changes arose. They are not abrupt anomalies or accidents in his view, but rather responses to the Church entering new contexts and responding to what he terms new "ethical horizons."[54] Much of his illustrative material either directly or indirectly implies a change that occurred at or was confirmed during Vatican II. This thesis is difficult to dispute. The stories of the contributions of Congar, Lagrange, de Lubac, Murray, and Rahner (see chapter 2, note 102) confirm that some significant intellectual shift in Catholic scholarship of the first half of the twentieth century anticipated the Council. Baum shows how the social and political context in the years following World War II influenced changing attitudes towards differences between persons and groups.[55] These "amazing" changes are therefore not "surprising."

Amazing Church reviews five major changes in Catholicism's recent history: (1) shifting toward emphasizing human rights in social teachings; (2) lifting the condemnations of certain thinkers based on new hermeneutical methods; (3) moving away from the neo-scholastic paradigm which subordinated social justice to salvation; (4) accepting conscientious objection in wartime; and (5) recognizing ecumenism and individual religious freedom, including reversals of statements that Protestants and Jews lived outside God's salvation. Among the many examples Baum describes, a brief recounting of the discontinuity between Pope Gregory XVI's 1832 encyclical "On Liberalism and Religious Indifferentism / *Mirari Vos*" (MV) and John XXIII's 1963 encyclical "On Establishing Universal Peace / *Pacem in Terris*" (PT) offers a sufficient demonstration of a substantial shift between old and new ethical horizons. Baum recounts how, in the context of responding to the threats Gregory perceived coming from the Enlightenment and post-revolutionary France's intellectual ferment, MV opposed liberal political society in favour of preserving the monarchical order. PT's contrast to this view is stark. In the context of a Europe that had just witnessed the horrors of World War II and the Holocaust, John XXIII was greatly influenced by the United Nations' 1948 "Universal Declaration of Human Rights" to formulate a teaching that promotes human liberty, religious rights, and even the impulse to revolution. Baum observes that where Gregory "define[s] public morality in terms of humble submission to the princes, knowing one's place in society and unquestioning fidelity to inherited values,"[56] PT, "by advocating freedom, equality, and participation" in the social-political order, "promotes aspirations that were condemned by MV."[57] Vatican II confirmed PT in GS: Baum identifies paragraphs 17, 29, 31, and 55 as outstanding examples.

So how does the Church recognize its passing from one ethical horizon into another? Baum observes that "Pope John XXIII introduced the idea of 'the signs of the times'" to "justify his bold new teaching on religious liberty and human rights. The Church may not continue to teach revealed truth," he continues, "as if these events had not taken place."[58] Baum observes that John's idea resounds in the explanation that GS offers for discontinuities like those between MV and PT:

> The Church knows how richly she has profited by the history
> and development of humanity. Thanks to the experience of past
> ages, the progress of the sciences, and the treasures hidden in the
> various forms of human culture, the nature of humans is more
> clearly revealed and new roads to truth are opened. From the
> beginning of her history, she has learnt to express the message of
> Christ with the help of ideas and terminology of various peoples,

and has tried to clarify it with the wisdom of philosophers ...
Indeed, the accommodated preaching of the revealed Word ought
to remain the law of all evangelization.[59]

This passage is helpful for explaining the fact of discontinuity in
teachings, but simultaneously begs the question of how the Church
straddles the threshold between two ethical contexts and "passes
from one inculturation into another."[60] Baum concludes that, in these
times of transition, maintaining a respectful internal disagreement is
proper and helpful to the development of teaching and Christian
self-understanding: "In certain historical situations, responsible
dissent expressed without anger or resentment renders a service to
the Church."[61]

The qualifications in Baum's formulation are instructive in finally
answering this question of how one dissents. Responsibility entails a
well-thought-through argument on a particular issue. In his example
of "Margaret's" dissent in the 1950s from the prevailing, pre-Vatican
II teaching on religious liberty, he emphatically states that she found
"an entire century" of papal teachings "on this issue" to be "wrong."[62]
He ostensibly employs Margaret's example because she intended neither to abandon the Church nor to discredit the institutions of the
papacy and the Magisterium in disclosing her arguments. Her service
to the Church descends from this disclosure; introducing divergent,
well-considered views ultimately has an effect upon the intellectual
and conversational rigour with which current practices are examined
and new ones adopted. The third qualification regarding "certain
historical contexts" presents a problem to those who might dissent:
how might one recognize these contexts so as to respond appropriately? On what authority can one say that a new context has begun?
Within a tradition that is wary of false prophets, and without any
intellectual guidance on the questions of how and when to dissent,
the dissenting actor might face Hamlet's dilemma, where both action
and inaction appear equally unattractive. So how does Baum release
the dissident agent from dithering paralysis?

Baum offers no direct incitement to dissent, but he does suggest
strongly that enough evidence is present in today's Church to show
that it has encountered a new ethical horizon, post–Vatican II. Specifically, he observes that notions of automatic deference to the Magisterium or one's social elders on matters of salvation and morality
do not obtain in today's context: "Catholics believing in God's revealing Word embrace the Church's teaching only when they are inwardly

persuaded by the Spirit dwelling in their own reflections." The trends of non-conformity he notices within today's Church reflect this attitude; likewise, some of the hierarchical Church's current credibility problems are symptomatic of the fact that it "has so far refused to review" them. Baum points to three places in Church teaching where this observation is especially relevant:

> The first issue is the Church's authoritarian centralism, which contradicts its official teaching on collegiality, subsidiarity, and the co-responsibility of people for their institutions. The second issue is the Church's refusal to review what the equality of men and women means in the light of God's revelation. It is puzzling to hear John Paul II, the great advocate of dialogue, tell Catholic women what their vocation is, instead of first listening to their spiritual aspirations and their painful experience of exclusion ... The third issue is with the Church's refusal to allow Catholics in their various cultures to review the meaning of sexuality in the light of their faith ... Inquiries into the behaviour of Catholics reveal that in matters of sexual love Catholics ... clarify their conscience independently of the Magisterium.[63]

These observations on the apparent disjunction between Church teaching and the beliefs of significant numbers of parishioners within today's Church can be interpreted to show that a new ethical horizon does not need Magisterial recognition to exist within the body of the faithful. At the very least, it overcomes deterministic views which would maintain that dissent in today's Church is not analogous to the changes Catholicism witnessed in the pre-conciliar era, or that the Church even stands outside history itself.

So what is today's context? In somewhat of a contrast to the sanguine view that Baum takes of dissent within the Church, journalist John Allen's book *The Future Church* offers a view that throws Baum's "ethical horizons" thesis into greater contextual relief. Allen notes that the worldwide Church is becoming increasingly uncompromising and deliberately different with respect to its identity *vis-à-vis* the secular world, which is in direct contrast to the attitude in the immediate aftermath of Vatican II, when anything that made Catholics seem different from mainstream society was frowned upon.[64] This trend of distinction coincides with a resurgent emphasis on natural law as the foundation of Church teaching. In its response to contemporary moral issues, the Church will insist strongly that its socio-moral teachings are correct not because they are based on the Magisterium's legislative authority, but because they are congruent with "real qualities that exist in nature."[65] The implication is that there will be further marginalization of those dissident voices who would maintain that Church governance and teaching are subject to the Church's own contextualized social construction. The trend among bishops will be to enact the development of distinction and natural law rationales by "boldly and courageously ... defend[ing] the Church's traditional teachings" as their primary function.[66] Dissident views which fall outside the Magisterial Church's use of natural law will thus be cast in terms that are less credible than what the mainstream institution promotes.

If one credits Baum with accurately observing major dissident trends within Catholicism, then due notice must also be taken of Allen's prediction that the Global South will dominate Catholicism in the twenty-first century, as the majority of Catholic persons will live there. Catholic attitudes in South America, Africa, and Asia are more doctrinally traditional and morally "conservative," and this trend will hold prevailing moral teachings steady.[67] This demographic shift will mitigate any change in the Church's moral teachings and block dissent on gender equity and sexual ethics; at the same time, however, Allen predicts it will be "liberal" and very politically assertive on social justice issues like poverty.[68] The Church will thus become a dynamic but divided entity that is increasingly alien to some Europeans, Americans, and religious "liberals."[69] From Allen's prediction one can infer that Baum's observations are likely most valid within the contextual orbit of Europe and North America; however, it would be unwise to hastily conclude that Baum has found a "tipping point" for twenty-first-century Catholicism worldwide. Allen does not discourage the kind of dissent Baum might support, but does show that the current ecclesial climate discourages its expression. Nonetheless, Allen's report concludes with a recommendation that aligns with Baum's own critical method: "Initiatives, movements, and campaigns in the twenty-first century will either be rooted in a strong sense of Catholic identity, or they will arrive stillborn ... They will have to phrase their arguments in the language of the Church, appealing to its own traditions and concepts, rather than drawing on secular democracy or corporate management."[70]

In chapter 5 I argue that true dissent draws from a group's own history and knowledge tradition, and in chapter 7 I integrate that claim into a pedagogical model for critical thinking about Catholicism.

In brief, there are two educational questions that emerge from Baum's and Allen's writings. First, how should Catholic schools imagine their role in responding to the different socio-moral religious perspectives students present; and second, what kind of pedagogical and social support should be afforded to affirm the religious freedom of *any* minority Catholic religious views in a school? These two questions anticipate philosophical and pedagogical treatments in chapters 5 and 7. For now, it is sufficient to connect these concerns with the statement by the Canadian Catholic School Trustees Association (CCSTA) on the Catholic school's proper role: "In the face of the cry for women's rights in the Church and the world, greater ecumenical openness, continued liturgical reform, wider theological plurality, and the call for authority to become softer or more rigid, the task of Catholic Education is ... to bring them together, to seek the good in all of them, to be critical of all of them and to love all of them into communion."[71] The Catholic School serves *all* Catholics, not simply a homogeneous few of them. If one takes the CCSTA seriously, the concern in response to this statement is how to articulate aims in terms that promote Christian unity but do not require uniformity of theological and ecclesial thinking on all matters.[72]

CATHOLIC SCHOOL AIMS IN THE POST-CONCILIAR AGE

The aftermath of Vatican II brought forth many questions about its influence on the Church, and with them many concurrent issues have arisen regarding the aims, missions, and performance of Catholic Education-Schooling. These foundational problems represent topics that are necessarily linked to the course upon which Vatican II set the whole Church. However, in many other ways, issues such as the relationship between Church and State in education and the influence of secular curricula upon the program of instruction in Catholic schools were already ongoing prior to the Council, and so it is fair to say that the Council has had a fair, although not exclusive, influence upon the ways in which these problems have developed and are interpreted.

While there is a great deal of variety in the ways Catholic schools appear and represent themselves, misperceptions about how much variety is tolerated leave Catholic schools vulnerable to stereotypes from within and without. A modern stereotype that Catholic schools are somehow more behaviourally disciplined, academically rigorous, charitable, moral, and pious than today's secular schools could be inferred to have descended from dominant pre-conciliar images and even caricatures of Catholicism. The religious and academic discipline in these stereotypes may legitimately be connected with certain discrete incarnations of these images, although many of them have fallen into disuse or obsolescence.

Consider the assertion that strongly ties a school's Catholic identity and the Christian formation of its staff to the traditional garb of the clergy and religious who used to staff them. Since Vatican II, it maintains, the fact that most teachers and administrators in today's Canadian Catholic schools are lay persons has weakened this identity. This assertion prompts three questions: (1) Can one assume that the level of Catholic identity, formation, and faithfulness among instructional staff has ever remained constant across time and place? (2) Are Catholic identity, formation, and faithfulness correlated with being ordained or religious and with the presence of clergy and religious in the school? (3) Does the act of asking such questions reflect prejudices about ordained, vowed, and lay persons, and is it even fair to be asking them?

Here it is helpful to resume using publicly funded Canadian Catholic schools as an illustrative example of historically, socially, and ecclesially conditioned institutions that currently struggle with problems of their internal constitution. With the advance of secular integration into Catholic schools, and the modernizing reforms of Vatican II, the question becomes relevant of what makes a Catholic school more than a secular school that teaches religion courses in parallel with the secular common school curriculum. The expectation for how these schools are to appear and function is thus a question of aims. To this end, the Ontario Institute for Catholic Education has published a list of "Catholic Graduate Expectations," which are listed in brief as follows:

1 A discerning believer formed in the Catholic Faith community who celebrates the signs and sacred mystery of God's presence through word, sacrament, prayer, forgiveness, reflection and moral living.

2 An effective communicator who speaks, writes and listens honestly and sensitively, responding critically in light of gospel values.

3 A reflective, creative and holistic thinker who solves problems and makes responsible decisions with an informed moral conscience for the common good.

4 A self-directed, responsible, lifelong learner who develops and demonstrates their God-given potential.
5 A collaborative contributor who finds meaning, dignity and vocation in work which respects the rights of all and contributes to the common good.
6 A caring family member who attends to family, school, parish, and the wider community.
7 A responsible citizen who gives witness to Catholic social teaching by promoting peace, justice and the sacredness of human life.[73]

Interestingly, Catholic schools around the world, Ontario included, admit and serve students who are non-Catholic or non-Christian, and also students whose identification with and practice of Catholicism runs from various expressions of "thick" devotion to a much "thinner" faith that is possibly more of a cultural identity. As any one school could be serving a student population which reflects this entire variety, it would follow that it is simultaneously providing various kinds of Catholic Education and Catholic Schooling (as described in chapter 1), depending on what the student's intentions are. The school may have a mission to provide "thick" religious experiences to some, but for others it may simply be providing the social service of improving their intellectual life. The ICE's vision, however, is strongly linked to a vision of *Catholic Schooling as personal formation*, which is especially evident with the leading statement that a graduate of the Ontario Catholic School is expected to become "a discerning believer" who is no less than "formed in the Catholic faith community."

If this list is intended to be internally consistent, and it presents no evidence to the contrary, then it appears that all of the aims which follow the first, even though some of them could be interpreted more "thinly," are intended to promote and sustain such a strong view of formation. These expectations, therefore, assume and point to a particular kind of Catholic Education within a particular kind of Catholic School in order to achieve this outcome. Now it might be conjectured that these aims have more of a strategic external political purpose than schools might be reasonably expected to achieve in practice. Consider that not all formation aims are the same, and so do not carry the same political meaning. The CCSTA articulates one such aim that is uplifting spiritually without mentioning *belief*: "The biblical saturation of Catholic Education is not merely about biblical information, but a commitment to biblical formation. We break the word open for our children, helping them apply it to their lives. We open the eyes of a new generation to the meaning and mystery of God's Word, so that they might see all the places in their lives where the word of the printed page wants to become flesh in their actions, behaviour, and choices."[74] If Ontario's publicly funded Catholic school system is under pressure to make explicit its distinctiveness from the secular public system in order to preserve its status and avoid the same fate as Catholic schools in Newfoundland and Labrador and Quebec, where publicly funded Catholic schooling stopped after 1998 and 1999, respectively, then the ICE aims do go a long way toward articulating such a large difference. And there is nothing wrong with these strong formation aims, so far as they represent one kind of service and outcome the school offers. However, in announcing the schools' difference in such an apparently narrow fashion, the ICE aims also exaggerate one aspect of the distinctiveness these schools have at the expense of subordinating and silencing other possible kinds, and misrepresenting the diverse kinds of Catholic Educational service which occur simultaneously within the same building and same classroom.[75] The CCSTA aims are relatively more inclusive of multiple services.

The Catholic school encounters a difficult problem when it attempts to deal with the perceived threat of creeping secularism. The school is, after all, charged with the dual demands of integrating within the secular society *and* remaining consistent with Church teachings. This observation provides a fresh perspective from which to re-evaluate the story of Canadian Catholic education as it began in and emerged from pre-Confederation Ontario. As Catholics became increasingly integrated into mainstream society, their dependence upon the Church for a social identity decreased as secular Canadian culture became a greater part of their identity. With the adoption of that integrated identity, however, came the perceived problem of corruption: Is Catholicism corrupting the secular state, is the secular state corrupting Catholicism, or is something else happening? The problem of integrating the secular and the sacred thus falls upon the schools, and in day-to-day interactions that problem becomes the Catholic school-teacher's concern of how to integrate the institutional requirements of the state with those of the Church, and then how to accommodate that integrated set of requirements (no matter how well-formulated they are) with the individual pedagogical needs of students.

Murphy's work provides an example of how a creeping secular dominance and de-Christianization of society troubles Catholic schools. He remarks that in contemporary Ontario, "Roman Catholics are no longer a tiny minority. They represent approximately 30 per cent of the population, and are neither economically deprived, nor without political clout." Things are apparently looking good for those who call themselves Catholics, especially in comparison with Catholics in Upper Canada's pre-Confederation era. While Catholicism is a numerically strong movement throughout the world, it seems to be in the minority so far as it perceives itself to be struggling against a prevailing secular view.[76] In a liberal democratic society like Canada's, the threat is that the secular liberal view will, by its very nature, lead inevitably to individualism in its various forms, and to a tendency for individual choice and self-definition to be based on arbitrary preference or self-interest, rather than on a view of life that is more coherent and other-regarding.[77] Good Catholic citizenship must therefore balance the norms of secular society with a religious attitude that on the one hand does not recognize the legitimacy of certain elements in the modern secular state, but on the other hand does not flee from it entirely and instead would aim to improve it. The integration of sacred and secular in the Catholic school must therefore balance a critique of the secular state with an acceptance of the elements that promote Catholic values.[78]

There is no doubt that Catholic schools provide an important service and do good work in the current context. However, in an age where rapid changes are the norm and the expectations for one's intellectual and social development carry a high degree of meaning in terms of the political structure of the school and other educative relationships, several questions and ambiguities exist in the ways in which the Catholic Church is structured and the place where Catholic thought sits *vis-à-vis* Catholic practice. Most importantly, these questions remain unresolved within an institution that struggles to identify and articulate the work it does and the goals and hopes it has according to the aims of Catholic Education and Catholic Schooling. The internal work that Catholic schools do is also a reflection of their desire to present an externally distinct Catholic identity. The context of publicly funded Canadian Catholic schooling can largely be reflected in the theoretical-political problems that have emerged in Ontario, although the degree and direction in which they are felt elsewhere will likely vary somewhat. These themes are of vital importance to any discussion of Catholic Education insofar as it represents the integrated, organic culmination of all these influences.

CONTEMPORARY CHALLENGES FACING CATHOLIC SCHOOLS

The current concerns of Catholic schools to develop, nurture, and assert a distinctively Catholic identity within the larger secular Canadian political-educational culture reflect a development and interpretation of their pre-Confederation history. Their own self-understanding wrestles with these questions, and academic theory has struggled to follow and support them. The very terminology that weaves throughout these institutions represents a very good example of this paucity. One such term, "Catholic distinctiveness," is unstable and its meaning continues to transform. Throughout history that transformation has had a profound effect on the self-understanding and hence the character of Catholic schools.

Since the nineteenth century, both Canadian and Catholic social climates have changed greatly. Nineteenth-century Catholic schools were established for reasons intimately tied to the ethnicity and religion of their supporters, but that social element of Catholic distinctiveness gradually waned and the *raison d'être* for Catholic Education took on a different flavour as Catholics were gradually assimilated into mainstream Canadian society. While anti-Catholic sentiment is by no means completely dead today, it has in large part been neutralized and does not come close to presenting the same external threat it did in the nineteenth century. As the relatively more intense climate of bigotry also gradually eroded with assimilation, the justification for publicly funded separate Catholic schools as a protection against social oppression came to be supplanted by an emphasis on the theological, spiritual, and philosophical elements of Catholic schools as the qualities which distinguish them from secular public schools. Today's rationale for Catholic Education is no longer based on the visibly external criteria that had characterized pre-Confederation Catholics as a socially marginalized religious minority; the focus instead is upon providing an alternative form of education in which the entire curriculum and socio-moral atmosphere of the school is markedly religious. Purely religious reasons for maintaining Catholic schools have thus come to supplant the religiously dependent socio-ethnic reasons under which the schools gained their public charter.

That shift in emphasis was only possible, however, because spiritual distinctiveness was omnipresent, if possibly only softly emphasized or tacitly taken for granted in the pre-Confederation era as the obvious *root cause* of bigotry. During the period of change between the nineteenth century and today, Catholics have had to shift their educational outlook from the perspective of a group that had been *told by others* that it is different to the perspective of one that today *is telling others* that it is different.

In this current age, James Mulligan's book *Catholic Education: The Future is Now* reveals several of the problems and challenges that Canadian Catholic Education faces. Some of these problems descend from the historical foundations of Catholic Education to the present day, but all are relevant to the present and future story of Catholic Education in Canada generally speaking. In the course of highlighting these problems, however, Mulligan makes several troublesome assumptions about Catholicism and Catholic Education. It is important to note that Mulligan is not alone in his problematic assessment of Catholic Education; however, the large audience he has attracted makes his treatment here central to a critique of current popular perceptions. His work is important for identifying several issues of concern and for implicitly revealing the framework under which he identifies them, but it is problematic in terms of how he interprets and responds to these problems. Instead of making a comprehensive syllabus of Mulligan's persistent philosophical shortcomings and the methodological limitations under which he conducted and reported his interview-based research, in this section I will treat a representative sample of the problems Mulligan raises and the problems with his assumptions about Catholic Education. Although Mulligan is not a philosopher, his discursive treatment of Catholic Education warrants philosophical examination because it ventures into political, moral, and epistemological issues that are also properly the domain of philosophy of education; hence, the validity of his assertions also depends in large part upon their philosophical rigour.

The crux of the problem that Mulligan picks up is that Catholic schools in the current age are threatened by a climate of secularism within Canadian society and a general lapse of enthusiasm and vigour among Canadian Catholics for their religion and for religious education – two trends which threaten to erode their distinct identity and possibly lead to their demise, as happened in Newfoundland and Labrador and Quebec at the close of the twentieth century.[79] His arguments suggest that the spiritualized identity and learning out-comes of the Catholic school have eroded in recent years because the socio-ethnic communal basis of the foundation of Catholic separate schools has been displaced, because Catholics have assimilated into mainstream society and its secular values, and because Catholic identity within the Church has been thrown into flux in the period since the Second Vatican Council. Increasingly, too, non-Catholics and non-practicing Catholics choose to attend Catholic schools: a fact which ostensibly mitigates or blocks any singular focus on "thick" catechesis or formation in the school.

Additionally, since the Second Vatican Council there has been a great decline in the number of clergy and religious teachers in the schools; hence the appearance of Catholic piety as the primary symbol of Catholic identity has changed and declined from its preconciliar days, as lay teachers currently form the great majority and the clergy and religious have been reduced to being at best a very small fraction of Catholic school staffs. Thus, any image of a Catholic school staff representing an elite spiritual cohort that stands in distinct contrast to the (rest of the) laity and the secular world is, in addition to being fanciful Catholic romanticism, lost in the assimilation of Catholics into mainstream Canadian society. Notwithstanding that Catholic teachers come from the same parish congregations that populate the school, Mulligan nonetheless laments that in the present day there is a significant lack of religious formation among teachers in Catholic schools[80] – a situation that for him ostensibly signals a decline from what he believes the Christian character in Catholic schools should be, but for which he does not assign any responsibility to the parish Church in the formation of its congregations. The mission of the Catholic school, which was founded on the distinctiveness of its students and maintained by the piety of its teachers, according to Mulligan, thus requires refurbishing. In the absence of the preconciliar images of Catholic piety to carry the weight of re-articulated aims and action, Mulligan calls in this age for a renewed theological and spiritual statement of the Catholic school's distinctiveness.

Mulligan's Catholic Educational critique is striking because it is well-meaning, but potentially a source of distortion to a fruitful discussion of Catholic Education's problems because of its philosophical weaknesses. One such weakness is his too-quick conflation of liberalism with relativism.[81] The root of his error lies in his ignorance of two philosophical approaches whose main commonality (as he frames them) is that they both fall outside the teachings of the Catholic Church. Being "non-Catholic," however, is no more legitimate grounds for comparing liberalism and relativism than it is for comparing Judaism and Islam. Here is an example of how Mulligan treats this topic: "In the last 30 years, the glitter and glamour of hardcore materialism have generally enacted ties to spiritual sensibilities, and the liberal ethic of individual freedom and relativism has relegated the teaching and preaching churches to the cultural sidelines."[82] Relativism is indeed incompatible with Catholicism, but this is no grounds for reducing any and all challenges to Catholicism to it. That is the root of a straw-person argument. Furthermore, there is no mention of secular liberal thought that does not fall into relativism, mistake freedom for licence, and degrade the value of community. Well-known liberal theorists like John Dewey and John Rawls, among many others, have developed modern conceptions of the individual subject that do not slip into relativism or atomistic individualism. Such treatments of liberalism and relativism are unhelpful for current educational projects that aim to explore the integration between secular thought and religious doctrine, because the secular approach to considering "truth" has been prejudicially anathemized. Unfortunately, such views do not fairly consider the possibility that that something other than a Catholic brand of "hard universalism" might contribute to an understanding of truth and the role of religion and religious authority in society.

Mulligan's treatment of postmodernism is a similar case in point, and more than anything else its value is limited to an exercise in the exegesis of a folksy attempt to apprehend the term. His analysis is overcome by nostalgia, a syllabus of contemporary malaise, and distaste for the ambiguity of pluralism: a triad of complaints that occupy the space where an analysis of the scholarly debate surrounding postmodernism's definition should be:

A modernist consciousness or approach to life is rational. There is a reason for things, a certain logic. Progress and rational development, while inevitable, are thought to be good. Things are always going to improve. This modernist thinking, which is very Western, prevailed pretty much through the 1960s. Then the modernist spirit seemed to peter out. Life and living became increasingly complicated. Plurality and diversity in thinking and doing became more prevalent in our culture. Certainty about our approaches and convictions gave way to ambiguity. No longer could we assume that the children of the 1970s and 1980s were going to be better off than their parents, especially in terms of employment opportunities and economic security. Expectations have now diminished. Uncertainty and insecurity seem to be built into the contemporary psyche, and they contribute significantly to shaping how we live.[83]

Mulligan's lament completely misses postmodernism's critique of the liberal subject as the centre of rational, disembodied thought, and its repositioning of Enlightenment truth so that the truth can be perceived from a variety of perspectives rather than a singular transcendent view. The "confusion" that Mulligan attributes to postmodernism is as a result of the longing for a single, "hard," universal truth, although the modernist perspective to which he nostalgically refers has also seen its share of criticism as an inadequate and incomplete measure of reality.[84]

Postmodernism might also represent a critique of the prosperity to which Murphy (quoted above) refers when he speaks to the Catholic Church's obligation to be a counter-cultural presence in the world. Secular postmodern critiques of the same social conditions would in this case overlap with Catholic critiques. Moreover, he also does not consider the chance that Catholic schooling might represent a postmodern approach to the nation-state's means of accommodating minorities. Catholic schools – and especially publicly funded Canadian Catholic schools – exist distinct from and outside the uniformity and conformity many modern liberal secular states (such as France and the United States) embrace. Canada's multiculturalism, accommodation of minorities, and acceptance of the "jarring note"[85] that disrupts cultural purity stand in contrast to the modernist European conception of the liberal nation state because of the inability for any one modernist vision to dominate the Canadian political landscape.[86] Separate Catholic schools are therefore both a contributing cause and a living symptom of Canada's postmodern condition: a condition where doubt and lack of affixed national identity is positively understood. "[What] makes a country of minorities interesting," writes historian John Ralston Saul, "is the doubt, the questioning, the uncertainty which is there to keep us focused on the idea of the society rather than slipping into the old nationalist certitudes."[87] Instead of considering what postmodern critique might have in common with or where it could benefit Catholicism, Mulligan stubbornly clings to notions of postmodernism as Catholicism's philosophical, political, and theological nemesis.

As the object of blame for much of what is wrong with the Catholic Church, postmodernism often becomes the scapegoat for the symptoms of an ancient institution's struggle to adapt and maintain itself in a (post)modern world. Partly because of this attitude, Mulligan misreads an adolescent disaffection with what young people perceive to be an outmoded medieval church, believing it to be instead a postmodern malaise that is in competition with Catholicism. In Mulligan's estimation, then, postmodernism is a theme of the liberal, secular society that threatens to subvert the Catholic Church and its people. Young people, especially, must resist "assimilation of the superficial, self-serving values of the [secular] culture." The role of the Catholic school is to use the Gospel to teach students "survival skills in the context of a spirituality of resistance" amid "a culture which advocates racism, consumerism, sexism, militarism, avarice, an unrestrained sexuality, a culture which reconciles massive inequality and creates the conditions for class conflict."[88] To his credit, here Mulligan has pointed to many important problems in liberal society that both Catholic and non-Catholic persons struggle to confront and reverse.

Unfortunately for Mulligan, though, his work misses considering the possibility that much postmodern literature is as concerned with tackling these issues as the Catholic Church is.[89] As for the malaise and fragmentation, he also fails to wonder whether they might be symptomatic of lay disaffection with clericalism. He does not consider the issue of whether Catholic teachings might inspire a strategic indifference among lay Catholics because open challenges to them draw negative attention and meet frustration. In response to this situation, the school meets the laity and the institutional church halfway: it presents the official teaching to satisfy the Church, but in order to satisfy its constituents it makes no intrusion into the lives of its students. The Church is thus left in a slow state of decay and the laity left to its own devices of resistance and dissent.

While Mulligan might have a legitimate worry that the Catholic faith has been marginalized by the dominant forces within secular thinking and secularism, his critique of those forces is weakened by its argumentative shortcomings and lack of factual depth. Some forms of liberalism and postmodernism may have potential contributions toward the development of Catholic thought and the interpretations of the aims Catholic institutions state. Unfortunately, Mulligan does not acknowledge or appreciate this nuance or possibility. His treatment might retain some merit as an oeuvre that accomplishes the long-overdue task of bringing controversial topics within Catholic Education to the public forum; unfortunately, however, even in this respect its helpfulness is diminished by a philosophical looseness that alienates and distorts the scholarly perspectives that sustain the quality of a debate which is neither polemic nor apologetic.

Not all commentary on Catholic Education suffers from lack of terminological clarity or scarcity of theoretical depth. Dennis Murphy provides a quick synopsis of some of the most urgent problems within the Church at large that also seem to threaten Catholic Education: "What is evident everywhere is a high level of disenchantment with the church by both young and middle-aged Catholics. These latter attach no great credibility to the teaching of the church, particularly on moral issues. Hardly anyone pays attention to church teaching on birth control; and this arguably is the reason for a lack of credibility in other areas, particularly areas of personal morality."[90] Murphy's synopsis raises the question of what role Catholic Education should take in tackling these problems.

Evidence from the American context confirms Murphy's observations, and suggests that Catholic schools in the current age face great limitations if they are to attempt to redouble their students' Catholicity. Sociologist Christian Smith reports that lower levels of Catholic adolescent religious involvement are strongly tied to their parents' low levels of religiosity[91] and that since Vatican II, contemporary adolescent and adult American Catholics tend to be "more acculturated, more individualistic, and more selective in appropriating elements of the Catholic worldview as they personally [see] fit."[92] Moreover, Smith reports that, for better or for worse, American Catholic schools are focusing less on socializing students in the faith than they are on providing basic educational needs for poor students and, more typically, on preparing students for college entrance.[93] These phenomena contrast with the sharply defined counter-cultural tone that John Allen observes as the hierarchy's posture *vis-à-vis* the secular world.

The philosophical problem of how to integrate all the school's constitutive elements is a major issue for which there is no cleanly defined resolution. If the school does its job of "teaching" (as in "presenting") what the Church directs but the students do not accept its validity, has the school done its job to meet the needs of these students? Likewise, if the school eschews any care for what the Church teaches and for expedient reasons of good relations with students and parents adapts and alters Catholicism to such a degree that it no longer accurately represents the Magisterium, is it doing its job to meet the needs of the Church? Moreover, in the latter case, if the school is not meeting the needs of the Church, is it arguably still a Catholic school, or has it forfeited its right as a dissenting entity within the Canadian federation?

This issue can be analyzed using a series of questions that would take a sanguine view of what the school is currently doing well, in spite of any laments commentators make. For instance, if the school is serving the Church, then what is meant by "Church," who is the Church, what is the role relationship between the hierarchy and laity, and (how) should the school be expected to remedy adult and youth disenchantment with the Church at large? If the Catholic school is to integrate secular and sacred, individual and institution, ordained and lay, and private and public so that these tensions do not slip out of balance in a way that oppresses minority or marginalized interests, a philosophically and theologically sound means of addressing these questions must be found. This means cannot be imagined, articulated, or implemented without some reference to the conceptions of Catholic Education and Catholic Schooling that are present within the aims and intentions that one finds in the institution, for otherwise it would slip into the trap Olson identifies, that of making reforms from the perspectives or in the interests of only one side within the school's constitutive partnership.[94]

Besides raising questions about the nature of the distinction and relationship between Catholic Education and Catholic Schooling, Murphy's and Smith's observations also bring forth at least two competing assumptions about the role of the home in supporting Catholic schools. The first is the assumption that Catholic schools should conform to a certain idea of a Catholic environment, experience, and curriculum that begins at a certain place where the responsibility of the (it is assumed also Catholic) home ends. The home is expected to provide all the private experiences of religion that will adequately prepare the learner to enter the institutional religious sphere at a level of fluency that enables the school to provide public religious experiences that the home cannot. It is interesting that neither Murphy nor Mulligan mention that the Second Vatican Council declares that parents are free to organize religious life in their households as they see fit, and according to the Catholic principle of subsidiarity, the family's primacy should not be supplanted, nor should educational interventions take place without "due considerations ... for the wishes of parents."[95] Nonetheless, what Murphy and Mulligan bemoan[96] is that when the religious expectations of the home do not match those of the school – say, when the school expects that all its pupils have the experiences of praying before meals at home and attending Mass on Sunday, but the home does not provide that experience – the school is thus put in a position to complain about a decline in Catholic values that the home does not provide. The school perceives that it is being asked to do the "private" work of the home, and so must divert time and resources away from what it perceives as its "public" function: that of working on a curriculum that presupposes a domestic foundation in Catholic life. When those apparently "private" learnings are not obtained in their domestic place, those in charge of Catholic Schooling become worried that the learners who come to, and help constitute, the Catholic school are in no way different from the learners who constitute a secular public school. Without such an obvious "Catholic character" inherent in the student population, claims that the Catholic school is distinct for housing a uniquely religious student body seem to become shaky and, it is feared, nullified. From this point of view, the decline in Catholic distinctiveness has begun in the home, and so it follows that the home must reassert itself, especially in places where Catholic schools receive public money. A kind of strategic essentialism is seemingly required in this view to maintain Catholic Education. The questions remain open, however, as to what precisely constitutes "Catholic character," and whether the home is being judged according to an appropriate ideal of Catholic Education-Schooling.

The second competing interest maintains that the home is being expected to do too much in maintaining the appearance and delivery of a distinctively Catholic Education. This contention proposes that the institutional Church has alienated many Catholics from their own religion and the home cannot rehabilitate what the parish Church has lost. Far from wishing for the demise of Catholic Education, Catholics in this theorized situation are frustrated and disaffected by the lack of flexibility within the political institution of their religion, given that it cannot keep pace with the secular advances in moral and political thought. Without recourse in formal public institutions, the family asserts itself against Church teachings in the private sphere because this is where it currently has the greatest ability to do so. The shift is from an outward public piety that conforms to the Catholic Church's explicit teachings to an inwardly muddy domestic righteousness that unfortunately comes at the cost of partially withdrawing from or even abandoning organized public expression at Mass or extra-liturgical parish functions and associations. The Catholic School and Church and their apologetic commentators are well enough organized to makes their complaints about the Home in the public press, but the Home's ability to respond to these criticisms is severely hampered because it is, by comparison, simply an aggregate construct of many competing ecclesial and theological views and has no collectively authoritative spokesperson.

In some way, the bureaucratic and clerical Catholic Church likely has an intuitively deep awareness of this shift from the outward piety of institutional religious conformity in the public sphere to the inward, isolated, and independently non-conformist righteousness of the private sphere. In an age where regular (weekly) church attendance is declining among the majority of Canadian Catholics,[97] the Catholic schools have become aware that in many cases they are the first and perhaps only place of regular institutionalized religious contact for students. The notion of "community" as an aspect of the Christian person is thus learned first and foremost in the school. As a result, the school takes on the pastoral task of evangelizing the "unchurched" Catholic, and, as Murphy observes, adopts the essence of the parish Church's function: "The Ontario bishops have mentioned in their 1989 pastoral letter 'This Moment of Promise' that for some students schools are already the primary faith community. Fewer clergy, the lower Sunday Mass attendance, less parish involvement, have in the last number of years exercised very negative effects upon parish life. My question is whether or not we can embrace a specifically Catholic understanding of community education which would offer new life and a broader vision to all our institutions and enable them to better respond to the needs of the future."[98]

Given the above concerns, it seems prudent to ask whether Catholic Education ought to rethink the assumptions that are inherent in its aims and the tasks it undertakes. It is unclear, for instance, whether the phenomenon of "unchurched" Catholic students in Catholic schools is symptomatic of a lack of disciplinary rigour and a weak, lackadaisical spirituality, or if it is rather a form of dissent from, resistance to, or disagreement with the Church, that is expressed via non-conformity to its public ritual. From the philosophical tensions within Catholic schools, the above concerns point to the larger questions about what exactly Catholic Education and Educational theory are in this current period following the Second Vatican Council. It is at least conceptually clear, though, that Catholic Education is struggling under the burdens of competing expectations of what it rightly should be doing. These expectations range from instilling a pre-conciliar catechetical programming; to providing a place of stricter discipline and academic achievement; to doing the Church's work of preaching the Gospels in conformity with the norms of Vatican II; to providing schooling in the name of Christian service to the community; to offering a kind of education from a Catholic perspective that makes intellectual growth in learning about and from within religion possible, but does not attempt to do the socialization work of the Home or the catechistic or evangelical work of the Parish. These are questions that need to be addressed with philosophical rigour if Catholic Education is to avoid the pitfalls of distorted perceptions.

A Catholic Philosophy of Education is Lacking

So on what theoretical grounds can one appreciate, criticize, and otherwise respond to commentators or make interpretations about Catholic Education-Schooling in a way that makes sense in theory and practice? The challenges facing Catholic Education in the present day are made difficult by the fact that there is no systematic or comprehensive philosophy of Catholic Education. According to philosopher of education David Carr: "It has been observed that, within contemporary philosophy of education, no distinctively Catholic systematic account of the major role of education has yet emerged."[99] This is disturbing in light of the fact that the whole Church is arguably still in a period of response, transition, and adaptation following the reforms enacted at the Second Vatican Council. With all the changes in the Church Constitution and teaching that were brought about at the Council, there has been neither the philosophical nor practical support to help enact the changes or guide the transition from the Tridentine to the modern church.[100] The Council made wholesale theological and philosophical changes with little or no practical guidance on how to enact and monitor them in practice, and this fact has resulted in confusion for lack of any planned integration of changes into the Church.

This general assessment of the Council and its aftermath most certainly holds true for the situation that Catholic Education faces. The Council published a short descriptive vision in GE, but then provided little else that is more substantive in educational theory and practice that would help schools adapt to the pan-ecclesial changes. Ellis Joseph observes that Catholic philosophy of education in the post-conciliar era is wanting for fresh insight: "While Vatican II is seen to have set forth the concepts of collegiality and shared authority, the 'Declaration on Christian Education' is described as not having a philosophical base and as being a document which breaks little new ground. There is little doubt that [post-]conciliar thinkers are wondering whatever happened to Catholic philosophy of education."[101]

In the absence of a firm philosophical footing upon which to guide executive action in the years since the Second Vatican Council, Catholic Education has experienced a variety of problematic and vague substitutes that emerge from practical working solutions. These practical interpretations, however, often lack rigour and self-reflection, and philosopher of education Terence McLaughlin describes them as "platitudinous rhetoric or edubabble."[102] Such rhetoric is the result of gratuitous selection and shallow interpretation of Catholic Church documents in ways or contexts that distort their meaning or do little to bring clarity to vague expressions. As McLaughlin argues, vague phrasings should be fodder with which to begin philosophical discussions about Catholic Education, and not a means of justifying a kind of executive power that clamps off their growth:

> There is a distinctive Catholic variant of "edu-babble" which is typically forged out of phrases drawn from the various educational documents of the church. Often these documents are "mined" for such phrases in a rather eclectic way. Phrases such as "The school should be based on the values of the Gospel" and "The Spirit of Christ should permeate everything that is done in the school" can sometimes bring discussion of the Catholic distinctiveness of the school to an end and give the impression that the matters at stake have been satisfactorily dealt with. But like "edu-babble" in general, such phrases are primarily useful as spurs to deeper discussion, not a substitute for it.[103]

In the context of publicly funded Catholic schools, the lack of a clear philosophy of Catholic Education and the imprecise justifications for the administrative actions that follow from that philosophically weak domain lead to further difficulty with explaining how Catholic schools are to approach the theoretical and practical tensions which permeate them. These tensions include the integration of secular and sacred expectations and the management of the distinctions between public-private, personal-political (personal-ecclesial), and individual-community that precipitate from these expectations. The last distinction in that series is probably the most important in terms of pedagogical approaches to matters of socio-moral dissent from mainstream Catholic teachings.

The lack of an adequate and comprehensive philosophy of Catholic Education that takes up the task of describing and proposing an integrated secular-sacred model leaves its institutions without an explicit direction for practice. Within the context of a modern-day Catholic Church that has much breadth of perspective among its members, this directionless momentum leaves many issues unspoken, unacknowledged, unaddressed, and unresolved in the public sphere. This strategy of non-acknowledgment, however, can be more harmful than helpful in the long-term interest of public institutions:

> The increasing heterogeneity of belief in practice among
> Catholics ... leads to a number of well-recognized and significant
> tensions within the Catholic community as a whole and in rela-
> tion to its educational work ... One strategy for approaching
> such disagreements and conflict is through a "culture of silence"
> about certain matters. This seems to be, at least to some extent,
> a strategy used in the Catholic schools studied by Bryk et al
> (1993). In such circumstances rhetoric, ambiguity and obfusca-
> tion can have a lubricative role in relation to the management of
> the school and elsewhere ... Such a strategy does, however signif-
> icantly undermine the aim of achieving clarity about Catholic
> educational distinctiveness.[104]

The lack of any adequate and comprehensive philosophical approach to Catholic Education thus contributes to the problem of mythologizing: problems, critiques, and commentary that are at the constitutive institutional heart of the theory and practice of Catholic Education have become submerged within a culture that leaves questions of its internal intellectual diversity – and diversity within global Catholicism – undisturbed in any significant public manner. Rather, this climate tends to reduce any debates to sharp binaries and the debating positions within them to polemic attacks or apologies. The same attitudes and rationales which attempt to shroud clerical controversy within a mystic aura of holiness[105] are enacted to defend Catholic Education by avoiding its philosophical self-examination for fear of potentially undermining its existence. This is the dominant or prevailing view of Catholic Education's attitude toward dissent. "Mythology often turns into a denial of complexity," writes Saul, and "[on] a bad day, mythology encourages the denial of reality [where] absolute answers and ideologies prosper."[106] The outcome is a telling lack of willingness and learned sophistication with which to correctly identify and treat some of the Catholic Education's current challenges.

Following from the lack of a systematic philosophical approach to discourse in Catholic Education is an inability to express precisely and clearly a critique of the modern, secular world in a way that does not distort secularity and damage attempts to integrate the sacred and the secular in the Catholic school. Moreover, misunderstanding the diversity of secular perspectives by conflating them under terms such as "relativism" and "postmodernism" – terms that are mistreated as catch-all categories to house non-Catholic anathemas – undermines any possibility that portions of these schools of thought might contribute positively to a refurbishment of the philosophy of Catholic Education. The unfortunate dismissal of entire secular schools of thought, for the singular reason that some parts of their doctrines draw criticism from the Catholic Church or are misrepresented in the popular press, is in fact a real problem that a clearly articulated philosophy of Catholic Education could address with a progressive generosity that would help, rather than hinder, an enunciation of the sacred-secular integration.

A THEORETICAL INTERPRETATION OF DISSENT AND CATHOLIC EDUCATION

All of the above discussion of educational and ecclesial issues is on the subject of the dissent a minority group makes from the dominant, mainstream society. Without a disinterested theoretical framework within which to interpret this dissent, however, one runs the risk of either succumbing to the ideological gravity that sustains binary characterizations of religion and religious education, or else being unable to interpret the statements of, and respond to, those who present their views from any polarized or other position within Catholicism and the theory and practice of Catholic Education. To this end, Canadian political theorist Will Kymlicka's model of "external protections" and "internal restrictions" provides a disinterested means of fruitfully describing the theoretical problems at play when a minority group demands or is granted rights within a liberal society. External protections are "intended to protect the group from the impact of external decisions (e.g. the economic or political decisions of the larger society)," and are maintained so that the survival of the minority group is not threatened by the decisions that the dominant culture makes. "Internal restrictions" describes the requirements a minority group often makes that its individual members conform to the social norms and rules that controlling powers within the group dictate. They are "intended to protect the group from the destabilizing impact of internal dissent (e.g. the decision of individual members not to follow traditional practices or customs)."[107]

This combination of "external protections" and "internal restrictions" is intended to protect the stability of the minority community within the larger society and to promote its integrity by preventing internal instability. Canadian Catholic Education benefits from external protection in the provinces where it receives public funding, and most especially in those provinces that grant it full public funding, because in those places it represents an actively state-sanctioned alternative to the majority's mainstream public education system. When translated into the Catholic Church and Catholic Education, the tension between maintaining a group right versus an individual right has surfaced at points such as the Church's censure of dissent on the topics of women's rights, artificial birth control, and Magisterial teaching authority, among other issues.

Although Canadian Catholic Schooling has achieved its minority status *qua* its religious affiliation, it stands as a model for both religious and educational distinctiveness. As such, the external protections for Catholic Education represent three things: (1) A template for minority dissent against the dominant culture's oppressive education system (whether it be based on secular common or hegemonic religious schools) with the aim of protecting a minority population. This was the main reason for the recognition given the separate Catholic schools in the 1840s. (2) A distinct form of religious education from the dominant culture's secular – but not necessarily oppressive – educational system. This represents the admittance and recognition of a spiritual or religious dialogue into the publicly funded schools, as such representing dissent against the bias toward the prevailing secular educational style or styles. (3) An alternative form of educational philosophy from the mainstream state schools. This alternative philosophical approach represents an aspect of pluralism and choice among various forms of education. One might argue that choice is good for democracy, and as such, more variety should be present in a democratic society's educational offerings. Any or all of these three reasons count for the maintenance of Catholic schools.

Theorizing Catholic schools' status in terms of macro-political dissent provides the strongest philosophical continuity between the pre-Confederation and post-conciliar eras. Publicly funded Catholic schools are exemplars of dissent central to the Canadian socio-political climate, and so what is sometimes dismissed as an "accident of history" is in fact an exemplary instance of the Canadian social contract. Today, in addition to maintaining publicly funded Catholic schools in three provinces and three territories, that contract is pursuing social justice issues in terms of civil rights for women, visible minorities, persons with disabilities, and the sexually marginalized. A point of conflict in theory and practice arises, however, between (1) those who support both wholesale external protections and internal restrictions to advance the cause of minorities, and (2) those who support external protections but recoil from most, if not all, internal restrictions. Debates between those who favour the former position and those who favour the latter are in fact debates on the question of whether the rights of the minority group are superior to the rights of its individuals and sub-groups.

The issue of to what degree internal restrictions against individuals should accompany external protections for minority groups presents a tension that is under-appreciated and under-explored in the scholarship on Catholic Education (and Catholicism more broadly). How can a philosophy of Catholic Education fairly balance the individual Catholic person's rights within the system against the Catholic community's right (at least as it is represented by its leadership) to maintain some normative distinctiveness from the homogenizing tendencies of a majority secular culture? And to what degree does the content of these issues influence these discussions? This is the point at which there is a current lack of publicly available theoretical language for criticizing Catholicism and Catholic Education from a faithful point of view. How might a Catholic person challenge his or her Church without (being accused of) anti-Catholicism, apostasy, heresy, or de-Catholicizing the institution? This tension between individual and corporate aims is the point at which teaching professionals and students meet to implicitly negotiate in practice the aims of teaching and learning in a Catholic school.

4

Foundational Aims and Concerns in the Theory of Catholic Education-Schooling

The previous two chapters on the Church's normative educational theory and on the particular history and concerns in Ontario's publicly funded Catholic schools have gone part of the distance toward encapsulating a view of the promises and problems that accompany Catholic Education. As a methodological reference point for this whole volume, the introduction of these global and local perspectives and experiences has travelled across the territory of theology, ecclesiology, historical context, and some of the current political problems that emerge for Catholic Educational experiences. For the purposes of proposing a reform of Catholic Education, however, these multiple views, while important, still require supplementary perspectives for the whole theory to achieve optimal validity.

A metaphor is helpful here. If educational reform is a wild animal that must be domesticated so that one can get close enough to understand it, then some boundaries need to be erected in order to keep that animal within sight and reach. The requirement, of course, is to use barriers on more than one or two sides (assuming they are not circular), in order to make the structure functional, for otherwise the animal will simply turn away from its obstacle and move unencumbered in the opposite direction. Arranging several barriers so that they enclose the animal is a more desirable design. The metaphorical implication is that any grasp on educational reform must be a coordinated multi-dimensional effort, lest a unilaterally flat proposal be ignored and its object slide back to the familiar, even if uncomfortable, inertia of the status quo. To simply make a theology of dissent and then throw it at an institution of education would likely result in the institution's dismissal of, if not recoil from the theory, and its turning back toward a path that would maintain its current practice.

Now all metaphors break down at some point, and with this one it happens at the point where "wild animal" stands for "education" or "educational institution" and "captive" stands for "conceptual clarity." There is no attempt made here somehow to characterize Catholic schools as unruly and undomesticated, or to surreptitiously claim that I am planning to take Catholic Educational theory prisoner for the purposes of asserting total control over it. The aim is simply to describe the momentum and inertia of educational systems, and in doing so to demonstrate an optimal way for thinking about reform proposals. The more comprehensive the vision of any proposed educational reform, the less chance it might falter.

This chapter places a view of Catholic curricular theory in sequence with its prior counterparts, so as to gradually bring the theoretical structure one step closer to honouring the complexities of the complete reality of professional practice. The focus is not on how Catholic schools represent themselves, but on the hopes and concerns that result from attempts at translating these representative aims into classroom instructional practice. This topic of translation is the domain of curricular theory at a higher level of abstraction than particular day-to-day "methods," but at a slightly lower level than the statements of institutional aims. The use of "higher" and "lower" in this context is by no means a comparative assignment of value. Returning briefly to the metaphor of corralling the unruly animal of educational reform, one could imagine that if curricular theory were one of the barriers which completed a single side of the working enclosure, it would have to be of the same strength as each of its counterparts, or else by design there would be a weakness in the pen. The burden of this kind of curricular theory is to connect (Catholic) education's larger social (and religious) aims with the contingencies of working with real people. By "curricular" in this chapter I therefore mean the theoretical construction of the teaching-learning relationships by which students have religious experiences, encounter and produce knowledge, and develop thinking skills.

The chapter begins with a general exposition of the hopes that Catholic Education has toward these ends. These hopes are seen as primary to its institutional foundation, but their primary place is by no means exclusive of other foundational matters. The second section, on the *concerns* that Catholic Education faces, enumerates several issues which are also inherent in the institution of Catholic educational relationships, and to which any theoretical proposal that hopes to prescribe a reform of Catholic Education must recognize and respond. As this volume is directed toward accommodating student dissent as a proposed pedagogical reform, the final section in this chapter integrates the work on hopes and concerns into a view that considers the aims of the student as a partner that education cannot do without.

HOPES FOR TEACHING-LEARNING RELATIONSHIPS IN A CATHOLIC SCHOOL

The temptation to present educative relationships in authoritarian terms is attractive for some who would maintain that knowledge is fixed, complete, and comes from an external source that schools and teachers access and then represent to students, whose job it is to learn it.[1] This transmission-of-knowledge model is by no means the exclusive property of Catholic Education, nor does Catholic Education itself necessarily use it or employ it all the time, but when applied to Catholic Education, this transmission would follow a chain from the Magisterial teachings of the Church through to the School as authorized agent "to teach" on behalf the Magisterium, and finally to the student as the receptor of these teachings. So long as the content of what is "taught" is correct, and if each member adheres to its appropriate institutional responsibility, then everything is in its proper place. Of course this system works best if everyone agrees with this model's ostensible aim to reinforce a system of knowledge and ecclesial authority so constructed; but even for those who would most rigidly adhere to the political-ecclesial, moral, and epistemic assumptions this model represents, two major criticisms are present which are arguably ideologically neutral so far as the Church is concerned.

First, the model raises questions about what it means "to teach." "Teaching" as such could be used to mean actions like to "tell," "present," or "direct," but as these are unilateral actions performed by one standing in the role of "teacher," there is no way to ensure causality; "telling," "presenting," or "directing" are not sufficient learning conditions. The transmission model depends upon student receptivity, but cannot guarantee it. When used in this hierarchical sense, "teaching" is a problematic term because it overlooks the student's role in learning *along with* the teaching. Basically, can an action be called teaching unless learning occurs?

Second, the model also presents problems for those who are concerned with procuring authentic learning results. One of the great challenges Catholic curricular theory faces is to present normative Church teaching in a way that respects the learner's religious freedom. The Second Vatican Council affirms that all persons have religious freedom, and so to coerce or otherwise dishonestly procure anyone's assent to faith would consequentially result in an inauthentic faith.[2] The political-ecclesial model of hierarchical authority descending from Magisterial Church through to School and student may loom large, but as a model for constructing educative relationships, it finds itself confronting or at least being tempered by its own teachings on the individual agency of the learner. By definition, education mitigates rigid authoritarianism.

The challenge for Catholic Educational theory is therefore to work within the seemingly murky territory between an authoritarian Church and the agency and needs of individual learners. A well-known way of positioning the teacher within these circumstances thus eschews direct transmission of knowledge, and the teacher is often metaphorically described instead as one who "opens doors," "provides opportunities," or "uncovers" (rather than "covers") the curriculum for students.[3] Mary Boys is a leading advocate of this ideal for education in the Catholic faith, which she presents as making invitations and providing access to the faith, opening the way for students to read, ask questions, overcome obstacles to understanding, and otherwise participate freely at their level of comfort: "To provide access means to erect bridges, to make metaphors, to build highways, to provide introductions and commentaries, to translate foreign terms, to make maps, to demolish blockages, to demonstrate effects, to energize and sustain participation, and to be hospitable."[4]

Such a view is far from any naïve insistence or caricature that the curriculum of Catholic schools is drilled into students by dour and firmly authoritarian teachers who rely exclusively on methods of direct transmission to promote student learning. This description might be enough for those who would be satisfied with the description of a teacher who is "more humane" or "approachable" than the one who adheres to strict authoritarianism, but it remains partial until one considers the parallel construction of the student that would complete it as a view of *teaching and learning*. The view of the student implied here is of one who is curious and actively interested in accepting such an invitation. Furthermore, in Boys' view, this student appears remarkable for having his or her own intentions, which implies that for him or her, any acceptance of this relationship and any learning that occurs will be of the kind and quality that is most personally suitable. The desired ends of teaching and learning religion in a Catholic school and of being socialized in the moral atmosphere of the same institution thus cannot be determined precisely, past what one would hope that the student will achieve in terms of knowledge and critical thinking skills; because the degree of any faithful commitment or kind of ecclesial dedication or attachment that might result remains supererogatory and personal.

If one is to assume that in this case religious education holds out some kind of personal transformation as a possible, albeit not a necessary result, then sensitivity to the student's self in the teaching-learning relationship emerges as an existential matter that, for the purposes of writing institutional and pedagogical aims, implies a possible suspension or even reversal of the authoritarian model and begins with students' needs and interests as the basis of religious education. Edwin Cox, writing from within the British context and toward a more generic philosophical end, nonetheless provides some helpful prescriptions on how learning experiences ought to be designed which would obtain whether or not one is within a devotional setting. He offers that in the interest of learning, religious education should "relate to the understanding of pupils at their various stages of development," "deal with matters that pupils feel are relevant and important to their lives (and consequentially interesting)," and "enable them to move toward coming to terms with their own life problems by means of a coherent and conscious set of beliefs."[5]

Those with sympathies for the authoritarian, conservative pedagogy and a concern for the unblemished authentic transmission of what the Catholic Church teaches as the school's curricular focus may object on the grounds that such a mitigation of distinctively Catholic teaching and character might distort the picture of revelation-based truth in the school. From within a more specifically Catholic perspective, however, and for the purposes of establishing a distinctively Catholic teaching-learning relationship in the post-conciliar age, Gabriel Moran presents a model of revelation that emerges throughout the whole Church, including, but not limited to, the Magisterium. This model allows him to imagine a theological, rather than simply a decoratively instrumental justification for beginning with students' needs and intentions:

There is no revelation except in God revealing himself in personal experience, [and so in] deciding on the basis of a religious curriculum it is simply not true that one should choose (or could choose) between the child or the revelation. One must structure the teaching according to the people precisely because that is where revelation is. Why do not catechetical writers take seriously their own profession that God's revelation is found in Jesus Christ and his brethren instead of immediately reverting to the identification of revelation with doctrines? In the teaching of religion one must begin with the students, not because this is easier psychologically but because this is better theologically.[6]

Beginning with students does not logically lead to any exclusion of the Magisterium and Tradition; rather, by demonstrating to students their personal involvement in the history of revelation, the teaching method obtains some congruence with the GDC's emphasis on the subjective participation of those to be catechized.[7] Moran observes that models which attempt to insert revelation from an authoritarian Church into what is assumed to be the receptive vessel of the student do not work; for him, the pedagogical solution is twofold. First, he advocates for a more modest aim in religious education. While he is "completely in favour of total Christian formation and commitment," he maintains that he "[does] not feel that schools can do these things" and should instead properly make a smaller contribution to the student's whole life experience. Second, they should do so not by abandoning a focus on knowledge and intellectual questions, but in fact by taking on the tough work of "appealing to children's intelligences"[8] and making intelligible sense of the concerns that descend from their interests.

These views of Moran's are taken from his work in the period immediately following the Second Vatican Council, but as schools and school districts continue to announce their aims in such strong ways that suggest personal change, his argumentative currency and freshness seem not to have diminished with time, and the fact that contemporary writers echo similar views confirms his strength of foundational foresight. Thomas Groome, for instance, enumerates an annotated list of what he claims is the optimal way of "engaging learners in the teaching/learning dynamic." The headings in this list are "Arouse and create interest in learners ... Build curriculum from and for learners' lives ... Pose personally engaging questions and questioning activities ... Challenge learners ... Imagine ways to arouse curiosity ... Have enthusiasm for what you are teaching ... Vary teaching methods ... Assign varied 'requirements,' favoring, when possible, ones that demand their own generativity ... [and] Help them make meaning."[9] If these items are mutually consistent, and there is no reason to suggest otherwise, then it appears that he is prescribing an existential path toward students' discovery of their own relationship with religion and faith, and, following this, if appropriate and desired, discovering their own place within religious institutions and so "appropriating" religious tradition for themselves.[10] Far from simply appealing to anyone with firm but superficial commitments to "student-centredness" or "more humane" methods of teaching, Groome's prescriptions are in fact practical extensions of Moran's claim that revelation is found within people themselves, implying that revelation is an ongoing social event from which pedagogical aims, designs, and strategies can be interpreted.

One can find further contemporary congruence with Moran in the work of religious educator Graham Rossiter. Rossiter is very clear in his view that while there is a cognitive component in religious education, beyond declarative knowledge and critical skills in analysis, synthesis, and evaluation there are also emotional, moral, aesthetic, and spiritual dimensions that accompany the critical responses students make to the material presented. Given the personal, internal nature of these responses, Rossiter prescribes the provision of much space for students to contemplate privately their response and the dropping of any requirements that they respond within a particular set time, space, or pattern. To do otherwise, he asserts, is a "stifling [influence] on students' personal involvement in religious education."[11] Like Groome, Rossiter also prescribes methods that would allow students to appropriate religious traditions for themselves and to "[make] judgments about the implications of their learning and reflections in religious education," the latter of which he asserts is intrinsic to learners.[12] Curriculum design in accord with these aims would thus allow students to experience faith development in terms of their own felt relevance and personal readiness. To follow these aims, Rossiter claims, is to benefit the entire teaching-learning relationship: "A sharper understanding of the place for faith in classroom religious education not only makes the teaching more purposeful, confident, and satisfying for the teacher, and more interesting for the students, but also makes the work more valuable as an opportunity for developing students' religious faith."[13] Any aims that the school has in its formal or informal curriculum for catechesis, evangelization, formation of persons, community, social justice, and critique of the modern secular world must bear in mind that students, as objects of these aims, will respond to these efforts with their own personal intentions and existential concerns.

So far as the practical task of "making religion accessible" is concerned, the issue of students' general fluency with religious language and specific fluency within Catholicism emerges, because it is one of the major communicative means through which they become exposed to, learn about, and create religious knowledge. Catholicism is a particular kind of religion, and so for classification purposes the larger domain of religious knowledge, thinking, emotion, socialization, and other personal response to religion might be called "spirituality." This classification is a helpful means of describing the breadth of cognitive and affective territory within which religion teachers and their students work, and how, depending on students' needs, they could oscillate between the specifically "thick" language of Catholicism, and the "thinner," more generic realm of spiritual experience more broadly and inclusively understood.

Carson notes that for Catholicism, spirituality in the post-conciliar era is generally defined as a "growth in Christian experience by all Catholics" who, according to the Council Fathers, are "called to the fullness of Christian life and the perfection of charity."[14] This expression is certainly Catholic, but also open to interpretation as to how one would enact it as a Catholic person. Groome retains such open language as a goal for education as well, naming spirituality as "the soul's preeminent expression ... [of] drawing us inward and outward through our own depths into relationships with others and with Other. The spirit in spirituality is the human spirit for relationship with others and with God."[15] Within a Catholic school, this condition would represent the grounds upon which "thicker" interpretations would blossom. The use of the term "spirituality" raises a particular problem, however, because it is conceptually very open-ended. Carson warns that "spirituality" has become a very generic rubric for all kinds of experiences and is an "applause word"[16] for pluralism or, in certain places, even an intellectually shallow syncretism[17] that is so inclusive of all phenomena and experiences both within and outside all religious traditions that it is impossible to exclude anything from it.[18] At two ends of a continuum, therefore, spirituality may be very "thinly" diluted or void of Catholic content, or else explicitly named in "thick" Catholic terms – acknowledging at the same time, so as not to entrench a dichotomy between secular and sacred here, that several varieties of "thickness" are possible. This variance exemplifies the very conceptual slipperiness of the term.

Nonetheless, in terms of curricular design these conceptual difficulties are at least repaid by the word's helpfulness for also describing and admitting the range of possible personal responses that would descend from the above alignment of Boys', Moran's, Groome's, and Rossiter's approaches to Catholic Education. Assuming that Catholic schools admit students of many religions or no religion at all, including Catholic students of varying commitment to the Church, it follows that among the range of potential personal responses it would be conceivable to discover that students present many kinds of "spirituality" which might reflect a range from extremely thin and generic to decidedly thick and (in many different ways) very Catholic. Moreover, as a general concept spirituality can also encompass both the personal experiences students have and the formal ways in which groups and institutions make collective sense of experience and describe orthodox ways of commitment. For Cox, in order to make the bridge between students' personal experiences and the questions they have about commitment, two things must happen:

[The teacher's obligation is to] first help his [sic] pupils appreciate that the experience of living raises questions of truth and meaning and life-styles that no sensitive and alert person can avoid, and that religions and non-theistic life-stances are concerned with dealing with those questions; secondly, to assist the pupils to understand the language that religions use in discussing those questions, a language that is not the straightforward descriptive talk that is used by the sciences, but a language of myth, story, parable, and allegory.[19]

In this inclusive sense, the conceptual term *spirituality* as such can be broadly and ecumenically applied to mean the generally transcendent realm of experience and questions of ultimate meaning in life such as one's relationship with a creator and creation, and extends to questions of "ultimacy [as] a general designation for such ideas as infinitude, absoluteness, the unlimited, transcendence, perfection, completeness, all-inclusiveness, the supreme, and many others."[20] In a less generic but still inviting way, *Catholic spirituality* can be described as a "life structure" that is "the systematic approach to the presence of God"[21] in one's life and the life of the community, which follows "life-orienting images [as] the tracks or road along which it runs, giving it direction"[22] toward the end of "liberation."[23] Liberation is also a very broadly defined word, but according to Warren, one major goal of liberation is to see God in all persons and things, thus overcoming the evils of denial and indifference to the divine presence in Creation.[24] This breadth of scope between generic spirituality and spirituality defined in strictly Catholic terms is required so long as the curricular aims of accessibility and nurturing personal interests are to be genuinely maintained. There may be a kernel or kernels of "pure" or "sharply defined" Catholic spirituality within the school or within the curriculum, but to use any narrowly understood spirituality as an exclusive model for the aims of Catholic Education is ill-advised because such models are inadequate to the existential aim and task of meeting students as they are.

CONCERNS ABOUT TEACHING-LEARNING RELATIONSHIPS IN A CATHOLIC SCHOOL

Rossiter observes that often too much attention is focused on setting aims or on making "wish lists" of desired outcomes, and not enough on actually providing the pedagogical supports teachers require in order to make these aims have meaning in the curriculum and to adapt them suitably the needs of their students.[25] The former is relatively easy to do in a short period of time and makes good fodder for representing one's organization in a superficial manner, while the latter requires much more administrative courage and effort but attracts much less popular or media attention. If an appropriate aim for Catholic Education or for the mission of a Catholic school is properly situated on a continuum between thinner versions of spirituality and decidedly thicker varieties that are either "more identifiable" as Catholic or at least are explicitly framed under a commitment to (and interpretation of) Catholicism, then acknowledging this appropriateness leaves the teacher with the massive job of mingling this vague institutional aim with the varied dispositions that students bring with them to school. This is a daunting task, and although it is important, the reasons it might get left unattended are, first, the amount of intellectual heavy lifting required, and second, the amount of work required to shift toward these aims and away from the familiarity of the *status quo*.

Unfortunately for teachers, the pedagogical wisdom of working on a spiritual continuum is often mitigated or undermined by interests that have unrealistic expectations for how much personal change the Catholic school can produce in students.[26] Rossiter makes very strong assertions that in this area of education it is (some) parents, the Church, and governments that overburden the school with the task of fixing all of society's ills and the problems within the Church, and in doing so, they cause the mission of the school (to attend to student learning of a curriculum) to become neglected. His criticism of parents and governments follows a standard line of thinking that would resist assigning to schools the sole responsibility for providing students with "life skills," solving all society's problems, or producing good citizens of upstanding moral character. This kind of talk, he claims, is naïve because it does not "acknowledge that one cannot expect a simple, linear causal link between the educational process and change in beliefs/attitudes/values in the same way as there are casual links between classroom teaching/learning processes and changes in pupils' knowledge and cognitive skills."[27]

His strongest criticism, however, is levelled at the Church in this respect. In addition to assuming the same causal relationship, these statements, he claims, are too strongly ecclesial in terms of what is believed and what the Church's mission is, and not appropriately educational in terms of how students learn and what the role of the school is in promoting learning. The distinction between Catholic Education and Catholic Schooling comes to bear here, for if written in too narrowly theological language that neglects the teaching-learning relationship in the school, then such aims can covertly or tacitly assume particular (and particularly congruent) kinds of Catholic Education and Schooling that only reflect a part of the institution's *de facto* constitution. His words are worth quoting at length in this regard:

> Words like mission, ministry, evangelization, inculturation,
> witness and catechesis, together with a range of spiritual words
> like praxis, empowerment, consciousness-raising etc. have

strongly coloured the language about aims for Catholic schooling. In addition, the spiritual development of pupils is framed
almost exclusively in terms of a personal relationship with God
and in participation in the life of the Catholic Church. While
these purposes are central to Catholic education, and are not in
question, they need to be complemented with aims that are more
directly concerned with education – and not just with the
Church's mission, religious development of pupils and Church
membership. I believe that a Catholic school culture has developed in which there is a felt pressure to write the aims for
Catholic schools with such an emphasis on formally religious
terms that there is a tendency to neglect the basic educational
aims of the school.[28]

This language, Rossiter continues, is "excessive" and "exaggerates
the religious expectations of the school" to produce personal changes
in those they serve. These overblown outcomes, he continues, are not
observed in the "discourses about the religious mission of Catholic
hospitals, Catholic aged care institutions and other Catholic agencies." The potential danger is thus in widening a gap between the aims
and the practice, and exacerbating for teachers a sense that the aims
are "religious rhetoric which has little impact on practice."[29] Possibly
even more worrisome is that if the aims of any school are supposed
to carry any descriptive implication for how it will serve students,
then part of the hyperbole Rossiter notices is that Catholic schools'
aims seem to be aligned with some purpose other than the needs of
students, and so are out of touch with the kind of educational theory
that informs practice. At bottom, these aims therefore do not accurately represent or helpfully inform the work of building teaching
and learning relationships, and at their worst may even be distorting
those relationships.

Moran's theological view of Catholic Education also confirms that
if strong aims such as formation, catechesis, and so forth are to be
present in the school, they need to be tempered by strong views of
student freedom and the importance of intellectual development:

The way in which the teacher respects the person of another is to
seek for a communion of understanding with the other that will
provide the possibility of taking up his [sic] own freedom. There
is no direct way to form another human being's freedom; all that

one can do is to provide the context and the love and the light of understanding. Much of the newest catechetical writing [during the immediate aftermath of the Second Vatican Council], instead of presenting the broad human context from which a Christian understanding could slowly emerge, is ridiculously direct in its attempt to mould people. There inevitably appears in this a thinly disguised salesmanship which seldom fools any of the students.[30]

Moran's views are certainly helpful for the ways in which they can inform curricular aims and techniques, but their inclusion here may be questioned because they are written in the immediate post-conciliar period and so are notably already a generation or more old. If Rossiter's admonitions are to be taken seriously, however, they support a strong conclusion that Moran's views are no less fresh today than they were four decades ago. If any criticism should be levelled, it should probably be redirected toward places that have not acted upon this well-established view.

To be fair, though, catechetical writing has certainly changed since the late 1960s. The 1997 *General Directory for Catechesis* (GDC) appropriately cautions that any effort to inculturate the Gospel message should "not simply [be] an external adaptation designed to make the Christian message more attractive or superficially decorative."[31] Today's catechetical documents demonstrate a superior respect for student freedom. As formal curricula and catechetics are still documents that sit within the constitution of a school, however, their technical merit can still be couched within the overall aims for formation that remain within them, and they most certainly do not exist without teachers re-interpreting them. If the overall aims exaggerate the goals of formation but the formal curriculum and catechetics are represented in softer terms, then it would appear as though the rhetorical stance in the curriculum is simply trying to re-package the aim of formation via some means that appears more attractive, but fundamentally carries the same over-burdening material.

The GDC quotes Pope Paul VI's recognition of this inherent tension: "Evangelization will lose much of its power and efficacy if it does not take into account the people to whom it is addressed"; however, "it may lose its very nature and savour if on the pretext of transposing its content into another language that content is rendered meaningless or corrupted."[32] The dilemma for teachers and schools as interpreters of curriculum is thus: they may follow a strong path toward formation and so succumb to the "salesmanship" criticism Moran levels, or else they may back away entirely from the curriculum and its aims, which would risk making any religion course or the religious atmosphere in the school a meaningless exercise. Within an institutional atmosphere ostensibly based on some kind and degree of Catholic commitment and/or social service orientation, the teacher and school are left with the problems of how to teach Catholic religion without exaggerated expectations or over-presentation, and how to deal with the ideologies, faith perspectives, and spiritualities that inform students' freedom but are in competition with the strong and dominant conceptions of Catholic formation.[33]

On the more practical side of teachers positioning themselves in response to this problem, Crawford and Rossiter remark that many students "may be prejudiced to some extent by anti-institutional feelings." Thus, instead of being inculcated or formed as Christian persons in accord with the aims of an institution, they would prefer "to explore and evaluate the meaning and relevance of teachings for themselves." Crawford and Rossiter continue with the observation that in spite of concerns which may be present about "the dangers of a spiritual eclecticism and relativism, it is inevitable that to some extent young people will build a spirituality in this fashion."[34] Clearly these remarks are consistent with a view that would place limits on the aims Catholic schools have for formation, and in fact Crawford and Rossiter follow this idea to the end of rejecting the fallacy of transmission in educational aims, "which seems to imply that by intention and educational interventions it is possible to 'inject' faith or values into students."[35] Consistent with Moran's warnings about "salesmanship," there is also a concern that in Catholic schools students should not treated as the captive audience which is the raw material for producing a future community of faithful persons:

> [The] objectivity that we consider should always characterise classroom presentations of religious teachings is essential if students are to see clearly that there is no hidden agenda to engineer their unquestioning acceptance. This does not mean apologizing for, or watering down, church traditions and absolute claims to truth; neither does it compromise the school's religious commitment. But it is a recognition that the classroom, with compulsory attendance, remains a public forum where respect

for the individual's freedom and privacy is paramount; the faith presumptions that typify a voluntary religious commitment group do not apply.[36]

Clearly, Crawford and Rossiter do not equate the School with the Church, and so would refrain from making the parish Church's aims and work that of the School.

Discussion of this subject – how student freedom and objective habits of inquiry into "spiritual" matters fit within a program of Catholic Education and within the aims of Catholic schools, more particularly, as public (and sometimes publicly funded) institutions of Catholic Education – leads to the question of how critical thinking and, most importantly, the teaching of critical thinking is theorized within Catholic Education-Schooling. Mary Boys observes that throughout the literature on religious education, even the subject of teaching itself is a "taken for granted" assumption and "underdeveloped as a bedrock element in religious education."[37] The reasons for this are numerous, although I maintain that a large part of it obtains from a general abandonment in pre-service professional programs of considering foundational key questions in education, including, of course, that of *what teaching is.*

Teacher candidates, in my experience, struggle to respond to these questions and to appreciate their relevance in professional practice through no fault of their own; their struggle is mainly because they have been under-exposed to questions like these, and because they themselves have spent sixteen or more years in a system of education that is mostly comfortable with adopting a few unquestioned assumptions and carrying on with the vicissitudes of dealing with the procedural and managerial matters which descend from them. Candidates are often hurried through brief professional courses without time to slow down and contemplate these questions, and therefore often as a consequence they are more concerned with the issues of their own professional safety and performative competence, and with shuffling persons and resources through time,[38] than with such weighty theory.

In short, the reduction of education and teaching to a technical-managerial role performed exclusively in the context of schooling omits the expert professional functions of knowing about how students learn, identifying how real students in time and space are learning, and making judgments in response that would promote further learning. Someone could present curricular content from a book in a "telling" fashion and make sure that everyone in the room appears to be listening and is well behaved, but without attention to or skill in the design and assessment of learning just described, that person is a poor teacher by professional standards, regardless of how "personable," "dedicated," "industrious," or "professionally appearing" he or she is.

The aims of teaching religion, according to James Lee, are a hybrid of its unique disciplinary quality within the larger secular field of instruction. So teaching religion from a religious perspective and in a religious institution is not a theologically pure activity, because by necessity it must draw the particularities of religious commitment and worldview together with the commitment-neutral and disinterested "theories, laws, concepts, and procedures" that obtain across the entire (inclusively secular) field of instruction. Boys summarizes Lee's basic premise thus: "To teach religion effectively is to use a social science approach rather than a theological approach."[39] Lee's work is important for showing that educators should not conflate the theological content of religious instruction with the pedagogical social science of teaching and learning. Similarly, Sara Little's assertion that "the content of subject-matter and the content of process must be consonant with each other if maximum learning is to occur"[40] reminds educators that a social science orientation to teaching, learning, and institutional organization must not be subordinated to a narrow view of religion as theological knowledge. The CC echoes this statement with its warning that "it remains easy to fall into a 'content-method' dualism, with resultant reductionism to one or the other extreme."[41]

The conclusion that one can gain from these interpretations of teaching is that just as much is learned from the instructional method as from the lesson's academic content: the medium of teaching, to give a pedagogical shape to media theorist Marshall McLuhan's famous aphorism, is most definitely the message students learn – or at least a major part of it.[42] If the content aims for education are overemphasized, the result is that this "consonance" or balance between what is learned and how it is learned becomes skewed in a fashion that subordinates students-as-learners to the subject matter. Such subordination represents the school's informal or "hidden" curriculum, which may in fact be so subtle that even some teachers would be surprised to have it demonstrated to them. This hidden curriculum also cannot help but be a reflection of the dominant ecclesiology in the school, meaning that the way religion is taught reflects a (subconscious) view of how the student-as-ecclesial-subject is theorized.[43] A causal-linear statement of aims or arrangement of teaching and learning relationships would therefore suggest an ecclesiology of transmission, where learners (or lay persons) only act in response to the intentions of those who author the aims.

The prevailing dispositions in theorizing about religious education, however, suggest that something besides a transmission-based pedagogical theory is preferable. However, Boys notes that speech acts which reject the transmission modes of the "teacher-depositor" are easily uttered, but these claims only bear fruit once the speaker adopts a qualitatively distinct method in their place, and only once one knows how the methods and content are being used and learned will something be accomplished that is both meaningful and distinct from such "banking."[44] In moving the aims toward student-centred learning, Groome maintains, the learning objectives should not require students to accept texts at face value, but should use texts as objects to open opportunities for thinking and conversation.[45] Groome's prescriptions are revolutionary because they make a "major shift toward an active/reflective and relational/experiential ways of knowing,"[46] and so reflect the abandonment of positioning the student in religious education as a passive and receptive subject. This pedagogical shift therefore has profound ecclesiological consequences.

Simply changing the pedagogy, however, does not naturally imply or even signal a new ecclesiology. Trading in the deductive, transmissional approach for inductive methods that begin with an active student's concerns and problems in religion instead results in a dynamic tension within the institutions of School and Church. Cox in particular notices that the dilemma is between the epistemic claims of students regarding their experiences, on the one hand, and on the other, formally institutionalized religions that place the most authentic sources of revelation elsewhere and the authority to interpret revelation and name religious truth, most especially in a political-ecclesial way that extends past the phenomenological sense of personal experience, beyond students' grasp. One might accept Moran's contention that revelation is ongoing and so present in the lives of students, but the helpfulness of this innovation only takes one to the point of having to question philosophically and theologically how what is revealed through students compares against the epistemic weight of Scripture, Tradition, and Magisterial authority in the

Church. If teachers are experiencing a dilemma as to how to relate to students, then this problem in theory should mirror the concern and ambiguity that students face when meeting supposedly student-centred pedagogy within an institution whose charter is blessed by an authoritarian Church.

It is from this dilemma and ones like it that Moran's call for an increase in the amount of theology – and there is no doubt he means *good* theology – that informs religious education should include or be accompanied by an increase in the amount of theologically informed ecclesiology and political theory that would describe and make prescriptions about the social construction of teaching-learning relationships, especially as they occur in the public spaces of religious educational institutions. Education in these theological-ecclesial-political questions for the sake of bringing students into relationship with the formal and informal/hidden curriculum is a matter of critical thinking in the Church and *with* the Church that cannot be put off once students ask for it; for as Moran notes, students need "someone to give them a truthful and respectful answer to their particular questions." If students have questions that relate to the aims and authority of the Church and School, then to suspend answers will only frustrate them at the point where they are most ready and enthused (even if by a desire to confront any nascent confusion or frustration) to explore these questions.[47]

Moran's governing thesis is that Catholic Education should prepare students for the adult experience[48] of the Church or of religious questions, and so he claims that such questions need intellectually honest answers: "They should be answered with the truth as far as we understand it and in terms they will understand. They should not be fed with evasions and downright falsehoods. There is a place for serious intellectual inquiry in Christianity that will not take place in college unless it has its beginnings in grade school."[49] If teachers encourage creativity and individual critical thinking on these questions, and embrace an aim to probe for student thinking operations[50] on such inquiries with the same vigour that motivates them to present a clear and accurate picture of *what* the Church teaches, then it can be said that the content of what is taught is congruent with the methods; for in thinking about these theological questions, students are indeed working toward the learning objectives of thinking religiously and interpreting and evaluating what is authoritative in Catholicism. Both of those objectives are ideal attributes of an educated person, generally, and of an adult Catholic person, specifically. Beyond the cognitive content they presuppose, the affective and devotional aspects inherent in both the content and methods are also appropriate to be freely chosen, but not imposed, within Catholic Education-Schooling.

The salient critical questions are not uncontroversial, either. For one instance, one might look to the Catholic Church's claim that it finds unity in its diversity.[51] It takes little philosophical imagination to realize that this apparent paradox raises conceptual questions of what this unity looks like, is *imagined* to look like, or *should* look like; moreover, it also prompts questions of *who* is performing such descriptive, imaginative, and prescriptive acts, and on what authority they are grounded. To ask these questions should in no way suggest that one disapproves of unity, diversity, or the Catholic formula that combines them. Rather, as a critical ecclesial act, it asks for clarification of how this statement is officially justified, how theologians outside the Magisterium interpret it, and what it means for the good of life in the Church. Critical thinking in religion and in Catholicism cannot logically be reduced to a descriptive reiteration of how the Magisterial Church thinks critically, for such an act is merely imitative and robotic. Such reduction is impossible, even if one's religious views and one's critical justification for them mirror precisely Catholic orthodoxy, for in that case it would be incumbent on the beholder to personalize the thought and rationalize how as an agent he or she has freely subscribed to such a position. But if a Catholic variety of critical thinking is to have any rigorous intellectual and political meaning, it cannot exist only in a vacuum or in this one particular kind of Magisterial sympathy, and so this fact raises the critical question for Catholic Education: How does individual agency sit next to the Magisterium on Catholic critical thinking? If personal, inductive approaches to the curricular content and methods are going to prevail, then some theoretical work on this question is required. This is a question for which, to date, there has been no meaningful philosophical reply.[52]

BRINGING HOPES AND CONCERNS TO THE STUDENT

This final section is dedicated to bringing the discussion of aims back to considering the student as he or she figures within the institutionalization of aims and development of content and methods. It bears mentioning that no matter how well the educational aims which descend from the State, the Church, the Community, or even the Profession itself conform to the standards of theoretical rigour, internal consistency, the educational ideology that inspires them, or the norms of the institutions and society in which they sit, if they are assembled without consideration of the personal intentions of students then it is very likely that they will be meaningful to everyone except those in whose service they have been proposed. Certainly not all students think alike. While some students may be more than pleased to conform to Magisterial teaching in some way or another, one must also account for the fact that a significant number of students meet certain religious educational aims with ambivalence at best.[53] Many of today's youth live within an environment which is secular and has secularized their spiritual concerns;[54] and statements of aims, delivery of content, or other classroom interventions cause limited personal changes, if any, for these students.[55] It could therefore strain the school's teaching staff and administration to wonder why these phenomena occur, whether or not their school is responsible, and to what appropriate end it might direct its service.

The argument proposed here follows the literature to concur that, given a hierarchical model where the School (which here means administrative and teaching staff) is theorized to be responsible for implementing the lessons that the Church (which here means the Magisterium) passes to it, and can therefore take the credit or blame for the degree to which students are learning what the Church teaches (or tells or directs), the School in fact cannot be held *totally* responsible because, in short, its responsibility is mitigated by student intentions.[56] If our working definition of "School" is expanded beyond staff and administration to include the students who constitute it, then it is similarly short-sighted for the Church and others to blame the School for being religiously deficient according to aims for Catholic socialization, because, as Rossiter observes, the religious climate in the School only reflects the climate of the Home and Church.[57] If the parish Church is declining, therefore, it is inappropriate to ask a teaching-learning institution to pick up its slack, as the two have fundamentally different orientations. Schools might be influential institutions, but they cannot be assigned responsibility for the work of the Church or Home, which are things over which they have no control. Moreover, beyond the influences of domestic and ecclesial environments, students' internal responses vary and are not uniform, in contrast to the ways in which the over-arching aims tend to be written. Personal approaches are a valid pedagogical method for bringing students into conversation with religion, but since students' responses to religion are also *personal*, the students cannot be judged according to how well they conform to the more abstract and homogeneous affective aims made at the level of policy-makers. Aims that are comparatively much more modest and sensitive to the vicissitudes of professional practice and student life are required.

Given the state of flux in which adolescent faith sits, and given that the use of an inductive, personal pedagogy which reflects students experiences will by necessity mitigate any strong Church or State intentions, Crawford and Rossiter are quite correct in their assertions that development of faith or other affect is better framed as a *hope* than as an *aim*,[58] and so should not be written in the same "outcomes" language as is used for knowledge and skills.[59] This reframing is not made to suggest that Catholic Education-Schooling adopt a defeatist posture that students are over-determined to be unbelievers and non-practitioners in this "secularized" age. Much to the contrary, religion remains a source of much interest as students search for ways of responding to reality and making meaning in their lives. As an institution of religious learning, and in some places a publicly funded institution, Catholic Education-Schooling is a prime stage for introducing to students the subjects and controversies that are relevant to them and are therefore meaningful points of pedagogical entry. Such a venue has the potential to overcome the alienation, depersonalization, and privatization of spiritual and religious concerns that are otherwise characteristic of much of the rest of society, and especially in those public institutions which function according to an idea that Church and State must remain separated. Formation of believing and practicing students is possible, but it is only one legitimate educational outcome among many as students learn about religion from within a religious institution.

5

A Theory of Dissent

It is apparent that fundamental disagreements are intrinsic to relationships in religious education, and that these disagreements obtain at many levels. Catholic Education is no exception. In tackling the problems of disagreement within Catholic schools, it might be tempting to be satisfied with simply naming the teacher-student relationship as the most important of these foundational levels because that is the place where these phenomena are probably most immediately apparent and explicit. However, to imagine that a reform to the pedagogical treatment of student disagreement can be considered at *only* this level is naïve, to say the least. Before considering the ways students present disagreements in the Catholic school classroom, one must withdraw at least briefly from the classroom relationship and work one's way along several levels of political, ecclesial, and pedagogical abstraction to the philosophical point of origin where the very conceptual idea of dissent sits. The chapters prior to this one, if read in reverse, map out this framework quite handily, as they delineate a theoretical treatment of relevant disagreements which are present in the ways curricular and classroom aims are written, the historical and political establishment of Catholic Education in Canada, the ways in which the Catholic Church understands itself to sit apart from the secular world while still existing within it, and the ways in which dissent is understood and responded to as a phenomenon within the historical entity of the whole Catholic Church: including, but definitely not limited to, its educational aspect.

All of these places inform the classroom relationship, but what comes still prior to everything just listed is the philosophical concept of dissent itself. It is this concept that allows one to make thorough descriptive, interpretive, and prescriptive sense of what these events mean. Ostensibly dissent is a salient aspect in many organizations, but to understand whether it exists (or should exist) for better or for worse requires a definitive analysis of this complex and possibly tricky concept. Most importantly, a treatment of how one can disagree in a substantial way while remaining part of a group is required in order to coordinate the gathering of all prior and forthcoming data into a pedagogical theory based on it. As the concept of dissent is central to the proposal made in this book's final chapter, this current chapter undertakes that comprehensive analysis as a meta-theoretical means of organizing and framing the entire argument.

Dissent is a multi-layered concept which defies simplistic explanation, and as some types of dissent are preferable to others, a reasonable depth of discussion is required in order to appreciate the complexity and significance of the concept in its optimal form, and to observe ways in which less-than-desirable kinds of dissent can be present in organizations and arguments. Now having just warned against short definitions, I will momentarily break that rule only for the heuristic ease of introducing the concept and establishing the grounds for further, more detailed presentation. Concise definitions of complex entities carry the weakness of reducing and filtering out the very nuance and complexity that makes them interesting, but that weakness is overcome if the brevity functions as a helpful entry into their analysis. It is in that spirit that I proceed.

The basic definition from the Oxford English Dictionary states that dissent is both a verb that "expresses disagreement with a prevailing view or official decision" and a noun that names an expressed opinion at variance with those commonly or officially held. Dissent is also defined as nonconformity with the official teachings or established orthodoxy of a Church. The etymological root of dissent is the Latin word *dissentire*, which means "to differ in sentiment." The etymology of dissent's cousin noun *dissident* also provides some further instructive fodder. A dissident is "a person who opposes official policy," and the root of that word comes from *dissidere*, meaning "to sit apart or disagree." Although the definitions and etymologies of *dissent* and *dissident* suggest a fractured whole, they also seem to allow that something remains in common institutionally or politically between the dissident nonconformists and the prevailing, conforming supporters of orthodoxy. The questions of what distance and quality of "apartness" dissent implies are of an open nature, and this fact allows that said opposition is not necessarily a complete dismissal or quitting of the group. It could mean simply sitting off in some other section of the same whole somewhere. The feeling or opinion within the institution may be divided, to be sure, but in these brief expressions, such division is not necessarily framed as a breakage, and so implies that differing sentiments or altered allegiances do not persist at the cost of dismantling or destroying the whole. One might disagree with the majority and make that disagreement known without resorting to rebellion, sedition, or abandonment of the institution or association. In summary, my basic definition of dissent maintains it as the condition of "sitting apart from those that one is a part of."

It seems baffling that the scholarship on dissent has advanced to date without a philosophical analysis of the concept.[1] In the tradition of philosophy, the importance of questioning the terms of discussion is one of the primary reasons for the early introduction of students to Socratic questioning. One might imagine that if one argued before Socrates that dissent is valuable for moulding citizens, Socrates would quickly stop listening to value arguments and interrupt with questions asking the speaker to explain exactly what this dissent is that has so much value. Fortunately, the arguments over dissent's value are not nearly so shallow as to have entirely neglected defining their terms. If they can be faulted for anything, it is simply that they do not assume the burden of making explicit a comprehensive discussion of dissent; however, these same arguments tend to be so well researched and calculated that in their collective discourse they implicitly provide much of the instructive fodder that can be assembled into a comprehensive analysis.

From that collection I present here a sevenfold description of dissent. The fact that there are seven distinct criteria underscores the assertion of the term's complexity; none of the criteria are reducible to the others, although certainly each criterion depends on the others in order to achieve a sense of the complete concept. The dependent relationship between the criteria is also tighter than that of a mere collection of descriptive puzzle-pieces which can be laid down in any order; because the criteria are also layered, which means that an understanding of each successive criterion is embedded within the summary context of its antecedent counterparts. They must proceed in the order as presented because each proceeds from a requirement to qualify the last. The seven criteria proposed here maintain that dissent is a condition that assumes: (1) enfranchisement; (2) an epistemological history;

(3) contra-hegemonic and (4) ethical purposes; (5) epistemological diversity within an association; (6) a public expression; and (7) persuasive argument.

I ENFRANCHISEMENT

Without a doubt, the bare form of dissent is problematic for many because of its very precarious and ambiguous situation between the poles of firm loyalty and adamant rejection. The problematic aspect of dissent, of course, is that it leaves undefined the point at which loyalty leaves off and open revolution begins. "Dissent is a troubling word," writes theologian Margaret O'Gara, "because it begins on a negative note and its meaning is ambivalent, suggesting to some a group wishing to secede from the community."[2] Something like an Aristotelian "golden mean" between the poles, or even a way of abolishing the polarity altogether, seems desirable in order to describe more fulsomely a type of loyal but fundamental disagreement and so avoid being bogged down in a binary narrowness. Those who argue for the importance of dissent suggest that it is the "truest expression of loyalty,"[3] and philosopher Wendy Brown proposes that dissent "not only presumes something of a stable nation-state population but presumes as well an investment from both critics and non-critics in preserving rather than overthrowing the state."[4] In Brown's formula one could substitute employer, institution, church, family, or any other association for "nation-state" and not lose the meaning inherent in the individual-group or minority-majority tensions.

Dissent as such assumes and maintains franchise in the group. Dissent emerges from and is performed by a person situated within a group (family, team, community, school, religion, state) who distinguishes him- or herself from the prevailing view in that group. The dissident does not abandon identification with the group or membership in it, and in fact uses his or her internal position as the starting point for reforming the association. Dissent is therefore not protesting from the outside. Michael Walzer's distinction between immanent and rejectionist critics helps to explain the difference between dissent and protest. An immanent critic aims to reform an institution within its existing structure. From this perspective, the material with which to fashion an improvement is thought to be already present, although it may be dormant. Change comes through reform of the institution. The rejectionist critic, by contrast, regards the institution as irrevocably tainted and incapable of improvement without resorting to open revolution and beginning anew.[5] For instance, Martin Luther was a dissident from the Church of Rome until he abandoned it and started his new church, which is aptly called a *protestant* and not dissident church. Not all protest is rejectionist, however, as some public expressions of objection might legitimately come from within the body politic. The popular notion of *protest* is therefore, in some cases, more like *dissent* in the technical sense described here, depending upon which group or organization defines the baseline for membership.

It is not always so easy. From within an ideological framework which demands firm and unquestioning loyalty, dissidents at best persist within the nebulous, ill-defined, and obscurely understood gap between traditional allegiance and outright sedition. Sarat describes the test of dissent in terms of negotiating a precarious threshold between dichotomous views: "The dissenter is neither a conformist nor revolutionary. She is at once within, but outside of, the community and its conventions. In part because of her liminality the dissenter is often accused of disloyalty and subject to sanction and stigma by the state and society. Pulled from the one side by those who say that dissent does not go far enough and from the other by those who demand acquiescence as the sign of loyalty, maintaining the 'in-betweenness' of dissent is very difficult."[6]

However, it could be argued that, since the dissident incorporates his or her critique within the bounds of the association, some sort of loyalty, respect, and acknowledgment of its legitimacy or importance is presumed. Love of or concern for the association and a preference for membership in it are crucial dispositional characteristics that separate such dissent from any charge of disloyalty. Classicist Garry Wills suggests that this is the choice facing disenchanted Catholics: "If you want the church to be reformed, you need a church to be reformed."[7] Implicit in Wills' statement is the double assertion that it is the people who constitute the association, and if the people do not stay within it to disagree then there will eventually be no association remaining.

Brown uncovers the tension inherent within enfranchisement through her interpretation of Socrates' speech in the "Apology." In response to charges that he has corrupted the youth of Athens, Socrates predicates his defence on casting his actions as loyal to the State, and thus attempting to abolish any assertions that they could be anything otherwise. His argument swings upon the claim that his critiques of Athenian social convention are good for the city and its citizens. Although the meaning of dissent is often distorted by attempts to view and measure it in terms of a binary distinction between loyalty and sedition, Socrates nonetheless begins his case from within that framework. This beginning, however, does not restrict his argument, and Socrates demonstrates his flexibility within the terms of discussion by crafting dissent as a brand of loyalty and thereby opening a divergent line of discussion that subverts the weaknesses of dichotomously framed dissent. In Brown's assessment, Socratic dissent is "not merely compatible with love and loyalty to a political community but, rather, is the supreme form of such love and loyalty ... Socrates makes the case for intellectual critique as the highest form of loyalty if and when this critique is aimed at improving the virtue of the citizens."[8] By shifting the focus of his defence away from narrower conceptions of loyalty and love for the state, and questioning the meaning of loyalty itself, Socrates has thrown the dichotomy into flux.

In a manner similar to Socrates' divergent depolarization and re-branding of loyalty, Karol Cardinal Wojtyla (later Pope John Paul II) treats the apparent tension between solidarity and opposition with an approach that opens more breadth for a comprehensive and inclusive reconsideration of opposition. In his reformulation of this relationship, he first insists that the two concepts must be considered together. "The attitude of solidarity," he claims, is in fact an integral means of establishing one's personhood and, hence, one's contribution to the community, because "the common good properly conditions and initiates participation, and participation in turn properly serves the common good."[9] His statement that "opposition is not inconsistent with solidarity"[10] frames dissent in terms of one's franchise because it broaches the subject of how one can challenge the desires for uniformity and purity within one's own group. Since the Catholic understanding of personhood depends upon establishing moral relationships with others in community, moral opposition is sometimes required in order to ensure that the balance between individual and group does not become skewed toward conformity. One does not necessarily have to sacrifice one's membership in the group in order to advance the cause of what is good for all against more narrowly conceived but popular views.

> The one who voices his [sic] opposition to the general or particular rules or regulations of the community does not thereby reject his membership; he does not withdraw his readiness to act and to work for the common good. Different

interpretations of opposition that an individual may adopt with respect to society are of course possible, but here we adopt one that sees it as essentially an attitude of solidarity; far from rejecting the common good or the need of participation, it consists on the contrary in their confirmation ... [T]hose who in this way stand up in opposition do not thereby cut themselves off from their community. On the contrary, they seek their own place and a constructive role within the community.[11]

Wojtyla's work is not completed with his statements aimed at protecting the individual, though, and he next turns his attention toward protecting the community from the errors that can be brought about by conformity. He claims that society and its institutions should be structured in such a way that faithful, loyal opposition and a culture of dissent can function for the common good:

More precisely, in order for opposition to be constructive, the structure, and beyond it the system of communities of a given society must be such as to allow the opposition that emerges from the soil of solidarity not only to *express* itself within the framework of the given community but also to *operate* for its benefit. The structure of a human community is correct only if it admits not just the presence of a justified opposition but also that practical effectiveness of opposition required by the common good and the right of participation.[12]

Far from supposing that dissent is antithetical to the development of group cohesiveness and hostile to communal and social solidarity, John Paul, like Socrates, re-frames the discussion by adding breadth to one of the existing terms in what is commonly conceived of as a dichotomous structure, thus abolishing the dichotomy. Rather than suffering the limitations of an established polarity by searching for a third or middle path, both Socrates and John Paul depolarize the apparent binary in a manner that admits diversity within the terms and suggests an alternative to a construction based upon opposites. Questions such as "Is the dissident either loyal or disloyal?" need to be replaced with others such as "How is this fundamental disagreement an unusual but important expression of loyalty?"

As binary structures have proven inadequate means of understanding dissent, a theoretical means more sensitive to plurality and less rigid in its view of loyalty is required. To this end, redefining dissent as a non-antithetical dialectical relationship is much more fruitful. This re-definition, transplanted from Edward Schillebeeckx's Catholic ecclesiology and theology, maintains that "unity is not created by overcoming opposition but by reestablishing irreducible and cooperative relationships which make up all of reality."[13] The non-antithetical and dialectical relational qualities are primary and central to dissent because they emphasize a complex unity that is born out of accommodating fundamental differences between people. Such relationships, moreover, cannot be reduced to associations of like-minded people, nor can the individual be abstracted from the community of relationship. It is wrongheaded to attempt to overcome the dissent of the minority, according to Schillebeeckx, but morally correct to bring that dissent into relationship.

2 COMMON EPISTEMIC ROOTS OR KNOWLEDGE BASE

Enfranchisement presumes knowledge of the institution, group, or society where one is situated. As an immanent reformer, one must be aware of the historical narratives and philosophical assumptions that constitute the prevailing and subordinated views in the institution. Dissent draws from the knowledge that is rooted in one's franchise and the corporate memory, and makes that knowledge available to the group. The dissenting view shares a knowledge base with the prevailing or majority view, although the dissenting view will by definition attempt to provide breadth to the prevailing scope and will offer alternative interpretations of what the data mean, what counts as factual, and how data stand as evidence for arguments. Such knowledge might be commonly known, not commonly known but easily accessible, or else extant but somehow suppressed, hidden, or dormant. Recalling Martin Luther, his dissent was based in his learned knowledge of Christian theology and ecclesiology, and this warrant supplemented his already prominent status as priest in the community.

As with many epistemic claims, the justification issue is a question of who or what is an authority or authoritative, and why. The "prevailing" view as such is therefore attached to the prevailing epistemological and political authors and ideology. A return to Walzer's distinction between immanent and rejectionist critics is helpful when considering the prevailing and dissident views' shared epistemic roots. As the immanent critic prefers reform to revolution, he or she will naturally seek improvements within the relationships and structures that already exist, and thus use the knowledge within that tradition in order to enact change. The degree of change or the size and quality of the framework may vary. For instance, one might observe the English tradition of challenging the various powers that the English Crown has held over time and altering the current monarch's role, so that he or she is more accountable to Parliament and less dependent upon public taxation for income. Alternatively, however, the dissident might wish finally to abolish the English monarchy altogether, and would thus appeal to the trend over centuries where England has gradually changed the monarch's role from direct governance to mere ceremony. Both kinds of dissent descend from within English political movements, even though the former works within a framework that has more tolerance for monarchy than the latter.

If dissent is something besides an act of rejection or abandonment, clearly its immanent epistemic warrant must be drawn from somewhere within a tradition broadly conceived. Tradition, according to John Elmer Thiessen, is more than just the dead weight of the past that one must throw off in order to achieve emancipation. He maintains that established norms and emancipation exist within a creative tension[14] that tempers each other's respective excesses toward stagnation and capriciousness. The kind of emancipation that would completely lift the person or community from historical context, moreover, is an illusory, impractical, and impossible ideal, because everyone is raised in a certain tradition that imbues a "permanent mark" upon subjects: "To pretend that we can entirely escape this historical and cultural context, as is often presupposed by those who urge us to be critical and open, is to delude ourselves."[15] From Thiessen's point of view, then, tradition is an indelible personal and communal quality from which one cannot escape, but it also contains the knowledge – including the prevailing and suppressed versions of history – from which comes the creativity required to make appropriate changes to habits, patterns, and customs. Dissent thus challenges traditional associations or ideologies to surmount an overemphasis on repetitive thoughts and actions and to explore areas where choice and innovation are helpful. Dissent, therefore, as with creative change, emerges from the same tradition that it critiques.

The immanent scholarly reworking of tradition within Catholicism provides a good descriptive sense of how suppressed parts of a corporate memory can be uncovered and possibly applied to current needs for reform. O'Gara notes that the activities of recovery and transposition have been and continue to be central to the activities of renewal within Catholicism.[16] Recovery is the act of accomplishing the background work that rediscovers the dimensions of a tradition that have been lost or suppressed over time. Historical and exegetical scholarship often provides the new knowledge or attitude toward knowledge from within a tradition. As an example, O'Gara remarks that the rediscovery of an ecclesiology of communion within the Christian tradition and the recovery activities performed on early texts have been "a major building block in [recent] ecumenical discussions on overcoming the divisions in the Church that keep us from a common mission."[17] Transposition is the complex act of removing one set of beliefs, practices, and customs from one age into another. The difficulty with transposition is that it always must consider the appropriateness of uprooting an object from a particular age or place and introducing it to a new context. A piece of music cannot be transposed from one key or octave into another without respecting the range, resonance, timbre, colour, intonation, and other relevant characteristics or limitations of the instrument or voice that will perform it in the new tonality or register. Likewise, transposition in other disciplines must not be blind or naïve to new circumstances.

O'Gara uses Catholic theological and ecclesiological terms that demonstrate the care one must take in order to lift and move new discoveries without distorting the essence of their meaning: "Recognizing the historicity of our formulations and of our conceptual frameworks, theologians and the Magisterium at last concluded that while the meaning intended in dogmatic formulations cannot change, the formulations themselves might need changing precisely in order to clarify, illumine, and deepen the same meanings, to transpose the song of Christ into a new key rather than lose the tune."[18] In more abstract terms, change within a tradition is possible even though there is a limit to the amount of it that can be managed without distorting the epistemological essence of the association. Claims that one has found the "authentic essence" or "core" of a tradition, custom, or issue must be carefully considered and tested with reasonable scepticism. Here it is essential to recognize that dissent begins within a political franchise that is itself situated and rooted within a recovery of the tradition's corporate memory. While it is clear that all epistemic criteria depend upon related warrants that either confirm or trouble the justifiability of that knowledge, within the following proposed criteria numbers 3 (that dissent is contra-hegemonic) and 4 (that dissent ought to be ethically justifiable), a framework for the justification of certain kinds of dissent and the disapproval of others will emerge.

3   CONTRA-HEGEMONIC

In spite of the fact that some traditions are stifling or some dominant epistemologies are oppressive, sometimes prevailing views are to be valued. The prevailing view in society that it is wrong to kill a person intentionally without a reasonable cause such as self-defence, for instance, *should* prevail because it is ethically sound and creates social conditions preferable to those in places where arbitrary killing is sadly (accepted as) the norm. In such lawless conditions it would be desirable to challenge the prevailing view, but in instances where the prevailing view protects justice and human dignity, it is preferable to leave it unchallenged and to focus one's energy on challenging something unjust instead. While not all prevailing views and traditions are harmful, clearly there are cases where adherence to custom, ritual, and habit for their own sakes can become an obstacle to meaningful social progress. Unless tempered by a social conscience, the danger of adhering at all costs to prevailing views within traditions is that such an attitude will marginalize subordinated but correct views, threaten the just treatment of some groups of people, and ultimately alienate a society from some of the most potentially desirable opportunities and means through which it might be reformed. As a contra-hegemonic act that challenges dominant claims to knowledge and practices within a prevailing view, dissent provides the conceptual and material means through which the desirability of alternative forms of association and social change are considered.

The third criterion of dissent is therefore that it challenges the leading ideological view in society. This criterion is especially crucial and relevant to cases where injustice requires remedy, fallacy requires the embarrassment of exposure, or error requires correction. Thompson underlines Schillebeeckx's position that an obligation to dissent is present when it is observed that certain practices and beliefs have misappropriated control of a tradition, warped its message, and misapplied that warped view to current situations that do not reflect the needs of that situation or context. Dissent's critical importance lies in its "obligation to unmask ideological language and praxis, [where] ideology [refers] to the manipulation, monopolization, and distortion of language by those in power to maintain that power over others."[19]

The obligation to dissent is thus relevant to any place where a dominant viewpoint has marginalized and silenced a "minority" dissident viewpoint within that tradition. I cautiously associate the term *minority* with dissident views, however, for as John Stuart Mill is careful to explain, there are occasions where the dominant viewpoint lies in a minority social elite that is "the most [politically] active part of the people"[20] and uses its power to oppress the majority underclass. Consider the dominance of the minority white population over black and other "coloured" people during South Africa's apartheid era (ca. 1950 to 1990) as an exemplary case that illustrates the wisdom of Mill's qualification. The hegemonic tendencies of the prevailing view to appropriate oppressive traditions and patterned social behaviour for its own benefit are not to be underestimated, either, for according to Samuel Fleischacker, the strength of a tradition's dominance is sometimes in direct proportion to its lack of self-examination and its intolerance for external examination: "'[T]raditions are first and foremost the sum total of what is not argued in the transmission of knowledge and practice from parents to their children,' [writes Fleischacker]. A tradition, in other words, is less an argument than an attempt to avoid an argument. It is an attempt to establish something as given – and then to use that givenness as a basis on which to build or maintain community, and to preserve the community's narrative into the next generation."[21] Thus dominance maintains itself by keeping its critics misinformed, uninformed, and outside the accepted critical discourse. In terms of social justice, this critique of hegemony implies that if a dominant viewpoint is marginalizing another point of view that is of independent interest, then harm is done both to the marginal view and ironically to the whole group, which will then lack alternatives to help it change and grow.

The notion that dissent is an important concept solely in its capacity to correct the harms inflicted and perpetuated upon oppressed minorities and possibly promote social justice through a framework of more participatory democracy is, while admirable, not the complete picture of what dissent is, could be, and, interestingly, *was*. Dissent's contra-hegemonic aspect is documented in ancient Athenian political texts: one of the Western world's earliest glimpses at democracy and its problems. While much reverence is accorded ancient Athens as the progenitor of modern democracy, classicist Josiah Ober reasons that many of the ancient Greek political texts produced during this time can be read as dissenting points of view produced by elite Athenians who were critical of the ideology of democracy. He argues that democracy flourished in Athens not because of some "Greek miracle" but because the Athenian elite (*hoi oligoi*) were unable to dominate the ordinary citizens (*hoi polloi*) as was done in neighbouring regions. The result was the birth of government by the masses and a corresponding rise in elite reactionism:

> Greek elites (those who were wealthy, highly educated, and relatively cosmopolitan in outlook) were well aware that their inability to monopolize public affairs was anomalous, and they sought by various means to "normalize" the situation. Their sub-elite fellow citizens typically resisted these attempts. And thus city-state politics were characterized by intermittent civil conflict and by incessant social negotiations between an elite few who sought to gain a monopoly over political affairs and a much larger class of sub-elite adult males who sought to retain the privileges of citizenship or to gain that coveted status. Those hard-fought political conflicts and complex social negotiations proved to be a very fertile ground for the development of philosophical speculation and literary culture.[22]

The main project of *hoi oligoi* was to assert its claims to power by arguing against the ideological aspects of democracy: that is, pointing out democracy's weaknesses while making and reinforcing a case for oligarchic rule. What if, the elites might argue, the majority made a decision that gave popular legitimacy to a rule that was unjust or inadequate to philosophical principle?

With a lack of sufficient non-democratic force with which to wrest civic control from *hoi polloi*, these elites were compelled to play by the rules of the democratic game, which, especially within the political debates in the *polis*, allowed argument and dissent from the prevailing view. Dissent is thus, according to Ober, arguably born from an elite that, despite its disenchantment with popular rule and democratic harmony, was also unable to appropriate control of the social order in its favour:

> In an atmosphere of profound disillusionment with practical attempts to establish a nondemocratic government at Athens, the elite Athenian critics of popular rule set themselves the arduous task of reinventing political dissent. This meant, in the

democratic Athenian environment, finding new grounds for explaining what was wrong with "the power of the people" and describing alternative visions of consensual and noncoercive – yet nondemocratic – political societies. The result was a set of robust and highly original approaches to political philosophy.[23]

In short, the elites were able and allowed to criticize the dominant democratic ideology for the sake of promoting their vision of an improved Athens; moreover, they were not presumed to be in any way "un-Athenian" or disloyal in this endeavour. Had *hoi oligoi's* persuasive arguments been successful, what was formerly a dissenting position would have become the prevailing view, thus establishing the democrats as a dissident presence. The instrumental intentions of *hoi oligoi* are in this case illustrative of how some varieties of dissent eventually aim to establish themselves as the prevailing view and thus self-disqualify as dissenters. This variation on dissent demonstrates that not all dissidents share the interests of other dissenters, or believe in the potential good that dissent *in general* and a climate of dissent might provide for the good of all – a point which confirms suggestions that dissent cannot be considered a good in and of itself unless its purposes are qualified. Additionally, it reinforces the irony that liberal and democratic societies are inherently troubled with the problem of how to accommodate the illiberal and undemocratic interests within them. And although the connotations of elitism in the above example might be distasteful to some, especially if these connotations suggest unjustly wrought class difference, the point remains that popularity does not always or necessarily confer justification. Ethical principle and popularity sometimes clash, and for those whose only recourse to justice was based on principle, it was particularly frightening that a political ideology had been established where ethical principles could be subordinated to popular assent.

The most just forms of democratic participation, however, should create conditions where ethics and popularity overlap, or at least come close to overlapping. If all members of a democracy are interested in creating a more just society, then an allowance and respect for, and an attempt to address, dissent should bring forth claims from the oppressed that the dominant view might otherwise subjugate and ignore. Dissent is not confinable to democratic associations, but from the perspective that promotes, maintains, and enhances social justice, dissent can be seen as a constitutive aspect of any participatory style of democracy that serves both individual and group enfranchisement, and as a check against the dominating tendencies of particular groups or persons. Dissent is more than nominal suffrage; its maximum social utility is realized when its best forms are directed toward the creation of an equitable culture that allows and encourages the expression of epistemically and morally legitimate points of view or grievances that might otherwise be ignored, neglected, or marginalized. The question thence arises as to the ethical quality of the dissenting points of view: Is it good dissent, or is it potentially harmful?

Finally, as a contra-hegemonic act, dissent not only expressly disagrees with explicitly stated prevailing views, but also takes on the task of combating the automatic, routine, and unthinking social habits that perpetuate the problems, errors, and even evils of the prevailing ideology. Sarat argues that for Socrates, "the best Athenian citizen was the critic whose dissent helped prevent an all-too-easy slide from thoughtlessness to injustice. Thoughtless conformity to convention was, for Socrates, the gravest danger of citizenship and the greatest temptation of belonging in a political community."[24] Socratic examination of all that conventional life takes for granted serves society by questioning and troubling its understanding of social cohesion. In Brown's assessment, the conventional prevailing view in Athens was blinded by slavish acquiescence to the temptation of power and was thus "inimical to the thoughtfulness that [Socrates] takes as both the basis and necessary content" of the love of Athens.[25] Brown's commentary is instructive, displaying how a terrible tragedy like genocide can result from blind acquiescence to conventional trends and a culture that perpetuates thoughtlessness: "In [Hannah] Arendt's study of [Adolph] Eichmann, she argued that the precondition for radical political evil is not some moral or ontological predisposition to evil but rather 'ingrained thoughtlessness,' and it is precisely such routine thoughtlessness that Socrates aims to disrupt. If citizen virtue consists in avoiding evil, and if evil springs from such thoughtlessness, then thinking itself becomes the penultimate citizen virtue."[26] Socrates' questioning of what counts as virtue, then, is no trivial academic exercise in parsing meaning and examining assumptions, because the object of these pursuits is a concern for civic justice and for developing a philosophical framework and culture that would maintain political safety by attempting to lift the cloak of ideological obfuscation. It is from this point that dissent can potentially challenge the conditions that encourage less adequate manifestations of justice.

4 ETHICAL

In its ideal form, dissent is an ethically sound action or condition that aims to promote more justice for all in society. Ethical principles can be used to evaluate the quality of the dissent's expression, and moral decisions establish opportunities for dissent insofar as they involve questions of justice or the good of all in interpersonal associations or group relations. The person who *could* dissent wrestles with the moral question of whether or not he or she *should* dissent: Would dissent in this particular case be helpful, and is it being communicated through a morally correct means?

Thomas Platt argues that "the grounds of dissent" and "the expression of dissent" govern the conception of a reasonable and responsible act. The first criterion therefore evaluates the content and timing of a dissenting action, which Platt describes as the "intellectual grounds which define the instances of dissent as responsible or irresponsible," and the second criterion oversees "a range of allowable actions to be utilized for the expression of dissent."[27] The dissident thus is in the position where he or she must consider whether dissent is morally required and in what way that dissent is best expressed. An important philosophical starting place for dissenting subjects and groups is to consider such questions as "Is dissent *required* in order to promote justice; is this *means* of expressing dissent the most justifiable in these circumstances; and is the *content* of this dissent morally correct?" If all three criteria in the above set of questions are not met, it is possible that the value of dissent could be eroded or neutralized. One might recognize that dissent is required to remedy the structural injustices against a minority group, but if the dissenting stance is supported by propaganda that promotes violence against innocent fellow citizens, then the lack of any factual base or expressive means or method of implementation that does not perpetuate harm can quickly overshadow the moral intent in which a response is rooted.

Sunstein notes that dissent is not always helpful and can lead to social disharmony. For those who count as honourable dissidents in his view – people like Galileo, Martin Luther, Thomas Jefferson, and Martin Luther King, Jr – there are corresponding dishonourable dissidents like Adolph Hitler, Vladimir Lenin, the defenders of American slavery, and Osama bin Laden.[28] The major difference between the honourable and dishonourable dissidents is that the honourable ones emphasize respect for all people while the dishonourable ones do not.

The kind of liberty and protection Mill describes is consistent with the honourable form of dissent. Mill's ethics, like Kant's, is centred about respect for persons and "the sense that [persons] must be treated with a due regard for the dignity that moral responsibility deserves and without which moral responsibility is impossible."[29] Dissent's ethical utility is not limited to the individual's good, but extends to the good of society, because a free flow of information is advantageous to everyone. It is unethical to enforce silence on those with divergent opinions because such force "does violence to the person who holds it and also robs society of the advantage it might have had from a free investigation and criticism of the opinion."[30] An ethically justified act of dissent is subject to moral standards for the correctness of its expression, and, like the ethically sound climate that respects dissenters in general, also has a utilitarian value.

The ethical value of any dissenting act or view is content-dependent. Shiffrin notes that since the Ku Klux Klan believes itself to be a dissenting, pariah, and marginalized social minority that challenges the foundations of the current social system, those who support the value of dissent in society might be discouraged and wish to constrict dissent if it is going to reflect a racist undertone in society.[31] Shiffrin is quick to point out that the Ku Klux Klan's actions, like the Nazi persecutions of Jews, Roma, Sinti, non-heterosexuals, the physically and mentally disabled, and those who challenged National Socialism, also "arguably silence ... those who would otherwise be dissenters."[32] The honour of Martin Luther King, Jr, by contrast, lies in his response to socially wrought injustice through leading a movement that, among other things, broke unjust laws with the aim of rewriting better ones that would promote justice for all. One could universally prescribe moral actions that emulate King's work, but could not universally prescribe actions that express the beliefs of the Ku Klux Klan. King's work is also exemplary in this analysis because it promotes the value of universally justifiable dissent *in general*, which the Ku Klux Klan does not. It is therefore possible to dissent from the ethical criteria that a society uses to establish acceptable political behaviour, although the value of that dissent will depend upon comparing the worth of both prevailing and dissenting standards for acceptability in the school.

The ethical criterion that regulates the content of dissent is thus governed by a concern for justice. If dissent promotes social justice, or at least does not constrict justice (in decisions or cases that are not primarily about justice), and actively encourages an environment in which more moral dissent can flourish for the good of society, then it has met its ethical criterion. Ku Klux Klan expressions of dissent do not meet this standard: "A cross burning directed at the home of a particular Black family is not an act of dissent against a powerful status quo; it is a threatening act of power against a victim. In a society in which race has been and continues to be used as a means of perpetuating inequality, the initiator of racist speech further aggravates the position of the subordinated."[33] Some views that are uncomfortable with dissent in society may object that to allow dissent only erodes the security and comfort of the status quo, and that a totalitarian system which restricts dissent may be preferable to a system which would encourage harmful relativism and nihilism. To refute objections that allowing dissent might encourage an environment of relativistic nihilism and an erosion of totalitarian safety and comfort, an ethical standard based upon justice constrains such excesses and injustice and error in the world. Neither relativism nor nihilism is a realistic response to injustice, because both are groundless in their evaluation of what is just and unjust. Perhaps some objections of this sort may emerge, but to suggest that all dissent would promote such kinds of thought is to make a straw person out of legitimate kinds of dissent, and to overlook its potential value for improving, rather than eroding, the *status quo*. Ethical responsibility trumps the need for societies to agree, according to John Ralston Saul: "Responsibility-disagreement has to do with an understanding of our obligation to society. Solidarity has to do with the artificial removal of difference."[34] Ethically adequate dissent is thus politically valuable and legitimate because it takes advantage of difference in order to promote justice.

A final note must be made regarding the grounds upon which one makes ethical decisions. One of the established tensions in ethics concerns whether one should act according to obligation and duty (deontology), or according to what the best outcomes will be (consequentialism, of which utilitarianism is one kind). In proposing this theory I take no sides in this debate when it concerns the particulars of persons dissenting in context. A deontological approach may be preferable in one context, and a consequentialist view in another. My concern is only that some rigorous ethical evaluation be made as part of any test of whether an action counts as "good" dissent.

While this theory remains content-neutral on the deontological-consequentialist question in the sense of adjudicating dissenting acts, it is decidedly utilitarian on the question of whether good dissent is beneficial for society. Administrative procedures, a social climate, and learning objectives which promote good dissent should exist so as to optimize the organizational performance of schools (and any institution). The utilitarian justification for promoting dissent within organizations maintains that the widest possible consideration of all information and ethical positions is the most promising remedy for correcting error and injustice.

5 EPISTEMICALLY SELECTIVE AND CONSTRUCTIVE

Meaningful difference of thought in the present tense of the political sphere implies epistemic diversity. The dissident takes one of many different epistemic paths other than the prevailing trail that is available within a tradition. The pursuit of meaningful difference as such explicitly espouses reform, because besides wishing for change, it actively explores the diversity of knowledge available within an established tradition and as such constitutes the "reasonable heresy"[35] that counters or at least provides a check upon the static forces upholding the prevailing view.

The difference between this criterion and criterion 2 above is that here there is a consideration for choices that exist beyond the conventions of a group, institution, or society, where conventions are considered as the set of established customs, beliefs, laws, and habits that reflect the prevailing view, but do not reflect the entire possibility of what might be. This criterion implies more the generative creativity of thought in new situations and less the transposition of established knowledge from obscurity to prominence. Insofar as dissent challenges the norms established by the prevailing view, it implies a broader choice than what might typically be allowed or even perceived to be possible under the prevailing ideology. It encourages a political environment of transparency and variety while discouraging mystification and a constricted flow of information.

When dissent is "reasonable heresy" it represents a constructive force, insofar as it takes advantage of a diversity of thought to make society more complex for good moral, political, or epistemological reasons. These reasons are of course qualified by the ethical criterion above; from the perspective of a Ku Klux Klan or National Socialist Party member, too much of what is, from their perspective, considered the wrong kind of variety is also grounds for dissent. It is important to remember, however, that the availability of choice should not be unproblematically open in any absolute or unmitigated sense to the degree that it is irrational, unreasonable, or unjust. According to philosopher of education Eamonn Callan, those choices and that rationality should, however, also exceed the orthodox ideology of neutrality and political moderation. "Reasonableness must extend beyond reasonable orthodoxy to include reasonable heresy."[36] As such, ethical concerns for justice are prior to an allowance for heresy and validate what counts as the subset of "reasonable heresy."

Epistemic diversity is a crucial criterion for dissent because it describes an ideal free flow of information that is helpful for challenging hegemonic and unethical trends. Deference to the prevailing opinion does not necessarily imply that one is subscribing to evil, or that one has abandoned morally right action or epistemically correct positions in favour of what is popular but immoral and incorrect; but neither does it guarantee goodness, moral autonomy, or epistemic warrant. Unthinking deference to ideological hegemony or popularity for their own sake is the worst and most dangerous sort of such acquiescence. Sunstein follows John Stuart Mill's warning that tyranny can take both official and unofficial forms, and that while protection "against the tyranny of the magistrate" is certainly desirable, such formal and explicit protection is insufficient to protect "against the tyranny of the prevailing opinion and feeling; against the tendency of society to impose, by other means than civil penalties, its own ideas and practices as rules of conduct on those who dissent from them."[37] Social coercion is thus made possible and maintained by hegemony of opinion and a climate of unthinking or unchallenged collective assent that is tacitly and informally enforced. Sunstein asserts that at its worst, such a climate of informal acquiescence can lead to errors that do more than lead individuals astray from good decision-making: "Knowledge falsification, bred by the natural human inclination to defer to the crowd, can create serious problems for the crowd itself. If members of the crowd are not revealing what they know, errors and even disasters are inevitable."[38] A free flow of information in the public discourse is thus to be preferred because it can protect society from the immoral practices and corruption that accompany, but do not necessarily imbue every act or aspect of, social convention.

The protective benefit of dissent is bound to the fact that a free flow of information is also a constituent element of educative experience. Freely flowing information is necessary (although not sufficient) for educative experiences because it enables the sharing of various interpretations of human experience. Edward Schillebeeckx follows a Deweyan proposition that persons are "co-constituted by their place in time and culture," and that the most objective and rigorous knowledge is therefore possible only through an approach that is contextually sensitive to historicity and hermeneutics.[39] The rooting of such contextualism in Dewey's thought is important because it lends itself to a participatory democratic framework as the ideal of human existence: the greatest amount of experiential information is likely to be contained in the assembly of all persons. Experience of an event, interpretation of that experience, participation in meaning-making, and bringing forth a variety of complementary and competing experiences in community is the avenue by which Schillebeeckx's educative aspect of dissent meets a democratic framework for politics, education, and personhood.

Finally, a consideration of dissent as reasonable heresy would not be complete without a consideration of Gilbert Chesterton's thought. In his time, Chesterton was aware that the Catholic Church was a diverse organization that coordinated many enterprises and maintained equilibrium among many points of view. Ecumenical Catholicism negotiated a multitude of contexts and was predicated on inclusivity. Chesterton's notion of heresy was likewise based upon appreciating the difference between (a) reasonable criticism of the Church that reflects its inclusivity and universality, and (b) heresy of the unreasonable, exclusionary variety. Unreasonable heresy in Chesterton's view is the sin – here interpreted as the rending of relationship – against inclusivity, and in his thinking, reasoned heresy turns unreasonable when it becomes too proud to admit its relationship with others: "A man [sic] does not come an inch nearer to being a heretic by being a hundred times a critic. Nor does he do so because his criticisms resemble those of critics who are also heretics. He only becomes a heretic at the precise moment when he prefers his criticism to his Catholicism. That is, at the instant of separation in which he thinks the view peculiar to himself more than the creed which unites him to his fellows."[40] The reasonableness of heresy, in Chesterton's view, is akin to Socrates' attitude of questioning for the betterment of society. If dissenting heresy is based upon exclusion, elitism, or snobbery, its ethical and epistemic adequacy as described above quickly erodes.

6 PUBLICITY

The social utility of morally and epistemically reasonable heresy is severely diminished if the view is reserved within the confines of the private self. It cannot truly be called dissent, nor can it be valued as such, until it is acted upon in some way that extends beyond one's own unshared private thoughts. Until then it is not a political act. That is a bold statement for some, who would argue that the existence of a dissenting thought within a subject is enough to set him or her apart from others, regardless of whether or not that rest of the group or society is aware of it. The point of contention might arise then that an individual's personal hypothesizing of dissident-like views qualifies them as a dissident even without their (yet) publicizing the substance of their disagreement.

Probably the most attractive variant of this critique is the existential view which locates individual differentiation directly within the self. The question is therefore whether publicity is a necessary condition. To this critique some points must be conceded. If one is able to fashion themselves apart from the conformity that others display, but nonetheless to remain near them, and to accomplish that repositioning of the self in accord with all the above criteria up to, but not including this one, then it must be acknowledged that some kind of dissent has occurred. Personally I find this view quite attractive on existential grounds, but my concession is not limitless. This view is certainly correct from the perspective of the existential dissenter and from the perspective of one who prefers an epistemology that is satisfied that the presence of a single thought inside a mind is example enough of a phenomenon.

The problem with these views is that they diminish dissent's value by abstracting it from the interpersonal, communicative social sphere. Aware as I am that existentialism is more complex than what I have allowed in this short example,[41] to avoid making a reductive gloss of its philosophical breadth I will say with great caution that the existential dissenter in this example is characteristically asocial because their politics is limited to a population of one. If dissent is withheld as an abstraction or a selfishly guarded secret, then its value cannot be scrutinized, its usefulness to the group cannot be ascertained, nor can it be the genesis of future helpful thinking for others. By all appearances, keeping dissent to oneself signals to the group that one is in fact cooperating or complicit in the prevailing ideology. There are legitimate grounds to call private actions dissent, but the best kind of dissent is publicized dissent.

The above argument considered whether publicity is a necessary condition for a conceptual ideal of dissent, but with that concern answered, another question arises: is publicity a *sufficient* condition for an ideal if the quality of the dissent is not known? Two sub-species of the concept demonstrate its range from ideal to less-than-ideal: disclosure and contrariness. A strong example of disclosure is to be found in the actions of the little child in Hans Christian Andersen's tale "The Emperor's New Clothes." Against the prevailing view in the community that the Emperor is wearing a beautiful new set of clothes, when in fact he has been tricked by some dishonest tailors and is wearing nothing at all, as the Emperor passes by in parade the child has the courage to announce forcefully that the Emperor is naked. Andersen establishes as fact that the prevailing view was created and controlled by a climate of fear that would neither dare nor deign to insult the Emperor, and within this environment contrasts the innocence of a child with archetypal contrarian social grouches conditioned by adult socialization. These properties in the story strongly reinforce the child's act as a public disclosure of fact in contrast to the prevailing view. The value of the dissent in this case rests on the indisputability of the revealed fact and its requisite relevance and urgency for correcting the woefully wrong prevailing view. The child's revelation is also helpful because it enables and encourages others to act based upon good reason rather than social coercion. In addition to its acute value in overcoming foolish sycophancy, the child's dissent in this case has also apparently set the stage for a change in the pretentious social climate that is currently built upon illusory assumptions and coercive practices.

A contrarian, in contrast to a discloser, is simply disagreeable for disagreement's sake and is hence either a social grouch or one who indiscriminately doubts everything he sees, hears, or reads. Contrarians are unqualified complainers whose public statements are based upon faulty or incomplete information or jaded opinion, and who therefore do not necessarily help the group with their dissenting public statements. By failing to disclose accurate information with any degree of consistency or relevance, the contrarian's esteem in the

community is eroded because he or she is perceived to be an untrust-
worthy complainer whose arbitrary, unpredictable, and dubiously
factual dissent is as likely to hinder the group as to help it. The discloser is thus to be preferred to the contrarian on the factual grounding and ethical strength of his or her statements. Contrariness is still
dissent, although its value as such remains questionable. Publicity
therefore cannot be considered a sufficient condition for dissent, since
some brands of it unhelpfully detract from efforts to promote the
good of all.

Since all dissent runs contrary to the prevailing view in some way
or another, the variety of dissent that Sunstein calls disclosure should
be reconsidered as a revelation of information and opinion that, in
addition to its contrariness, also passes the tests of justice and truth.
What Sunstein calls contrariness is therefore wanton disagreement,
alarmist gesturing, and selfish posturing that lacks ethical and epistemological rigour and is made merely for its own sake and not for
the good of all. Since disclosure as such is to be preferred because of
its factual and ethical superiority over selfish contrariness, it becomes
apparent that the most adequate form of dissent must include this
sixth criterion that describes its political position and posture within
the community, institution, or group as a public entity. The best and
most performatively complete kind of dissent is therefore a public act
aimed at countering the harmful or limiting effects of the prevailing
public view.

Sunstein argues dissent is an optimal feature of public political life.
He acknowledges that it could either be private or public, and then
argues that the public variety is to be preferred because it improves
the chances that legitimate counter hegemonic information and opinion will be given fair political hearing, be recognized for its value,
and, he hopes, influence society for the improvement of the common
good. Publicity is a requirement for dissent because withholding or
privatizing information is equated with tacit approval of and acquiescence to the *status quo*. If the pressure of conformity acts as a filter
that sifts out (silences) the competing information that might correct
error or improve mediocrity, then the entire group risks stagnation
as a result.

The pressure to conform, however, is strong: "In the real world
people silence themselves for many reasons. Sometimes they do not
want to risk the irritation or opprobrium of their friends and allies.
Sometimes they fear that they will, through their dissent, weaken the

effectiveness and reputation of the group to which they belong. Sometimes they trust fellow group members to be right. These points help explain why people are especially reluctant to dissent during war or when national security is threatened, but the same pressures are felt in ordinary times."[42] In Sunstein's argument, when dissent is present in its fullest conception it contributes best to the common good by drawing information from the privacy of individual opinion into the public world so as to challenge and overcome conformist pressure. He maintains that in addition to a free flow of pertinent information, privately held opinions also need to be freely circulated for the good of society. According to Sunstein, "those opinions are of independent interest" and are valuable because "individuals and governments do better if they know what their fellow citizens really think." Perhaps more importantly, though, "people with dissenting opinions might have good arguments," and if those arguments are not expressed then it leaves the remainder of the community, including those who tacitly concur or who conform only for lack of alternative information and opinion, vulnerable to the effects of privatization.[43] The utility of encouraging dissent for the good of all, as expressed above, is in concert with Mill's admonition that dissenters look beyond dissent's instrumental value as a concept that advances their own interests and appreciate its value *in general* for the good of all.[44] Again, publicity fails as a sufficient condition because it does not guarantee the promotion of the good of all, nor does it guarantee that the dissent will have been expressed without attempting to coerce others.

7 PERSUASIVE

Finally, dissent is a persuasive rather than an intimidating force that seeks to convert opinion through free reasoned argument, rather than to enforce change through violence or coercion. The roots of rational persuasion can be traced to the democratic government in ancient Athens. Since, according to Ober, the Athenian elite was unable to gain political control and establish an oligarchy through traditional coercive or physical means, it was compelled to adapt to the city's democratic culture and attempt publicly to demonstrate on rational grounds why oligarchic values were worthy of popular assent and support. The elites were therefore separated ideologically, although not politically, from the democratic majority, but the elites nonetheless remained Athenians.

Sunstein expresses his support for the persuasive feature of dissent with his assertion that where majorities produce begrudging compliance, minorities, in contrast, procure willing, autonomous conversion. He suggests "that people obey majorities but are not really convinced by them, while people are persuaded, at least some of the time, that minorities are right."[45] Persuasion by the intrinsic value of information and reasonable argument is thus preferable to coercion by external forces that compel acquiescence or compliance. While compliance results from the use of unilateral power and ideological mystification as a means of coercing choice, conversion results from the offer of rational persuasion within a dialogical framework that genuinely respects agentic choice. The Athenian elites made their case for oligarchy through the power of reasoned, credible argumentation and justification rather than attempting to enforce a change of belief through coercion.

The Athenian emphasis on individual liberty remains throughout Western political philosophy and is at the heart of its commentary on liberal democracy. A well-functioning democratic society should not merely tolerate individual agency and divergence from the dominant view (while in truth silently perceiving it as an annoyance), but should positively evaluate and incorporate rational divergence as the mark of an advanced concept and practice of social harmony, akin to philosopher John Rawls' conception of accommodating social difference: "Political liberalism assumes that, for political purposes, a plurality of reasonable yet incompatible comprehensive doctrines is the normal result of the exercise of human reason within the framework of the free institutions of a constitutional democratic regime. Political liberalism also supposes that a reasonable comprehensive doctrine does not reject the essentials of a democratic regime."[46]

SUMMARY

The Athenian elites provide an illustrative secular test case for the seven criteria of dissent. First, dissent began with an exercise of their political franchise in Athens; in fact, their enfranchisement germinated in feeling entitled to govern the city themselves. Second, they were aware of the epistemic history in Athens and the culture of Greek city-states, and as such were arguing from a perspective that suggested it was normal and traditional for oligarchies to govern these political units. Third, as the elites were aware that the ideology of democratic governance would continue to diminish their aspirations, they attempted to devise forms of non-democratic governance as reasonable alternatives. The fourth criterion is related to the third in this case because the elites were aware that an ethical weakness of democracy is that popularity does not necessarily confer factual and ethical correctness or wise decision-making. If the lovers of wisdom and those suited to encountering the forms of rightness, like the guardians and golden philosopher kings in Plato's *Republic*, were to rule, then it was agreed that the city would be less prone to the errors of unwise persons. The ethical weakness of their argument, of course, lies in the fact that it prejudicially reduces the franchise of the so-called "sub-elites," which itself is a dubious category. Fifth, the elites' selective and constructive proposals for ideal governance were non-democratic heresy that nonetheless attempted to maintain a thriving community. Sixth, their arguments were expressed publicly as reasoned alternatives to democracy and did not wither in significance due to isolation in the non-influential sphere of private opinion. Finally, their arguments attempted to persuade, rather than coerce, their fellow citizens that the democratic experiment was inferior to oligarchic alternatives. Certainly this part of the test is also tainted by the weakness that the elites only employed rational argument out of instrumental necessity. It was not employed for its own sake – which would have been the best rationale – and likely would have been bypassed had coercive and physically forceful methods been available.

Charles Curran provides an excellent example of dissent within the Catholic context. He is enfranchised by Baptism, and thus makes his critique of HV from an "insider's" perspective; he remains a priest and faithful Catholic who loves the Church. In fact he frames his dissent as being "in and for the Church," with the attitude that it is "the highest form of patriotism," which "speak[s] the truth in love."[47] His critiques rely on the same historical and theological tradition that the prevailing view acknowledges, although he draws warrants from this tradition that do not support the dominant viewpoint. As such, he proposes his criticisms – including a view that dissent is possible – as reasonable departures from the mainstream within Catholic thought. His view of dissent's general value is notably revealed through his critique of "triumphalists" who would foist their views, whether "liberal" or "conservative," upon the whole Church and thus obliterate its productive tensions.[48] To this end, he has maintained his public expression and support for dissent, all the while respecting the freedom of those who do not agree with him to hold their views.

CONCLUSION

Dissent possibly remains a more complex entity to define than an action to perform, but in both concept and action it describes the liminal space and action where one awkwardly retains full member-ship in a group while also sitting apart from the leading attitudes in that group. Perhaps the next most significant difficulty that emerges from the analysis is that dissent encounters the same problem that liberal and democratic societies face when they attempt to accom-modate perspectives that are themselves illiberal or non-democratic. Not all dissenting views are concerned with the value of dissent in general beyond its significance to their own causes. Some would even prefer to strangle other forms of dissent that are contrary to their own. The ideal of dissent proposed here is a utilitarian variety that will admit the perspectives of these narrowly selfish and totalitarian views to the point that they can provide an ethically sound alternative to the prevailing view, but that ultimately rejects them beyond that point in their purported desire to usurp control and establish them-selves as *the* prevailing view that would tolerate no more dissent. The ideal of dissent admits more dissent and sympathizes with the value of dissent for societies in general. It is this factual ideal and the seven criteria behind it that I will carry forth into prescriptive notions for a reform of religious educational pedagogy.

6

The Limitations of Current Practice

USING PRACTICE TO INFORM THEORY

A theory of dissent in Catholic Education-Schooling depends on the relationship that Catholicism has with the theological and philosophical concept of dissent, the history of the Church's own dissent from secular society, and the Church's record of responses to internally dissenting currents as part of the way its teachings change. This theology, philosophy, and history are essential in establishing the theoretical and practical grounds from which anyone would respond to a discrete dissident view, reconsider pedagogical "best practices," develop a general institutional policy for meeting student dissent, or advocate on someone's behalf should their dissenting view encounter resistance. The same trio is required for proposing a theoretical pedagogy of dissent.

It might be attractive to stop here and consider the preceding discussion sufficient grounds for proposing a model that would reform the pedagogical justification for how educators treat issues that are controversial *within* Catholicism. To do so, however, would be short-sighted, because the discussion is not yet informed by a theoretical perspective on the actual practices that educators use when encountering students with dissenting views. So while this book proposes a pedagogy of dissent for Catholic Education generally, Catholic schools are nonetheless particularly interesting in this context because to propose a pedagogical model exclusively out of pure theology, philosophy, and history would be to commit the fallacy of ignoring the professional context in which students and teachers interact. Dissent is possible in theory, but several factors in the practice of Catholic Schooling currently keep it from achieving greater prominence as an approach to curriculum. These include the lack of Catholic Schooling's own pedagogical theory that would justify its inclusion, but also, and perhaps most importantly, any views that Catholic schools should focus exclusively on the prevailing teaching. At the same time in any one school it is likely that students will hold disagreements of some sort, such as those in the three examples from the introduction. In practice, without a formal pedagogical model for engaging dissent, the Catholic school finds itself facing the question of how to respond in a way that does not alienate its constitutive members.

Since it is generally religion teachers who most directly and most often encounter student dissent from Church teaching as part of their professional work, it makes sense to ask them how they respond, given the current practical context and theoretical lacuna on this topic. Religion teachers find themselves challenged to give students the space to air their individual views while attending to the prevailing culture in the community and adhering to a responsibility to present and model Church teaching. The professional challenge is to keep as many of the constituent members within the educational relationship as possible satisfied with the curricular *what*, *why*, and *how*. To alienate any constituent member by discrediting or even silencing them would cripple the relationship.

Among the many possible ways this could happen, the Church would have grounds to protest and withdraw its sanction from the school if its teachings were perceived to not be taken seriously, or students would become disaffected and possibly even move to another school if their concerns were dismissed as "mere rebellion." The goal of teachers is therefore to find ways of keeping conversations alive and interesting for the purposes of including all partners in service of the ultimate aims of student learning. In this task teachers have a tremendous burden and responsibility: teaching religion in a Catholic school can be rewarding, but that reward is also a function of being able to perform and master a very demanding and complex assignment. What do they do when students dissent?

This chapter displays a range of expectations and practices that teachers currently use when students disagree with prevailing Church teachings. It reveals some of the major ways in which teachers and schools accommodate dissent within the current approaches to teaching and learning in the Catholic school, and in so doing illuminates the limits of the best professional work teachers can do when faced with tensions in curriculum, community, and Church. Each of the three procedural concerns, two pedagogical stances, and six peda-gogical techniques examined in this chapter was illustrated in its professional context during private interviews with religion teachers. These illustrations accompany the descriptions of the concerns, stances, and techniques, and then each description is examined for its benefits and shortcomings. From the examination of uplifting and limiting features inherent in the current approaches to dissent, one can therefore recognize the good work that teachers are currently doing, while at the same time appreciating the need to develop for them a more rigorous grounding upon which Catholic Education-Schooling can encounter and respond to dissent. There are good argu-ments for dissent in the theological, philosophical, and historical abstract, but their practical rationality is enhanced when they are supplemented by an understanding of current pedagogical context and professional practices.

The presentation in the pages below demonstrates both the peda-gogical benefits and the systematic shortcomings within the range of currently accepted practice. The responses these teachers offered were examined within the guiding assumption that their approaches to teaching and learning are employed in good faith for the benefit of students, and that they reflect the most politically prudent and intel-lectually generous means currently available with which to engage the problems that the teachers encounter. The problems that emerge signal tensions within Catholic Education in general, and do not indicate a teacher's personal professional grace or weakness, as that is independent of institutional determination; it would be callous, to say the least, to draw a conclusion that teachers are professionally deficient for using techniques that have drawbacks when they have little other reasonable choice. The speech within the interviews that reveals and suggests the actions of the participants within the class-room is certainly shaped by teachers' own beliefs about teaching and learning, but also by several factors that are beyond their control, including the constraints of curriculum, the professional climate within their school staffs, and the expectations of students, parents, clergy, and administrators within the school division. In turn, every factor that influences teacher practice is also shaped by its place in the larger Catholic world; hence a continuous process of mutual shaping reflects Catholic Education's hegemony. The examination therefore assumes that much of what shapes teachers' responses is a reflection of the structured pedagogical climate within the school and the political-ecclesial society outside the school. It is because these teachers find themselves doing their best and still encountering systemic shortcomings that this chapter can conclude by recommending that a systematic pedagogical model for the justification of enabling student dissent be developed.

While individual teachers have many important responsibilities within the Catholic school's dominant practices, their responsibilities for its radical reform are understandably much lower, or even nil. All teachers may wish that they could do things differently but find that the current hegemony subordinates these wishes to the maintenance of the current rule. By candidly illustrating the limits of their work, however, the participants have provided material for a philosophical discussion of the problems within Catholic Education; this material has validity as "best practice" within the professional pedagogical context. By candidly discussing the systematic shortcomings of the practices they illustrate, I wish to remain generous to the participants' professional integrity and sincerity in contributing to a study of Catholic Education's pedagogical climate. I therefore assume that all participants have the best of professional intentions as they work within an environment informed by a theory of Catholic Education that is, unfortunately, poorly debated. The evaluations made here of certain stances and techniques are therefore meant to represent judgments of generalized illustrations that suggest the current limits for the practice of Catholic Education.

The critical commentary in this chapter is offered with the intent of improving Catholic Education through a theoretical discussion that recognizes the foundational value of its existing religious institutional context. Although explicit acknowledgment of the tensions and weaknesses within Catholic Education might not be favoured among some constituencies, especially those with strong commitments to the *status quo* in Catholic Education, it is nonetheless a requisite step before proposing reform to a system that has difficulty in adequately responding to concerns regarding legitimate student dissent. This chapter shows where Catholic Education-Schooling *is*; the next one shows where it *might* go.

A final word is offered here regarding the relationship between the choice of interview participants and the audience for this book. I selected teachers because they are the professionals who take up the *public* task of responding to dissent on a regular basis.[1] This public role is conditioned by an institutional responsibility to coordinate the student's dissent with a presentation of Church teaching. All the partners in Catholic Education hold religion teachers to account for their responses. At the same time, since parents also occasionally find themselves counselling their own dissenting children who attend Catholic school, one could reason that parents might also have some interesting perspectives to provide. After all, since this book applies to dissent in *Catholic Education* generally and is not limited to the dissent that is expressed in *Catholic Schools*, their views might be helpful. This is true to a point, but ultimately parents do not have the same public ecclesial-political accountability as teachers in this respect: parents are free to organize as they wish within the private, domestic sphere.[2] Politically they are responsible to themselves, and spiritually to God. Since this theory is concerned primarily with dissent as a public expression and the value that "good" dissent and the proper treatment of "good dissenters" confers on societies and organizations, I have deliberately focused only on teachers. However, I do not wish to discount the important role parents perform, and I hope that parents will find the examination of teachers' pedagogical responses to be an instructive way of knowing and appreciating what systemic limitations their children encounter in Catholic institutions. I especially hope that the insights here will be informative in planning the next steps in conversations they have with their children, their children's teachers, their clergy, and each other, and in other settings outside the school.

TEACHERS' PROCEDURAL CONCERNS

Even if they would reject or be highly sceptical about a pedagogical model based on dissent, all teachers do their best to accommodate what they would term legitimate student disagreement with Catholic teachings. The "best practice" of engaging with this difference is conditioned by the several responsibilities to all partners in Catholic Schooling; as well, it involves upholding a disposition (which is also inherent in secular institutions) to maintain good academic habits and respect for persons and the school. In fact, teachers' willingness to engage pedagogically with students' dissident views is in large part determined by these latter behavioural and procedural concerns. The first *classroom* test of legitimate dissent tends to consider not the political-ecclesial and moral meaning of *what* is said, but rather *how* the student expresses it.

It can be surmised that all Catholic school teachers are concerned that dissent not be used as license to promote ignorant, misinformed, prejudicial, or disrespectful ideas in the school. Dissident students will generally be accommodated so long as they demonstrate an understanding of Church teaching and do not dismiss the Church outright or present their views as superior to those of the Church. In positive terms, Participant Four states that students should be given the appropriate information, tools, and space with which to present themselves and their dissenting questions in such a manner that they receive a fair hearing: "Students should be able to ask questions that I think are legitimate questions, but I don't think that they should ask questions that are meant to embarrass people or to evoke a response from the class of humour: I think they should be serious, legitimate questions, and probing questions. I think that if they can meet that criterion that you are pretty much open to what emerges. And I think you can tell when students are genuine in their efforts to do that."

If good behaviour is the first step toward a desirably expressed disagreement, then the responsibility to provide a rationally sound argument naturally follows. Students are not permitted to simply disagree on relativistic grounds. Good pedagogy requires their teachers to prompt them to provide substantiating evidence for their views. Participant Fourteen demonstrates her desire to promote this habit: "[I]f they are going to dissent with me, have a good argument to back yourself up. I don't want to hear them say, 'Oh, I disagree with you because I disagree with you' … [My response would be:] '[That] is not a good argument. I want to hear *why* you don't believe.'" Independently of the *content* of students' opinions, the pedagogical imperative here is developing students' skills in assembling, judging, and presenting rational evidence for the perspectives that they have developed. Often, in practice, this task entails students developing reasoned positions out of their initial intuitions. Teachers who take this imperative seriously also discourage pre-critical repetition of the opinions students hear through the media, at home, and elsewhere, and so encourage students to engage with appropriate sources and styles of argumentation in order to move past any flimsiness in popular thought and support their views more thoroughly.

Finally, teachers are concerned with creating a classroom environment where students have freedom of religious choice and thought.

While Catholicism is naturally emphasized, teachers do not expect or require belief in Catholic Church teachings. They do, however, remain aware that some students arrive with an expectation that the purpose of the Catholic school is to indoctrinate them into Catholic belief. Although the Church forbids coercion and inauthentic formation, in a fraction of instances some students may legitimately carry this concern; much more common is that students are simply put off by doctrinally sound but overly earnest invitations, or else by their own misperceptions about what the school hopes to accomplish regarding their faith. These perceptions – and a teacher's inability to assuage them – can easily become a major barrier to building classroom rapport.

The conversation with Participant Thirteen presents an interesting example of how some classroom interactions take place over the question of indoctrination. He demonstrates that he would like students to consider the school's role in terms of extending an invitation to accept Church teaching freely. In his experience, however, the teacher needs to nurture this attitude toward doctrine and the religion program in the school:

> There are always some kids who have a chip on their shoulders about the Catholic Church and they always assume my role there is to tell them what they have to believe, and I always try to tell them right at the beginning of every course that I teach: "My job here is not to tell you what you have to believe. That is your problem: you have to figure it out. I will teach what the course says, what the course content is, what the Church says: I will teach you that. And I will invite you to consider the faith and the Church teaching and to take it seriously, but in the end I can't make you believe anything. You will believe what you do, period. I can't *make* you believe something." [emphasis his]

In this way, the religion course is presented as an academic subject that is also an intimately personal matter with the potential for further positive spiritual consequences.

Participant Two demonstrates an interesting variant of this pre-emptive manoeuvre to dispel misperceptions about the school. She frames her approach in arm's-length academic terms that focus on presenting the official, Magisterial view. While she would be open to the possibility of students adopting Catholic belief, and would actively encourage those who choose to adopt it, she explicitly states that she does not require it: "My biggest goal, and I tell them this the very first week, is that they'll just learn to open their mind. That's what I say. I'm not here to push religion on them; I'm not here to push the Catholic faith on them. I remind them that it is a Catholic school and I'm going to reference the Catholic Church when I'm talking. My beliefs will never be referenced in this class. Whether I believe in something or not is irrelevant." In this presentation of a learning relationship, the Church is situated as the authority providing subject matter of normative belief and the teacher presents herself as providing pedagogical approaches to learning it.

Importantly, these stances against indoctrination remain impartial to the teacher's personal beliefs on the topic being discussed due to a dual aim to (1) relieve any pressure for students to believe *as the teacher believes*, and (2) emphasize a common institutional Catholicism. Teachers present and follow this common, public approach to the faith as a strategic (and sometimes strategically agreed-upon with colleagues) means of minimizing any differences that may be perceived between individual teachers. The embodiment of a teacher's personal beliefs therefore may be present in the classroom, but not necessarily; if so, they would ostensibly only emerge subconsciously.

In the final analysis, the student is invited to receive religion class as an academic service toward breadth and depth of knowledge, as an exposure to a publicly agreed-upon Catholic identity, and as an invitation to consider religious and Catholic belief further. As a presentation of how teachers exercise professional power in the service of students who present dissenting views, it can be seen that while these pre-emptive discussions are helpful for affirming students' freedom – and so nurturing a deeper level of participation in the class – they also do not venture past that point of accommodation to address the academic question of *how* one would dissent. In sum, it appears that after these allowances are made to provide students with a forum to express pedagogically un-nurtured dissenting views, the students are left to discover and decide for themselves *how* they will respond to the teachings they find troublesome.

In addition to communicating "non-indoctrination" as an academic and spiritual hope for students, such pre-emptive manoeuvres seem intended to win student cooperation and "authentic" participation in class, thus decreasing any resistance that is based upon mistrust of authority or organized religion, or preconceived fears of indoctrination. These actions are intended to create a classroom atmosphere in which students can feel comfortable that their intellectual and religious freedom will not be threatened by attempts to make them conform to a religious code or belief set that they do not freely embrace. So while the teacher may very well be a "believing Catholic" and exactly the kind of person the Magisterial Church desires to be teaching religion, the teacher presents him- or herself impartially to avoid imposing a tacit expectation that students "be Catholic in the way I am Catholic."

The above illustrations are helpful for describing some of the features of a positive student dissent. Notably, they raise a parallel standard for teachers to meet, should they desire the disagreements presented in their classes to be academically solid. Unless one works on the assumption that the best kind of dissenting habits are not nurtured but occur naturally, the next pedagogical question concerns how dissident students might best be directed to the proper intellectual supports for their views, including authoritative sources and models of inquiry and argumentation.

PEDAGOGICAL STANCES

Once all the procedural concerns are lifted, teachers find themselves facing the challenge of addressing student disagreements from theologically, philosophically, and pedagogically rigorous points of view. Before adopting specific techniques of responding to students, they often first consider what *pedagogical stance* they will take in these discussions. A *stance* as it is considered here is the way in which a teacher positions him- or herself between fulfilling the requirements of the curriculum, school, Church, parents, and community on the one hand, and the pedagogical needs of the students on the other. As his or her foundational approach to teaching religion, it reflects an aspect of the teacher's professional mission that describes *what* he or she hopes to accomplish in the teaching-learning relationship, as opposed to the technical tasks that constitute *how* that mission will be performed.

I discuss two major stances here: (1) the *mediator between Church and student*, and (2) the *neutral facilitator*. These two stances are significant because they show substantially different ways in which teachers represent themselves to students and to the broader educational community in their effort to meet the needs of all parties within the school's educational relationship. The difference between the two stances is as follows. The *mediator* position suggests a stronger affinity with building bridges between the formal institution and individual students, and so is more congruent with strong evangelization and formation aims. It presents the teacher as one who extends an invitation for students to choose to learn about the faith with the intent of being drawn progressively closer to it. The *neutral facilitator* stance, by contrast, presents Catholic knowledge to students without explicitly extending an invitation to the faith, and so presents Catholic Schooling as the provision of academic service to students who may have other interests than understanding the Church but who might, just the same, have the independent volition to choose Catholicism. Both stances respect that religious affiliation and reception of Church teaching is a matter of the student's own free will, but the mediator extends an invitation to the positive freedom of following doctrine, while the facilitator steadfastly emphasizes impartiality and the negative freedom from the encumbrance of external expectations.

Stance A: Mediator Between Church and Student

The mediator stance fashions the teacher as a liaison between the Church and students, and regards the teacher as a guide for the students' formation as spiritual beings. It presumes that students who dissent or become frustrated with the Church do so as a natural consequence of their ignorance about its teachings, and so are in need of remedial understanding. It is the teacher's role to restore the relationship between Church and student by inviting the student to learn more about Catholic teaching and so return to an amicable relationship with the Church. Knowing the Church means loving the Church – a pattern of thinking that is rooted in Plato's philosophy[3] – and so the mediator believes that if the authentic and authoritative knowledge is accurately and effectively communicated to students, its naturally persuasive power will be best established to attract a learner's free choice.

Participant Twelve speaks of the professional challenge for teachers to *appropriately mediate* between the Church and student in a way that engages more than just the students' cognitive dimension: "[F]inding the curriculum that really is able to speak to the kids and speak to the Church in that relationship has been a bit tricky. You really need, in my view, a teacher who is able to do that, be that mediator, be that liaison between the kids and the Church in a very loving but powerful way: a real way. That is the challenge. Otherwise you can just be a person who just delivers curriculum and then marks it." As a mediator in this sense, the teacher presents him- or herself both as a pedagogical model who brings Church and student together, and as a model of concern for the whole person, not just for his or her cognitive dimension. In this view, the teacher withholds his or her positions on moral issues and issues of belief, but expresses a bias toward the Church by following the stated aims of evangelization and formation while attempting to bring the Church to students and developing them as whole persons. Each of these tasks brings a theoretical and practical challenge to the aims schools develop for teaching about what Catholicism *is* and *how* one is Catholic – even if only implicitly and through the hidden curriculum. Theoretically, the question remains as to whether it is possible to present anything besides a one-to-one correspondence with orthodoxy.

The benefits of this stance, according to the current aims of Catholic Education, descend from the ease with which it enables the teacher to ensure that the Catholic faith and teachings on socio-moral issues are presented fairly and concurrently with evangelization and formation aims. It reinforces the teacher's display of loyalty to the Church because he or she is always seen as its representative, offering its academic enlightenment and spiritual fulfillment. From this stance the teacher also avoids charges of indoctrination, since his or her actions are restricted to extending invitations and explicitly avoiding coercive tactics; the allowance for personal freedom and religious liberty means students' individual pedagogical needs are given space for expression and consideration within the classroom.

The major drawback of the mediator stance is that it discounts the religious experiences of students and their families as relevant contributions to knowledge about the Church. Students are perceived to have an intellectual deficit with respect to the Catholic Church upon entering the school, and it is seen as the school's and the teacher's responsibility to erase that deficit by beginning the journey to remedy ignorance. While it is generally accepted that all students have some degree of immaturity that is appropriate to their age and corresponding cognitive ability,[4] sometimes immaturity becomes improperly confused with a disposition to disagree. Specifically, if students disagree with Church teachings on female ordination or homosexuality only because of their exposure to these issues through the popular media, but are unaware of the specific Church documents that promulgate these official norms, for example, the first inclination of teachers in this stance will be to try to have the student reconsider his or her opinion through an examination of primary documents rather than a version that the popular press or conventional hearsay represents. The *mediator* stance downplays the breadth of students' moral agency with the intent of alerting, focusing, and conforming that moral agency to the comprehensive truth of the Church's teaching. An agent who will not conform is initially presumed to be ignorant, uncooperative, unready, or *unreceptive*.

The mediator stance can provide intellectual reinforcement to those who already agree wholeheartedly with the prevailing Church teaching, and a persuasive alternative offer to those who completely disagree with it. However, it leaves those faithful whose commitment is troubled by disagreements on non-infallible teachings with no further support beyond a reiteration of the invitation to reconsider official teaching. For these students, the mediator's response begs the pedagogical question on controversial issues, because a balance between revealing Church teaching and developing individual critical agency is skewed in favour of the Church's own epistemology; hence the pedagogical flexibility of this stance is limited to revisiting an array of persuasive arguments that all point back to the same official view which inspired the disagreement in the first place.

Stance B: Neutral Facilitator and Information Provider

Unlike the *mediator* stance's emphasis on an open invitation for the student to come closer to the Church, the stance of the *neutral facilitator and information provider* emphasizes instead the learning of curricular knowledge for its own sake. Catholicism is presented as the prevailing view which the teacher is responsible for presenting, but the emphasis tends toward dispassionate understanding more than spiritual reception of Catholic teaching. The teacher's concern is that students should be familiar with Church teaching as a matter of fact, but he or she eschews the expectation that this knowledge necessarily will or should influence their spiritual relationship with the Church. Correspondingly, the teacher's own beliefs remain in the background as he or she emphasizes Church teaching and its application to life in personally impartial terms.

Participant Two reports that she withholds her own opinions from students with two aims in mind. The first descends from an administrative concern that the students in her school should not receive conflicting messages from two or more teachers. The second is a cognitive concern with bias. She hopes to challenge students to form their own opinions without copying those of their teachers: "I want them to form their own beliefs. My beliefs don't matter. I just want to create an opportunity for them to discuss it, give them background, give them history; I want them to start thinking for themselves. They have to start – they're not thinking. I keep my opinions out – all of us keep our opinions out – professionally, because many of us, really in the Religion department, last year there were eleven of us there and you have eleven teachers coming from different backgrounds, all with their own beliefs." The felt institutional imperative for unanimity among the staff in the Catholic school strongly suggests that enough diversity of privately held beliefs exists among teachers to arouse significantly conflicting views. There is ostensibly also a felt concern to shelter students from any official or public acknowledgment that they live within a variety of adult responses to Catholic teaching. Without a theoretical framework for responding to controversy in a way that suspends closure for educative purposes, anything besides what Participant Two does in her setting would be very difficult.

The major benefit of *neutrality* is that, as with the *mediator* stance, the teacher can allow for a great degree of student freedom by presenting Catholic teachings as intellectual academic requirements rather than personal spiritual obligations. However well neutrality is achieved in the classroom, the student's academic needs are nevertheless generally well met by providing them with an approach to Catholicism that is intellectually adequate for all, regardless of their degree of commitment to Catholicism. For those with strong, partial, or no commitments, this intellectual fodder might either reinforce or disrupt their attitudes toward spirituality, religion, and Catholicism in particular, but there is no expectation that any particular change in faith be the outcome of this learning; that matter is left to the private discretion of students.

The primary drawback of neutrality is that it does not overcome the systemic overexposure to prevailing teaching in the school, which occurs at the expense of subordinating what Bernard Häring calls "the other information"[5] that supports legitimate ecclesial pluralism and moral freedom of conscience. The instructor's 'neutral' presentation of prevailing knowledge thus does not overcome the fact that the religion course curriculum and the school's institutional ethos are not content-neutral. Presenting critiques of Church teaching with an impartial attitude – even if these critiques are known within the Church's history and theology – could be interpreted as a challenge to Magisterial authority and therefore a violation of the teacher's claim to "neutrality" or "impartiality." One particular example concerns the controversy over HV, the report of the Papal Birth Control Commission, and the CCCB's "Winnipeg Statement." The neutral stance does not necessarily bring to students any information of the kind contained in the Commission's Report or the CCCB's statement. Given the lack of legitimately Catholic alternatives to the prevailing view, the epistemic stage is also set here to perpetuate a major shortcoming in the area of exploring how an individual agent's moral authority works in coordination with Magisterial teaching authority; unfortunately, this stance's major effect is to reinforce students' perceptions that there is no Catholic way of disagreeing with controversial teachings, and hence strengthens their thought that all disagreement must originate from a binarily opposed secular source. Without knowledge of the Birth Control Commission and "Winnipeg," for example, one might falsely conclude that finding complete adherence to HV impossible is an "un-Catholic" act. In theory, notwithstanding the influence of lessons on conscience, the pedagogical stance of teacher neutrality has a high likelihood of leaving the impression that anything less than a complete match between a person's practice and Magisterial teaching represents a deficiency in the individual's reception. This impression is a misrepresentation of Catholicism's history, theology, and culture.

There is also the issue of any religion teacher's claim to neutrality. Complete neutrality is impossible in any context, and that reality becomes immediately apparent in the Catholic school should a teacher attempt to appear neutral and publicly silent on non-infallible ordinary teachings (such as contraception), but then encounter problems when asked to publicly profess belief in the Nicene Creed (Jesus as fully human and fully divine), for instance, as an infallible core of the faith and as a usual condition of employment.[6] "Neutrality" as such exists equivocally: the teacher is simultaneously known "to believe" as an ecclesial condition of holding office, but for pedagogical purposes also to remain "impartial" as a professional condition of good curricular management. Religion teachers must persistently negotiate a great tension between public belief and private faith. It ultimately befuddles a student (or anyone else) to believe that a teacher would have strong opinions on non-controversial issues, but no opinion on controversial issues: or, similarly, a strong view on infallible teaching but no view on non-infallible teaching.

When teachers shift between neutral and biased positions without acknowledging what they are doing or why, student frustration intensifies on these moral topics. This observation does not imply that "shifting" must cease; rather, its continued practice should open the opportunity for students to learn how the difference between the levels of teaching authority carries real-life consequences in the Church. In the public forum of a Catholic school, this consequence would entail a demonstration of assent to infallible teaching as the core of faith, and then (sometimes) *obsequium* for (some) non-infallible teachings. The Catholic teacher's religious freedom to display *obsequium* thus constitutes the warrant for his or her option to reserve his or her opinion on non-infallible teachings. The student's right to know the difference, and, where appropriate, to see this response demonstrated, offers a second pillar of support to this argument. And whether or not one agrees with teacher neutrality on non-infallible teaching, it remains the responsibility of the school, its teachers, the curriculum, the Church, and the home to be informed about and to communicate the difference between non-infallible ordinary teachings and the infallible teachings of popes, councils, and the universal ordinary Magisterium. When non-infallible teachings are conflated with infallible teachings, it suggests that there is either ignorance of the different levels of teaching, or else an unwillingness to revise the personal spiritual or political-religious commitments that are shaped by such conflation.

TEACHING TECHNIQUES

Teaching techniques are the means through which teachers adapt to their circumstances and perform their missions so as to meet their professional purposes and aims. *Techniques* are ways of engaging with students from within a pedagogical stance, but no one technique fits exclusively within any particular stance. The six techniques described below represent typical ways in which teachers prepare for and respond to student dissent. Just as the pedagogical stances are not entirely unproblematic, each of these techniques also has varying degrees of advantage and disadvantage for engaging students on controversial topics. Each technique, like the teaching stances, is presented as an aspect of the professional engagement with students that currently "works" or is "effective" toward delivery of a curriculum and development of a teaching-learning relationship. The discussion of each technique is therefore made according to its philosophical and theological adequacy rather than as an appraisal of its apparent social and religious acceptability within the classroom, the community, and the Church at large.

1 Omitting Offensive Material

In certain circumstances, teachers decide to omit material that they judge to be potentially offensive or damaging to their students' psychological well-being. Such omissions could occur for pastoral reasons on topics like abortion, divorce, or homosexuality if it is felt that students with parents, relatives, or friends who have had abortions, experienced divorce, or are non-heterosexual – or if it is the students who themselves are non-heterosexual or have had an abortion – might feel alienated from the Church because its teachings on these subjects are perhaps too stringent or even harsh-sounding to be heard in certain circumstances. The advantage of having the option to omit certain material is that it allows a teacher to delay the material's presentation in circumstances where sensitivity to students' psychological welfare is paramount, or where it is determined that a student's level of cognitive or social maturity is not yet well suited for these lessons. Teachers can exercise compassion for their students to the degree that, within their classrooms at least, certain facts will not be presented in any untimely way that might offend or emotionally overburden them.

Aside from the occasional exercise of sympathy during emotionally demanding circumstances, the option of omitting material on the grounds that it is circumstantially offensive is inadequate to inform a general approach to controversial topics, because it incompletely presents the curricular knowledge required of the Church's socio-moral teachings. Whether certain teachings are perceived to be offensive or not, students are required to know them as important socio-moral aspects of Catholicism. Since this approach presents only a partial view of Catholic life, it cannot claim to provide sufficient data to inform one's conscience of the Church's teaching on a subject. The pedagogical consequence is the impediment of students' personal growth, because they have been removed from situations where they might have to coordinate moral conflict, and so are maintained in a state of cognitive, spiritual, and moral naïveté. If applied consistently throughout the curriculum, omission thus only replaces one problematic situation with another.

2 Understanding Before Criticizing

The second pedagogical technique that teachers use to engage with student dissent, dissatisfaction, or disagreement is their firm insistence that students understand the Church before criticizing it. When a student presents disagreement with a Catholic teaching, this response engages in a focused examination of that teaching so that the adequacy of the student's knowledge that supports his or her criticism can be tested. The presumption is that some partial or total misunderstanding of the Church is the source of this criticism. While the teacher recognizes that it is fair for the student to hold and express this criticism, and at the lesson's end to remain in disagreement with the prevailing Church view, the teacher ultimately wishes to ensure that any criticism is based on a fully informed understanding of Church teaching.

The two possible kinds of engagements with students that this posture can sustain mirror the distinction between the contrarian and discloser versions of dissent (see chapter 5, section 6: Publicity). The first kind of engagement is with a contrarian student who is genuinely ignorant of Church teaching and whose criticism is uninformed, replete with fallacies, and possibly made merely for the sake of expressing a defiant posture against an established adult institution. In some cases the difficulty is simply intellectual because the contrarian student is merely ignorant and stubborn. In other cases this sort of expression is possibly (also) the manifestation of the attention-seeking and peer-conforming behaviour that some people (adolescents and adults) display.

The second kind of engagement is with a disclosing student who has at least partial knowledge of Church teaching, recognizes something morally or theologically troublesome through that view, and expresses dissatisfaction with it on those grounds. This sort of expression, to be fair, is also typical of certain adolescent interactions with the adult world in general, although it is also the case that students may repeat views which prevail in their homes regarding morality, salvation, social justice, and so forth. Engagement with the contrarian requires that he or she be informed in order to be able to make responsible statements, and for the sake of improving the epistemic adequacy of public discourse. Engagement with the disclosing student requires the kind of knowledge that will refine a concern for fairness with the best information to support his or her persuasive arguments.

Fulfilling the requirement to properly represent Church teaching in curricular content and experiences is not merely a token gesture which is undertaken so that students can move on with their disagreement. Church teaching *is* the curriculum around which learning is structured – notwithstanding whether the outcome is strictly cognitive but affectively disinterested, or moves to a position of either assent or dissent – and ignorant or incomplete knowledge of the teachings and their history can lead to caricatures and ill-informed opinions. For example, all the teachers interviewed remark unreservedly that they have encountered students who are frustrated with the Catholic Church, and many suggest that some of this frustration is the result of an ignorance of Catholicism's teaching and authority structure. The job of any religion teacher, therefore, is to convert this ignorance into understanding. As the examples below illustrate, some teachers expect that students who achieve understanding will either have their concerns satisfied by discovery of authentic Church teaching, or else will at least be able to disagree from a position that is not ignorant, biased, or prejudiced.

Participant Eight speaks well about this technique. She confirms that it is the teacher's responsibility to bring forth the Church's position within an academic atmosphere that evaluates all perspectives fairly, but that the primary task is making a responsible presentation and generous evaluation of Church teaching. Although she contends that she herself can see good reasons to disagree with the Church from time to time on certain issues, a professional responsibility for informing and challenging her students to consider the relevance of this information by themselves and for themselves precludes these views: "My job as a Catholic educator is not to give my own personal opinions but to give the Catholic Church's doctrine and say, 'Look. Take a look at it from [the Church's] point to view. This is why they're saying this. Don't just say, 'They say no,' because they're actually sometimes not saying 'no,' they're saying, 'this is *why* we don't believe this should happen.'"

Participant Three likewise reports that a relevant foundation of information must be laid before any meaningful approach to critical thinking can be undertaken. She insists that using primary sources so as to get a direct and, she hopes, unfiltered and unbiased account of what the Church says and stands for is an essential task that must be undertaken before any responsible critical perspective on the Church can be established. Incomplete, un-nuanced, and biased representations of Catholicism in the popular media have, in her view, contributed to the difficulties many people have with the Church. Moreover, she emphasizes, since the popular press and secular society are such strong forces in shaping students' worldviews, it becomes the role and responsibility of the Catholic school to properly represent the Church so students can have a perspective from which to evaluate it fairly:

> The Church has become an obstacle in terms of how people want to live their lives and they get this information through second, third hand [sources] – through the media, but no one ever actually picks it up and reads it and tries to understand why was this put out? Why would the Church even speak out against this issue? So that's where I think a lot of the critical thinking comes, is *to understand*. You don't have to agree, but at least understand where it's coming from, what's the motivation, what are the outcomes of people following and not following – personally, globally, kind of thing and that's where the major critical thinking comes in. Because they already understand secular society: they've got the message, and bringing the two together, but they don't really sit and take apart what the Church has to say.

Ultimately, Participant Three illustrates a perspective that attempts to meet a responsibility to the Church and to the religion curriculum, while also meeting the needs of her students for cognitive and spiritual growth. She also concurrently models a practice of constructively *delaying* or prompting *reconsideration* of decisions about one's relationship with the Church, for in taking the time to "sit and take apart" Church documents, one is forced out of a situation where he or she might impulsively abandon the Church without having given that decision an informed and fair treatment. She does not, however, raise the issue that all curricula are mediated through and interpreted by the teacher; hence, the question of what kind of bias she or any other teacher presents toward the Church and what this means in a teaching-learning relationship remains unexplored in her example.

Participant Three's interview suggests that if the learner's ignorance of the Catholic Church is overcome, then it is possible for him or her to see the diverse scope of a religion that is synthetic of multiple – if sometimes contradictory – perspectives. She asserts in this vein that one's Catholic being is not definitively related to full agreement with Church teachings, and that one can disagree with the Church and remain Catholic because the Church is a diverse entity that is always in a state of change. Disagreement, in her view, constitutes part of the process by which the Church changes. Her personal perspective on the current Catholic Church teaching on homosexuality demonstrates that the breadth of scope and tensions inherent to Catholicism allow it to be criticized *from within*. The form of her criticism illustrates how one Church position might be criticized because of its apparent incongruity with another:

> A lot of people misunderstand that the Church embraces everyone, and everyone's allowed to be a part of the Church, and that means whether you're straight, or gay, or married, or single: everyone has a place in the Church, but the major limitation is that [non-heterosexual persons] can't get married … So I find that unjust and I find that any Church document works on the basis of dignity of human life, and that's why a lot of times I understand and support what the Church has to say because a lot of times it is based on dignity of human life, but if you're denying a person the potential of getting married and enjoying fully what everybody else gets to enjoy I think that violates dignity of human life.

Participant Three's position on marriage, which is predicated on an understanding of the breadth of scope in Catholicism, is also expressed in terms of her belonging within the Church, as evidenced by her use of the first person plural construction when commenting that such a point of friction is not going to affect her belief in the Church and in God, because homosexuality is an issue "that not even society has a full grasp on, and secular and Church are trying to deal with the whole concept of homosexuality. We haven't even come close to dealing with it properly, and so our policies, our laws, our encyclicals, our views are all skewed, and out of whack." For Participant Three, therefore, working through the philosophical, political, and theological tensions behind social injustices is an intrinsic part of being Catholic, even if that work takes place as a critique of one's own community. The fact that this issue is so difficult within the Church at large only directs a brighter light upon the fact that the same issue receives a less-than-adequate treatment in Catholic Educational theory. Within this theoretical environment, this technique satisfies the bare cognitive requirements *vis-à-vis* the prevailing view, but it stops at the point of dealing with any of the larger controversial issues as they are part of public life in the Catholic school or the Church.

The benefits of this teaching technique are that it maintains a firm stance of responsibility to the prevailing curriculum in the religion course, and it directly engages student interest with relevant course content. Teachers who wish to ensure that they meet all the curricular requirements for the course, and that they present as comprehensive a picture of the Church as possible, can take advantage of students' expressed disagreements as opportunities to explore their interests for their own sake and exploit them for the pedagogical purpose of engaging with Church teaching. With this technique, teachers can firmly demonstrate support for the Church while simultaneously allowing students an occasion for self-expression, and thus make a reasonable and responsible coordination of the requirements set by (or felt from) both their employers and those they serve: at least in terms that are acceptable within the current prevailing environment in Catholic schools. In addition to the learning outcomes that are to be had from moments of self-expression, students also have the opportunity to gain a more adequate knowledge of the prevailing view within the Church, and thus improve the epistemic adequacy of their expressions. The preferred results of such improvement would be threefold: (1) to correct contrarianism or partially informed disclosure, (2) to upgrade any surprisingly promising kinds of contrarianism to disclosure, and (3) to advance the epistemic adequacy of justice concerns that were based upon correct sentiment but only partial knowledge. This stance thus demonstrates a high concern for pedagogical accountability to the prevailing standards of Catholicism and the *status quo* in Catholic Educational practice.

In spite of its success and apparent desirability according to the prevailing view in Catholic Education, this pedagogical technique has three major philosophical drawbacks. These drawbacks are highly symptomatic of the systematic repression of dissent within the Church as a whole, combined with a very thin philosophy of Catholic Education.

The first drawback is the technique's presentation of a one-sided view of debate in the Church. Because of a systemic suppression of dissent within the Church, a lack of resources concerning dissenting Catholic views, a thin philosophy of Catholic Education, and the prevailing Catholic theology's intellectual bias toward a concept of a singular, unifying truth, there is very little with which to guide teachers outside an exclusive presentation of the prevailing view. As the result of this systemic shaping of the academic and institutional milieu, Catholic Education is strangely, although at the same time perhaps not surprisingly, committed to an intellectually restricted representation of Catholic thought. Consequentially teachers are left with little in the way of pedagogically satisfying recourse, other than refining students' understandings of the prevailing view in balance with an allowance for airing personal opinions. Unlike an intellectual approach to political questions in history courses (as one example) that exhibits a concern for revealing and overcoming bias with a balanced presentation of competing views, the religion courses, even when considering issues *within* the Catholic paradigm, are epistemologically narrowed by a focus on the prevailing Magisterial view that is unaccompanied by any competing *Catholic* views or scholarly criticism of these views. Because this technique's interpretation of student disagreements reduces them to mere immature individual opinions that cannot compete with the epistemological weight of the Church's institutions and historically developed customs, students (and adults, including students' parents) are left without any legitimate theological or other theoretical support to develop their views. Religious disagreement is implicitly reduced to a private matter between an individual and the Church, and is seen as as the result of stubbornness, intellectual deficit, and/or secular influence, rather than morally adequate decision-making and rationally legitimate examination of underlying principles.

The second drawback of this posture is its presumption that a deficit in students' knowledge is somehow the entire root of their concerns that there is injustice in the Church. When a generalized approach to practice is sincerely justified by this sort of thinking it reflects an illogical causal argument. While it is fair to expect that students should know Church teaching as a requisite step in articulating their concerns about it, not all concerns germinate or sustain themselves due to ignorance. While some genuine concerns may be put to rest as the result of gaining more information about the Church, it begs the question to presume that acquiring greater and more sophisticated amounts of Church knowledge will always resolve disagreement. A student may be very well informed and still disagree. The deficiency observed here exists in this technique's overemphasis on the content of Church teaching, an overly optimistic estimation of its intrinsic persuasiveness, and its relative inattention to how students respond to it.

Above and beyond the epistemic deadlock to which the privatization of individual expression leads, the third drawback with the technique of promoting understanding before criticism concerns the practical matter of what to do next. Should a student come to a point where he or she fully understands the Church's teaching but still disagrees with it, the teacher and student find themselves in a pedagogical vacuum and moral deadlock that cannot tackle the problem of how to coordinate one's disagreement with the prevailing view. This is a problematic state of affairs, because although it leaves students in the more intellectually desirable state of knowing what they disagree with and why, it offers no direction beyond the achievement of that step. Students quickly discover that they are left little other choice than to convert their hearts and minds toward the prevailing teaching, leave the Church, or somehow uncomfortably live with an unresolved and apparently unresolvable disagreement. Should they wish to disagree but remain Catholic in any way that is more spiritually satisfying than what this third option allows, there is no intellectual support given that places their thoughts within a tradition of dissent in Catholicism. This technique is most problematic if taken to an extreme that leaves the impression that Church teaching is not a dialogue in which one might participate but a monologue to which one must assimilate. "Agreeing to disagree" leaves many moral questions in an intellectually frustrating state of suspension.

This "understand before criticizing" technique is particularly significant because it raises the question of how the pedagogical aims in Catholic schools differentiate between pre-critical, unsubstantiated, and relativistic stances of disagreement on a first level of engagement, and informed disagreements and well-considered arguments on a second level. Tackling disagreements with the aim of refining students' knowledge of the prevailing view suggests an approach that would subordinate an intellectual breadth and depth of support for dissenting interests to the aim of reinforcing and clarifying the presentation of the teachings with which they are already clearly concerned. Such an approach is neither genuinely student-centred nor balanced between the needs of students and curriculum, because it simply capitalizes on student concerns as an entry into one-sided acts of refining prevailing content knowledge.

The limitations of the "understanding *before* criticizing" technique as an approach to Catholic Education are nonetheless heuristically promising for a theoretical refurbishment of Catholic school pedagogy, because they open the path to the suggestion that the focus on controversial religious topics might shift to one of "understanding *through* criticism" instead. Rather than treating dissent as a marginal problem that is to be remedied through clarifying the prevailing view, an alternative pedagogical approach could be founded on a view that dissent is an intrinsic existential feature of being Catholic, and that Catholicism's theological and cognitive complexity does not obstruct its relevance to the experiences of many Catholics. Possessing intellectual superiority need not, after all, be a requirement to justify one's moral rights and existential freedom.

If students arrive in the classroom presenting serious moral questions that already tend toward dissent, the task of the teacher and the school could be to avoid a habitual attachment to doctrinal clarification and to bring them through the intellectual material that supports a responsible dissent. In the process of learning about dissent, however, doctrine should still be learned as a key academic component that grounds the franchise and epistemology through which the dissent occurs. The best dissent must necessarily have an ample knowledge of the doctrine or practice from which it sits apart. If students are already approaching their studies from a point of confusion and frustration about the Catholic Church and its doctrine, I suggest that the gravity of their feelings cannot be compounded by a clear admission that the way with which Catholicism has and continues to encounter dissent is itself confused. Perhaps most importantly, this pedagogical approach would have to be regarded in a developmentally heuristic sense. The dissent students exercise and express might not always match its philosophical ideal, but, as with other Catholic teachings and secular topics, the school is the means by which practice helps them approach more morally and intellectually adequate approximations of it. Adding dissent as a pedagogical approach within a curricular and extra-curricular environment where the Catholic ideals of marriage, human reproduction, Mass attendance, and other matters of obedience are tested, contested, and often not met hardly seems like the admission of a corrupting agent into students' experiences.

3 Attitude of Questioning

One general aim in teaching religion and promoting the development of religious thinking is to promote the thoughtful *questioning* of what students discover and learn about their own faith and the beliefs of the Church. Given that disagreement with Church teaching is a common phenomenon among Catholic adolescents in the School (and among adults, no less so), promoting an attitude where one *questions* the Catholic Church is, given the current conditions in which Catholic Education takes place, a pedagogical approach which many teachers employ. As even those who agree with the prevailing view come to their agreements through interrogative reflections, questioning Church teaching presents a promising way of leading *all* students through the intellectual acts of composing good questions and seeking legitimate reasons to support the replies to them. These reasons can themselves be the focus of a next round of questioning, and so this technique ultimately leads to a dialogue about the teaching. It is not a direct exhortation to adopt faith or any particular cause, but it does give students a means of encountering curricular material and issues that are the stuff of faithful contemplation.

Some educators are wary about the meaning or impact of dissent, but since all faithful persons question their faith as a normal part of its growth, they instead encourage *questioning* as a means of accommodating student concerns at a high intellectual level without risking the institutional fracture which they worry dissent might produce. In his current practice, for example, Participant Six finds dissent to be too strong a term to introduce to students. Simultaneously, he nonetheless encourages the expression of intellectually legitimate student opinion in situations of moral conflict and frustration, and maintains that persistent questioning is an appropriate attitude and attribute that teachers can bring to students. In his view, persistently encouraging students to ask informed questions is a fruitful means of engaging controversy: "There are some times you bring up terms that the kids will use to question further. You just bring up the term 'absolute truth.' What is absolute truth? And they will respond by saying, 'Does the Church say this is absolute? And is this absolute, and is this absolute, and is this absolute?' Which is great. To me that is legitimate – if they are questioning and saying, 'Is that something that can change?' And you hit it right on the head: it is women in the Church, it is homosexuality, there is a lot of things." Interestingly, at this point Participant Six observes that there is a definite difference between the way students respond to the Church's moral stances on issues surrounding family life and sexuality that are directly relevant in their own lives, and the way they respond to topics such as the Trinity, Jesus' divine and human natures, or His presence in the Eucharist: "They never question the practices within the Church, though. They never talk about, 'Is this ever truly the Body of Christ? At what point does it really become?' They never question that; they accept that. It is all issues of morality, which is very interesting. It is controversial, it is in their face, and they are experiencing it quite often. It is all family life issues as well." The nature of *what* students question and *why* and *how* they question is therefore illustrated to be an equally important issue within the subject of student disagreements, and of what one considers to be legitimately Catholic in this domain. There is a marked difference between the way students respond to what are considered core Catholic beliefs and what are moral instructions on family life, which, although they are important, are secondary in terms of defining one's Catholicism. Any difference between what it means to *question* one's faith versus what it means to *dissent* from it is a problem that is informed by a consideration of where within Catholic theology that difference exists. Generally, questioning is a more inclusive term because it also includes instances of the prevailing view challenging what it considers unorthodox. All dissent may be questioning, but not all questioning is dissent.

The benefit of this approach to the teaching and learning relationship in the Catholic school is that it appropriates an accepted custom of normal faith development into the pedagogical practice of accommodating, legitimating, and addressing student concerns. In pedagogical terms, promoting questioning as part of the cognitive and spiritual growth of students is entirely appropriate within the current theology and philosophy that informs Catholic Education. As faith has a different meaning to children than it does to adolescents and adults, it is considered natural over the span of a lifetime to question one's faith as part of its growth and the exercising of one's freely performed encounter with the Church and with God. Consistent with this critical engagement through a religious institution and experiences of the divine is a Christian-informed critical perspective on the entire world and the relationships contained within it. Hence if a student has a moral objection to or difficulty with the Catholic Church, the student's teacher legitimately adopts the technique of asking questions and exploring the range of possible moral responses that a discussion of them raises. This technique is thus pedagogically sound for its incorporation of students' academic needs within the norms and practices of Catholicism.

The *attitude of questioning* has no intrinsic flaws as a teaching technique and aspect of Christian life, and in the classroom it should be considered a generally helpful means of engaging with morally difficult issues. Beyond its usefulness in this regard, however, it has limitations when used as a substitute for dissent or to offset propositions that favour dissent. Questioning can accomplish much for people in faithful and faithless contexts, and it can even describe the attitude of one who dissents, but ultimately it is too generic a term to correctly substitute for dissent. Since questioning is a normal attitude and practice within Christianity that is required for growth in faith, it also describes the actions of those who subscribe to the prevailing view. Those who subscribe to the prevailing view question the grounds of their own faith and would question any dissenting view without dissenting themselves. *Questioning* is also a vague term. Not all questions are dissenting questions, nor necessarily designed to cast doubt on something. Some questions are posed to gather information, procure explanations, or ask for clarification. Those who are committed to the prevailing belief could certainly ask questions of their faith within these categories and feel comfortable that they are not challenging the prevailing orthodoxy. Any suggestion that questioning as a pedagogical technique be thought of as a *replacement* for dissent therefore stalls.

Finally, questioning does not necessarily substitute for the step of making a persuasive argument against the prevailing view. From this point of view, questioning could be considered a constitutive attitude of dissent that is weakly descriptive of a dissident's intent, but is certainly very little more than that. The suggestion that dissent might be assimilated into (or might already subsist in) current practice under the rubric of "questioning" raises the issue of what pedagogical aim the encouragement to question Church teaching currently has.

Does use of "questioning" follow a specific aim with respect to a desired attitude for one's membership in the Church and the quality of one's contribution to it? Or, is it meant to be confined strictly to the classroom, possibly as a means of privatizing and confining disagreement to the relatively powerless individual – even possibly for the narrow managerial reasons of controlling students' discontent by offering them some intellectual analgesic? The answer to this question is perhaps best considered elsewhere in empirical or conceptual terms, because the question of *why* it reflects an aim or likewise *why* teachers employ it diverts too far away from considering the conceptual adequacy of the technique itself.

4 Leaving Alternatives to Students and Families

A fourth technique is the encouragement given to students to ask for more information from places beyond the religion classroom. Some participants report that in the course of discussions on controversial topics, they will encourage students to extend their information-gathering and intellectual consideration beyond the space of the classroom and the formal curricular time allotment. Students are encouraged to inquire of their parents and guardians at home to receive perspectives and engage in discussions that might be beyond the limit of what the school can accommodate, engage, or impose.

One technique in this respect is to encourage students to ask more questions, with the final pedagogical goal ostensibly being to form an attitude of perpetual questioning. This technique is used with the assumption that there is, both in theory and in practice, a separation between Church teaching (which the school can openly support and convey) and the views expressed privately in the home. It is important because it respects, mirrors, and follows the theological distinction between Magisterial teaching authority and personal moral authority, while in concert with the principle of subsidiarity it also leaves a portion of the pedagogical responsibility for a student's moral formation in the hands of the home, the parish, and other sources which the student may be exposed to or discover. The school does not monopolize responsibility for the student's moral formation. In theory and practice, at least, it seems able to accommodate "all sides" in any debate. However, in doing so it also leaves no doubt as to the epistemic authority of the Magisterium as the official public voice on Catholic morality, and the prevailing voice in the school.

Participant Five presents this pedagogical technique in a creative way that subtly suggests moral plurality through its open acknowledgment of the many legitimate stakeholders in students' education. The explicit recognition is that the Church, school, and home each have a legitimate stake in a student's moral formation; the strongly implicit suggestion is that discussions can take place in the private sphere of the home that would have a much different quality from the teacher's public presentation of the Church's and school's views in the classroom. Participant Five reports that sex education is a major tension point in her classroom. Her method of handling this problem is to point students in the direction of their families as a potential source of further information: a method which also directly reveals the dimensions of her own Christian self that comes to bear in different contexts:

> I feel that there are restrictions for me as a teacher. Sometimes I will say to them, "You know, I'm a mother too, I'm not just a teacher. This is what the Catholic Church says and I have to teach you this, and for the most part I agree with most of what they say. But as a mother who has compassion for my children and who would never withdraw my affection for my children for whatever reason, especially if they were in trouble or if their sexuality was an issue for them – that kind of thing – as a mother I'm telling you to go home and talk to your parents about this. I want you to go home and have a frank discussion with your parents about what we talked about in class because we need your parents' input and I'm not the only person who can inform you on sexuality." So that's sort of how I feel I can cover it. But whether or not they actually do go home and talk to their parents about it, I don't know.

Participant Five models this approach to controversial issues by temporarily stepping outside her professional role to draw upon her social position as a mother to communicate to her students that there are conversations they can have at home that may provide information that would not be presented in the school. Besides her exhortation that students inquire at home, Participant Five states that there is little, if any, further pedagogical space where she can propose alternatives to the prevailing view, and there are certainly no resources available in the school to support dissent.

There are three main benefits that this technique enjoys. First, by holding open controversial moral questions, it recognizes that the school's curricular obligations and expectations within the classroom carry some practical limitations. With the recognition that students have awareness and experiences of moral options outside the formal curriculum, the school meets students' needs by acknowledging their concerns and respecting their possible desire to include a wider variety of information. If the school wants to communicate both formally and informally that it is not attempting to indoctrinate students, then an open gesture of encouragement to seek more information than is available in the classroom accomplishes much toward that goal.

The second benefit is the acknowledgment that families have a role to exercise in educating Catholic youth. If the school is working with the assumption that it shares responsibility with the home and the parish for the Catholic education of youth, then the encouragement to seek out information at home is also a sincere gesture that respects the autonomy and responsibility of the student's family. The family's autonomy is respected through an acknowledgment of its negative religious freedom. Without this freedom the family could not be said to have a legitimate experience of Catholic faith, nor could it genuinely be responsible for its educative role in the lives of youth. If students' dislike for "being told what to believe" is a product of a domestic attitude, then attempts to impose moral duties in a manner that bypasses acknowledgment of and respect for the family's autonomy would likely strain relations between home and school.

The third benefit is that this encouragement to seek information outside the school acknowledges students' personal freedom apart from the autonomy their families exercise. Students are not imposed upon to seek immediately, if at all, for this information, and have the latitude to engage with their families on controversial topics when they themselves and even their families are intellectually, emotionally, and spiritually ready for such discussions. In this way the school and home do not impinge upon the students' moral dignity, freedom, judgment, rights, and autonomy. Again, the school asserts itself in an important, although not monopolizing role in the intellectual, social, and spiritual development of students.

In spite of the advantages that this technique has in its allowance for epistemic breadth and its respect for the negative freedom of students and their families, leaving the consideration of alternatives to the prevailing Church view solely in the hands of the home and other influences outside the school ultimately has major limitations as a pedagogical strategy. It is limited because it passes the school's responsibility for teaching about the intellectual adequacy of this alternative information, and for forming the cognitive capabilities on how to judge it, to the family or home. These are institutions whose missions are different from the school's, and who thus do not necessarily have the same professional capability that the school has with which to address these issues.

Descending from this problem there are accordingly three major difficulties with this strategy: (1) There is no reliable means of ensuring the epistemic adequacy of the information families provide; a fact that consequentially implicates (2) the school for avoiding any responsibility to teach students the means of how to judge this information; and (3) it reinforces students' frustration when encountering the prevailing view, by reinforcing their lack of any credible means with which to challenge it in the public sphere.

The epistemic adequacy of information gathered at home or from other sources, and the discussion or interaction that accompanies it, cannot be ensured to be on par with what is presented at school. Without adopting the undue prejudice of applying this concern to all Catholic homes, the problem with leaving alternatives to students and their families, however well it includes the home in these discussions, is that the home potentially has limitations or even deficiencies in its knowledge and interpretation of the Catholic faith. Several participants remarked during their interviews that students in their classes echo opinions from within their families that are ignorant, indifferent, opposed, or even hostile to the Catholic Church. While there is no quantitative data on how frequent and intense this problem is in all Catholic schools, the participants' remarks nonetheless illustrate real instances where the question is fairly raised of whether the average Catholic family can provide information that is on epistemological and moral par with the prevailing view presented at school.

Concerns about this issue are not completely alleviated even if one assumes that all families are intellectually sufficient in this area; because that assumption leads one to question the appropriate role of the school and its professional academic obligation to students who, presumably, could receive their Catholic religious instruction on both prevailing and dissenting views exclusively from the home. Surely any supporter of Catholic Education would not suggest that the school's mission and experiences offer nothing of unique value that differentiates it from the family, or that it merely substitutes for work that parents could easily do themselves. If the home and school had the same mission, it could be argued that there would be no need for Catholic schools; moreover, the need for professionally skilled religion teachers would also be cast into doubt. If the school indeed offers something of unique value to the presentation of the prevailing Catholic view, then certainly leaving a major part of the discussion in the hands of those outside the school does an epistemic and moral disservice to students whose pedagogical needs are focused on these areas. If students can be expected to go home to find, understand, and responsibly adjudicate between dissenting views without any pedagogical guidance, in addition to understanding an apparently advanced concept like dissent, then the justification for institutionalizing students with the purpose of teaching and learning the currently conventional version of Catholic religious curriculum is thrown into jeopardy. Ironically, the school system and its social environment are currently set up to ensure that professionals are in place to transmit and inform students about the prevailing view, but the school still leaves to non-professionals the more advanced intellectual task of teaching students to think critically about the validity of other dissenting options.

The major deficiency of deferring to the home is therefore due to the fact that the validity of extracurricular[7] information and the quality of accompanying critical discussion cannot be guaranteed. For example, assuming that the school presents (a) the best intellectual justifications for a controversial Magisterial teaching, one cannot know whether the home will provide (b) the best refutations for (all or only certain parts of) the same, or simply (c) an example of indifferent, uninformed dismissal. Both (b) and (c) are possible scenarios, but even if the school upholds the truth content of (a) it still prefers the intellectual act or method of (b) to that of (c) as an example of critical religious thinking.

This technique works under the pretext of respecting the home's autonomy and religious freedom, but also allows the school to thoroughly divest itself of its academic and ecclesial obligations to the public in this area, thus leaving students with very little, if any, opportunity to receive professional pedagogical supervision as they gather and engage with the material. If the situation in homes is as impoverished as the participants I interviewed and mainstream commentators on Catholic Education maintain, the implications for student

knowledge and moral judgment are quite worrisome and the pedagogical situation in schools quite unfortunately ironic. The participants' responses suggest that Catholic Education sadly perpetuates a
popular deficiency in dissenting knowledge through systematic under-
exposure to it.

This pedagogical issue is also a controversial political issue of
academic and ecclesial responsibility, for which a removal of obligation to the home seems, under current conditions, an agreeable but
insufficient compromise. The home does not have nearly the same
public responsibilities to the Church and community that the school
does, and so in theory can adapt with greater ease and flexibility to
tackling controversial questions, whether adaptation means deference
to the Magisterium, defiance of it, or abandonment of the question
entirely. Since the prevailing view regards dissent as a private matter
between individuals and the Church, under these conditions the private domestic sphere is the most adept at accommodating dissent, so
long as it remains within "private" boundaries. Although the home's
response might be less philosophically and theologically stringent
than any view that the school and Church could tolerate as a public
stance, without a sufficient guiding pedagogical theory with which
to address this matter the relative epistemic and political tranquility
that the school obtains for its institutional self through this divest-
ment seems well worth that intellectual price. In fact, without any
philosophically satisfactory theory upon which to base a valid and
publicly acknowledged address to dissent on controversial issues, the
institutions of Catholic Education remain dependent upon the home
in this matter, or else, in exceptional cases, upon a particular teacher's
creativity and charisma. This latter option is unfortunately also limited for being non-generalizable beyond specific contexts, and also
because it begs the theoretical question. Since neither the school nor
the home has the philosophical or theological equipment with which
to address these matters beyond settling at the above compromise,
the home remains the ultimate *de facto* educational authority on how
to coordinate the institutional Church and the individual will. Sadly,
although the home's political clout is very strong within its limited
domain, such strength accomplishes very little on the outside against
the Church's practice of weakening dissent's impact by isolating and
containing it within the private sphere.

The second drawback is that, by divesting responsibility on controversial issues, the school situates itself almost exclusively as an agent

of disseminating doctrine, rather than presenting the full range of intellectual options for "thinking religiously" within the culture of faith. A variety of intellectually valid options for the student on moral questions, it is presumed, are best achieved through inquiries at places that do not have the same strict public responsibility to doctrine. This approach reduces the roles of the school and home to those of owners of competing positions or mutually reinforcing transmitters of doctrine; hence it mirrors the error the entire Church makes, in regarding the teaching Church and learning Church as descriptors of *sub-populations* rather than *processes*, by not acknowledging that it is the responsibility of both school and home to engage in the process of considering the range of views within the Church. In cases where the school's and home's views match each other and this problem disappears, this defect is only replaced by the problems associated with reinforcing and perpetuating epistemic narrowness on controversial issues. Ideally, if school and home are partners in Catholic Education, then both should engage with the educationally valuable *process* of teaching students how to coordinate competing views, rather than setting themselves off each other as opposing representatives responsible for their presentation of those views. Such an approach reduces the purpose of Catholic educational institutions to the narrower aim of presenting and reinforcing the prevailing Catholic *content*, and so impoverishes the intellectual *process* of Catholic life and the potential that a student might have professional guidance in how to think religiously about his or her dissent. *How* one learns has become subordinated to *what* one is learning. The use of this technique also opens the question of what, if any, other public space besides the parish Church and School is available for discussion of alternatives to the prevailing view within Catholicism.

The third drawback of this technique is that, by reinforcing the prevailing view's dominance, it potentially leads to a perception that a limited freedom of religious expression is exchanged for student cooperation. The offer of negative religious freedom allows the school to claim that it disdains indoctrination and instead promotes the authentic reception of the Catholic faith. This conception of negative religious freedom is an intrinsic part of Catholic thought and life in general, however; as a foundational feature of the person before he or she even enters a religious school, it cannot be re-cast as a negotiable part of a conditional offer through which the Catholic Church and students agree to enter an educational relationship or ecclesial contract. The prevailing view's place of privilege is accordingly not, and cannot be, obtained through allowing negative freedom to students in exchange for their willingness to be subjected to a narrow epistemology.

If this perception obtains and/or this situation is widely practiced, then true religious freedom is arguably not being respected for a lack of attention to its educational and philosophical dimension. An authentic respect for religious freedom in educational settings *constituted* by religion must be accompanied by a curriculum and social environment that support the intellectual means with which to learn what that freedom is and how to exercise it. Claims that students will not be required to believe anything in particular and that they only have to respect the prevailing view as it is taught, along with a similar display for the opinions of their peers in the class, do very little to overcome students' knowledge that they are in a Catholic institution that will follow an agenda determined by a system that will not change as the result of debate among lay persons. The pedagogical option of leaving students with any such conception of negative freedom is therefore philosophically inadequate to the task of providing them with a sound basis upon which to explore their differences of opinion. The question of what to do when students disagree with the prevailing view, but do not wish to abandon Catholicism, remains unresolved here.

5 Holding Questions Open for Critical Examination

Critical thinking is one of the essential aims in religion class, even if all teachers do not have similar conceptions of what critical thinking is, or even if some of these conceptions are stronger than others. The cross-curricular aim of critical thinking does not necessarily suggest disagreement. "Critical" is a broadly inclusive term that suggests questioning, gathering and evaluating information, and, in the context of religious studies, raising one's Christian consciousness with the aim of applying one's spiritual awareness to the world at large. It does not necessarily imply disagreement, because it could mean a critically informed assent. The pedagogical objective of critical thinking in the spiritual domain aims to have students interpret their sociopolitical spiritual experiences, which in turn carries the further aim of promoting a disposition toward engaging students in the shaping of their society.

Critical thinking is an inherent feature of religious knowledge because it is implied throughout the phenomenon of having a religious experience, the act of making meaning of it, and then the process of making a "meta-examination" of the reasons why meaning was shaped in that particular way or ways. Participant Four illustrates this triadic process as the foundation for justifying the inclusion of critical thinking in religion courses: "So to me critical thinking skills were very much at the heart of religious education, and I think as we started to learn more and more about how people think and how they know and to what extent the social context shapes our thinking and our experiences it required students, more and more, to develop those kind of skills that allow them to critique their society, critique their culture, so that they don't simply become products of it, but so that they can take some ownership themselves for the kinds of choices they make." The pedagogical objective of critical thinking, in Participant Four's view, is that students must learn appropriate use of critical skills in engaging with the Church and the world so as to give their arguments legitimacy and so as to respect their personal development and the development of the Church. At the same time, he inserts a caution that critical thinking should not be confused with contrarianism, and that a healthy critical attitude should be balanced between looking for both the uplifting and negative aspects of things:

> Critical skills are an important part of any teaching and learning, so let's make sure they have as good critical skills as anyone else has, but that doesn't mean we should be looking for all the things that are wrong with the Church. We should also be looking for the things that are life enhancing and allow us to go out and work on behalf of life. And if we can do that I think we will create very balanced young people who are quite prepared to recognize, as we all do, that there is a degree of paradox and ambiguity that is a part of life and it's a part of relationships.

Critical thinking can thus be considered a core intellectual and spiritual attitude of Catholic life, including the assent to faith and the coordination of tensions that are inherent in human living.

In the more specific terms of classroom learning, critical thinking is upheld as a spiritually enriched cognitive reflection upon one's self and social life. Participant Seven's remarks exhibit critical religious thinking as an act which subsists within the pedagogical aim of promoting cognitive growth. He points to exercises where students work on interpretations of Biblical text as a means of unpacking spiritual and historical-religious meaning from Catholicism's foundational narratives. The stories about Moses and the parables of Jesus provide an excellent opportunity, he says, to ask students "to look beyond what they just see on the surface of the story. Getting them to dig a little bit deeper ... to think beyond what they hear or what they see there," and then for them to consider its meaning in their present-day lives. For Participant Seven, critical thinking represents an interactive opportunity to explore layers of meaning and to challenge common assumptions and conclusions in real life. He uses a social justice lesson on poverty, for example: "'You have all of these things, but down the road your next-door neighbour may not have enough food on their table to eat. As a Christian what are you called to do? How are you called to respond to that?' It is getting them to think about the bigger picture. What does it mean for me to be engaged in life? What does it mean for me to be engaged with my neighbour? Who is my neighbour?" Critical thinking in the religion classroom thus encompasses the pedagogical act of developing one's insight into the social significance and consequences of one's actions. It may or may not be accompanied by an action component.

When spiritual perspectives are reflected into certain issues, there is an inevitable socio-moral conflict that arises between the Church and the secular world. These problems therefore constitute an intrinsic part of teaching and learning in Catholic schools, and teachers embrace the opportunity to consider them because of their potential value for promoting cognitive, moral, and spiritual development. Participant Seven's words openly acknowledge this tension: "We live in a world," he says, "where moral questions ... [have] developed as a result of our consumerism, materialism, and individualism. The world is full of it. Our classrooms are full of it." These conflicts between secular society and Catholic teaching create opportunities for teachers and students to explore the history, philosophy, theology, and politics of ecclesiology behind moral issues. Moral conflicts therefore provide entry points to lessons that promote critical thinking and an expanded knowledge base on Catholic issues as they intersect with the secular world.

The aim to teach critical thinking is sometimes misunderstood among teachers generally, whether in a Catholic school or not. One

common misunderstanding separates critical thinking from any disciplinary roots, and as a result adopts the practice of trying to teach
critical thinking as a discrete topic: sometimes by doing puzzles or
playing games that have no direct relevance to the curriculum and real
life outside of school. A better understanding of critical thinking considers it in the disciplinary terms of curricular subjects and real life.
So while there may be some common cross-curricular critical habits
associated with such domains as creative problem-solving and informal logic, the thinking exercises are ultimately situated within real
topics and subjects. So as one learns to think scientifically or historically
under this model, in religion class one also learns to think religiously.

Critical thinking in the form of thinking religiously about the
spiritual and temporal order seems to come naturally to the religion
curriculum. One can imagine that no religion teacher would think
of their role as being to oppose a nurturing of students' critical thinking; the Church poses several of its teachings as critically informed
challenges, and students tend to bring critical questions to class
about issues concerning them. In fact, the greatest barrier to nurturing critical thinking might be imagined as the teacher's under-
appreciation of its importance and preparation with appropriate
means of engagement.

None of the teachers I interviewed, however, evince this flaw in
talking about their practice. Participant Seven illustrates well the aim
to promote religiously informed thought with his example of using
the moral conflict over same-sex marriage to lead students through
coordinating a real-life example where Catholic Church teaching
and Canadian law diverge sharply. He describes his method of handling this issue in the classroom, which is to consider as much relevant background information as possible, such as how relations
between religious institutions and secular states have evolved over
time: "You get them to do a little bit of history and they see that
marriage at one time was all done civilly – the Church ... was never
in control, it became a phenomenon later on. And then that raises a
whole different pile of questions for them. There is lots of stuff there
to get them engaged." Critical thinking in religion classes is thereby
a process of exposing students to a variety of information so that
they can become independently sensitive moral agents, while recognizing that the goal of critical thinking is to promote cognitive,
spiritual, and socio-moral growth.

In the process of facilitating the flow of information to students and attending to their learning needs, Participant Seven and his counterparts all report that the critical thinking component enters the interaction once students have taken all possible perspectives and reasons into account and then begin coordinating that information into a moral decision. The pastoral concern is not least among these considerations. In relating an example of discussing abortion, Participant Seven illustrates how sensitivity to contextual factors is an imperative component of critical thinking that brings it from a discussion in the abstract to a concrete discussion about a real-life problem: "We need to know the person involved" to make an accurate critical assessment, he says; "We need to know the situation. If we don't know the context then there's no way that we're going to be able to help that person make a good decision. [Their pregnancy] might be because of a rape – that's something that they may not want to share: May not *have* shared!" (emphasis his). Adding this step into lessons and discussions of whether abortion is right may or may not come to the same end as prescribed by those who hold firm views either for or against it, but as a learning opportunity it adds both breadth and depth to the pedagogical approaches to this topic. As a model of critical thinking being an all-encompassing activity, therefore, a consideration of context and how learning about the tension between doctrinal legalism and pastoral care for persons can be one such imperative for inclusion.

The appeal to critical thinking is related to deferring to parents on controversial issues, because both acknowledge that a variety of opinion exists on controversial questions within Catholicism. As a pedagogical practice, though, the appeal to critical thinking diverges from directing students to parents (or sources outside the school) by more explicitly making space within the school to acknowledge and contemplate the tensions between competing views. This acknowledgment implies a commitment to the cognitive value of publicly examining these questions, and so devotes classroom time to developing students' knowledge and their ability to articulate arguments from a variety of points of view. The benefit obtained from this technique therefore follows from meeting this public commitment to a degree of loyalty that satisfies all parties. In the process of accurately and fairly presenting Magisterial teachings, this technique also fairly attempts to coordinate them with other perspectives that challenge the prevailing Catholic view. Achieving a breadth of perspective minimizes student (mis)perceptions concerning indoctrination.

The obvious drawback of this technique lies not in its implication that there are open religious questions that can examined through several legitimate arguments, but in the fact that it unfortunately risks leaving students without examples of the kinds of Catholic knowledge and skills with which to examine them. One common critical thinking technique is to have students "examine both sides" of an argument.[8] This technique is helpful for prompting students to think outside any narrow views they might hold, but it is also quite unhelpful because it can default quickly to perceiving socio-moral issues in binary, rather than multiple terms. In an institution where Catholic teaching is the prevailing view, *the other side* of an issue can quickly become *the opposing secular side* in high contrast to Catholicism, which obliterates all other critiques. For instance, this binary may obtain if the critical examination of contraception is limited simply to contrasting HV with the prevailing secular view that permits contraception. If HV's status as a non-infallible ordinary teaching is not recognized, the attitude of *obsequium* not introduced, and information about the Papal Birth Control Commission and the "Winnipeg Statement" not included, then students might quickly perceive that the only way to critique the Church is to stand completely outside it. Unless critical thinking methods present options that do not elide the plurality *within* Catholicism, they risk presenting a distorted picture of it.

A second drawback with this technique is its limitations in terms of students' participation in the Church. If questions are held open only as abstract exercises, and it is not acknowledged that they are also at the epistemic core of the Church's political structures, then a false impression can be created that their discussions will be of consequence, when, for practical purposes, the question is often closed. A classroom can debate in great detail and at great length the Magisterial positions on female ordination and salvation's importance relative to social justice, for instance, without the outcome of those discussions having any impact on social action in the Church. The standstill which results suggests that students are expected to learn what the Church teaches and to enact it in the world, but any critical learning which might apply to a critique of Church teaching and structures should be considered only for its academic merits. This difference thus reinforces a dichotomy between the abstract lessons at school that have no immediate application to real life, and the concrete lessons of the world outside school that have a high degree of relevance to real life in the Church.

6 The Informed Conscience

A sixth technique for accommodating dissent is reference to the informed conscience as the model of Catholic moral decision-making. The informed conscience allows that there are sometimes greater divine moral principles than those found in Church law, and so this reference suggests to students that moral judgments which sincerely follow one's relationship with the divine sometimes can be more correct than institutionally codified rules. The informed conscience is one way in which a student could legitimately disagree with a prevailing Church teaching and still remain faithful.

Teachers generally have no difficulty considering the informed conscience as a means of accommodating student dissent, so long as it is legitimately informed. The patterns of justification used by the teachers I interviewed suggest that since dissent is an integral option for decisions of the informed conscience, and the informed conscience is taught in the classroom as an integral part of Catholicism, then the religion curricula directly accommodate dissent by design. Participant Thirteen suggests that in the teaching on the informed conscience, there is even more theoretical accommodation for dissent that what is currently built into the curriculum and classroom practice. In Participant Thirteen's formulation, like in Participant Seven's, the emphasis falls upon the person who chooses to make a particular decision:

In a way I teach that to every Grade Twelve class when I teach conscience. Church teaching is that we are required to obey our conscience, even if it disagrees with Church teaching. I teach my kids that because that is Church teaching. Ironically, Church teaching sometimes obligates us to disobey Church teaching. It is kind of a strange thing there ... I always tell them, I say, "When you are in a position of making a moral decision you are obligated to follow your conscience, but your conscience has to be formed; you have to be informed. You have to know the Church teachings and why. Have you prayed about it?" And so I go through all of these things.

An explicit treatment of dissent, however, does not carry any further than this in the current official incarnation of the curriculum.

The chief benefit of using the informed conscience as the means to accommodate dissent is that teachers can appeal to the prevailing view in order to justify their inclusion of options that would normally stand in contrast to Church teaching. The teacher therefore explicitly promotes and uses Church teaching to demonstrate that while doctrine should inform one's conscience, it should not monopolize one's thinking, nor unilaterally dictate one's response to a moral problem. While ensuring that the Church retains its privilege of place in the school's moral discourse and the students' consideration, the teacher concurrently admits students' experiences into the address of moral problems and so affirms their relationship with God and their agency to make decisions on controversial matters. By putting into action the concept of dissent's criteria for (a) grounding objections within the Church's internal epistemic history, and (b) making divergent reasonable choices, it approaches philosophical and theological adequacy as a means for addressing controversial issues that serves the needs of all partners in Catholic Schooling. By enabling a balanced Catholic judgment, the best use of the informed conscience avoids the polarization trap (i.e. sacred-secular) to which some critical thinking techniques are susceptible. At its worst, if it uses a critical thinking technique like "examine both sides" to organize the "informing" act, it strongly risks reverting to the limitations of binary constructions.

It is notable that lessons on the informed conscience seem to imagine dissent residing exclusively within the individual and his/her conscience, so if one is to dissent it is seen as a decision that only he or she is responsible for as it sits against the prevailing view of the group. While some dissent can truly be exclusively individualized, not all is. Here is where a crucial curricular decision comes into play. The observation about dissent's "exclusive individuality" can easily be taken to the logical extreme, regarding dissidents as disconnected and marginalized outliers. To treat their dissent seriously within the curriculum would thus afford a disproportionate amount of curricular time and resource to the counsel of one or two private disagreements that are not relevant to all persons in a class. If all these conditions obtain, the chief drawback of this decision is that it neglects the potential benefits that are to be had if all students learn to receive dissent well. What is at one time an unpopular view that has problems with its intellectual grounding may, with some assistance, achieve greater epistemic and moral adequacy and so increase its persuasive value. And even if non-dissident students still are not persuaded by this better-developed dissent, they would still have exposure to the benefits of learning how to receive views which are different from their own and to appreciate the value that they can bring to the group.

A second drawback with the lesson of the informed conscience is that it does not resolve the epistemic imbalance between the long-established doctrinal and political history of the Church on the one hand, and the nascent moral agency of the individual student on the other. This difference in epistemic weight in an important way mirrors the contrast between one who legitimately makes the Church's public expressions on religious matters, and another whose relative weakness by theological training and official sanction leaves him or her to dissent privately. Balancing Magisterial authority and individual agency within the realm of the informed conscience, while an important lesson for students, ultimately does nothing to overcome the political-ecclesial privatization and concentration of dissent to the lone individual. Since the resources to support the Magisterium are plentiful and those that support dissenting Catholic views are non-existent in the school, at least insofar as the aims for Catholic Education are written and as the participants illustrate, allowing for dissent as a matter of individual conscience is insufficient by itself as a means of overcoming the marginalization of dissenting Catholic scholarship and the problematic privatization of dissent.

However significant the limitations of appealing to conscience as a wholesale means of addressing student dissent, they do not undo the benefits and foundational importance that it brings to considering dissent in general. The concept of the informed conscience is central to any Catholic idea of dissent and is constitutive of the means by which a person dissents, notwithstanding the current practical deficiencies that Catholic educational theory has in using it to justify a pedagogical approach and to shape the curriculum and the school's administrative action. It does not logically follow from these facts, however, that the intellectual means by which an individual dissents must be achieved in isolation from others and without support in the school, the Church, and the discourses of educational theory. The Catholic conception of the human person, after all, relies heavily on a communal anthropology. As the informed conscience is an integral part of Christian living, if Christian persons are to learn how to exercise their consciences to dissent properly from within the Church, then any theoretically sound educational theory should prescribe that this learning must be supported in a manner equal to the support that is accorded to learning about the rest of the faith, which, paradoxically, is a personal matter that cannot be considered in isolation from others. The practical good of dissent cannot be optimized if its productive outcomes are suppressed and students' practice in the procedural development, reception, and treatment of dissenting views (one's own and those of others) is constricted.

If the Catholic community of faith and scholarship is to take seriously the pedagogical implications of the religious freedom inherent in persons and to respect the informed conscience as a means of exercising this freedom, then an admission of support for a rigorous theory and content that informs the dissenting conscience is required. In existential terms, one might wonder if students are truly free if the possibility of responsible disagreement is acknowledged but the pedagogical way not nurtured. Morally speaking, an educator or educational institution cannot use the concept of negative freedom to justify the neglect of a pedagogical interest which partially constitutes the relationship. The outstanding question is what, if any, are the unexplored possibilities that could extend from the benefits of what is being done right now with the informed conscience.

THE RAMIFICATIONS OF NOT LOOKING BEYOND CONVENTIONAL PEDAGOGY

Under the current circumstances when teaching religion in Catholic schools, and especially in the publicly funded variety, teachers weigh a variety of interests in choosing their pedagogical strategies and adapting them to meet the needs of all partners in Catholic Education-Schooling. If the stances and techniques above represent the most significant approaches for accommodating student dissent, it stands that, given their reflection of the shortcomings in Catholic pedagogy, an integration of further Catholic theological, philosophical, and historical thought into the way religion courses are conceived, designed, and delivered is called for so as to reconfigure the epistemic balance of competing perspectives within the Church and school.

Concurrent with wishes for dissent's socially desirable expression is a parallel concern that dissent could scandalize the faithful because it might psychologically disrupt their faith. This concern reflects a theoretical problem within the whole Church that could properly be the subject of its own book with a scope wider than the topic of education; however, here it simply raises the question of whether particular scandals might in fact be morally desirable. What if, for instance, it were to disrupt an infantile faith or ecclesiology with a gesture toward addressing the injustices that marginalized groups experience in the Church? While the school does well in presenting to students the intellectual tradition with which Church teaching was developed (like the natural law justifications), this current method falls quite short of presenting suitable ways to critique the Church's arguments and its standards for evidence. Dissident students have no legitimate theoretical recourse with which to overcome their frustration, and under these conditions those who disagree are left to struggle from a point where their intellectual and spiritual needs are high but the pedagogical care they receive is low. Most importantly, students are also left without any theoretical guidance on the issue of whether disagreement requires them to separate from the Church.

Teachers can exercise some pedagogical authority of their own to make sure that students know what they are criticizing, are able to ask important questions of the Catholic faith, have a breadth of knowledge from influences beyond Catholicism, and involve their families in making decisions. This authority, however, encounters several structural barriers should it attempt to venture beyond the bounds of conventionally accepted content and strategies. The consequence for students is that their concerns are left in a state of pedagogical limbo that is marked by philosophical and pedagogical mediocrity. Catholic Education does many good things and represents an important development in Canada's development of a pluralistic society, but in addition to those goods there is a need for some theoretical remedy to the limitations of the current framework.

An approach to teaching and learning based upon a genuine consideration of students' pedagogical needs therefore ought to be developed and considered as an alternative means of religious pedagogy and a proposal for reform of Catholic Education. That proposed reform should undoubtedly retain the benefits of the current teaching stances and techniques and tackle the philosophical and theological questions that sit in territory currently uncharted by theory and practice in Catholic Education. In addition, it should be guided by a disposition to mollify dichotomies and use the fact of the philosophical tensions they produce as a means of exploring the breadth of purpose in Catholic Education, rather than making an attempt at refining it according to a more rigorous application of the current model.

So how does dissent get privatized, and what are the ramifications of privatization? This can be demonstrated through a scenario describing how schools receive dissent. Suppose that a religion class is discussing same-sex marriage (for example), and a Catholic student in that class holds a view that reasonably dissents from the teaching that homosexual unions are contrary to "God's plan for marriage and family" and cannot be approved under any circumstances.[9] The teacher will not try to dissuade the student from holding that view, nor will its expression be discouraged so long as that expression conforms to the school's norms of polite public speech. *Prima facie* one observes that the dissenting view's publication in the classroom is not suppressed and is even welcomed so long as it conforms procedurally in this way, but simultaneously the limits of publication already apply here, even if their presence is only felt softly. This expression is welcomed because it is understood as an individual student's classroom dissent within the primary aim of learning about the Church's views on human life. The school freely yields *this* public space for dissenting expressions, but rarely any other. Dissenting expressions are not welcome in any other organized public forum outside the classroom; such expressions include both the publication of views and the organization of dissidents. Dissent is not expressed in any school-wide media, and if any indication can be taken from the controversy which arises when groups intending to provide social and emotional support for non-heterosexual Catholic youth attempt to organize in the school,[10] any group that attempts to organize for the expressed purpose of directly challenging a prevailing Church teaching is not tolerated either.

This restriction of dissent's publication to individuals in the classroom contrasts sharply against the ease with which the prevailing Catholic view is publicized throughout the school and its community. Students who support the Church's prevailing view receive authorization to organize and resources to publicize their views outside the school.[11] Students who dissent may receive a polite hearing and the opportunity to air their views in a debate in front of their classmates, and may possibly search out Catholic scholarship that critiques the Church's views on homosexuality and marriage (in this example),[12] but little else. Depending on the skill with which the teacher facilitates these learning activities to optimize the benefits of the techniques treated above, the individual outcome might be very good, but ultimately the student would find that the efficacy of this work is limited to his or her own individual-level growth as a conscientious decision-maker, and not directed toward any sort of socio-ecclesial action. Public legitimacy of ecclesial expression and school sanction is limited to institutional models which restrict notions of the Church to its Magisterium and the School to its administration (with ordinary approval). Students attend the School and Church, but the exercise of their administration does not recognize students as constituting these bodies. Dissident students therefore can easily perceive rhetorical motions to the Church as "People of God" and "School community" as illusions. The effect of these restrictions is to rule out any public role for a lay person that does not depend on the Magisterium, thus opening a gap between the matters of how one thinks about the Church as an academic exercise, and how one acts in it. If the School is to have some role in developing all students as "ecclesial agents" – including those who assent to all Magisterial teaching – then by restricting dissident students in the exercise of their constitutive public place, the School unfortunately hinders them in this regard. The effect of obstructing their public ecclesial participation in this regard can, as I state elsewhere, lead to their disaffection:

Students who agree with the Magisterium, critically or not, will remain well served. Those students who do not agree with the prevailing Church teachings on controversial issues will continue to find little or no meaning in raising their objections, unless that is they are prepared for (a) a conversion of thought and/or practice toward the prevailing view; (b) to be drawn into dialogue under the pretense that their opinion matters in the public ecclesial space, when it ostensibly does not; (c) undertaking an exercise in theory or thought that is divorced from real life; or (d) to be frustrated and alienated from the Church.[13]

The ramifications of ignoring or confining students' dissent range from frustration and alienation to group polarization. If students leave the Church as a result of perceiving that their concerns are not taken seriously, the intellectual diversity within the Church will slowly be truncated to include only those who adhere completely to Magisterial teaching. Again, *prima facie* one might be tempted to conclude that the result of this phenomenon would be a refining and strengthening of the school's Catholic identity. Ironically, however, one might reasonably predict that the opposite effect would obtain. Catholic schools already thrive by serving Catholic children whose parents enrol them for many reasons that are not restricted to Christian formation. When one considers that large numbers of non-Catholic and non-Christian students also attend, it becomes apparent that one cannot logically conclude that any incongruity between home and school is enough to drive all dissidents away. What is more likely is that the trends Murphy and Rossiter notice will continue: students will continue to see the school's academic service in positive terms, but will remain "unchurched" and uninterested in ecclesial participation.[14] If a means of meaningful critical engagement and ecclesial agency is continually denied to dissident Catholics, the most likely outcome is that disaffection will feature in the rearing of their own children who, in the future, will attend Catholic schools. The socio-ecclesial gap between the "adherents" and the "dissidents" would then only grow wider and exacerbate the difficulty of meaningful discourse across intra-Catholic religious differences. If they only listen to the voices that they ostensibly wish to hear, the School and Church in fact will contribute to the erosion of their own inclusive catholicity.

A significant concern with the current theory of Catholic Education is that the *public* legitimacy of critical thinking, and especially new varieties of critical thinking, is left outside the School and in the possession of the Magisterium. This allocation does not mean that students cannot express or practice divergent critical thinking in school, but it does mean that their only option to have their critical concerns publicly recognized and legitimized within the Church is to mimic and defend what the Magisterium has already critically thought. This model implicitly communicates to students that *what* is thought has priority over *how* it is thought. Without doubt the Magisterium's views should be expressed, but if these expressions are not contextualized within the Church's history of thought and its current internal debates, then an intellectual injustice is done to students. Moreover, if caricatures are made of challenges to these views, then the intellectual breadth within Catholicism is constricted and the awareness that breadth even exists is diminished. If on controversial issues students are made aware of Magisterial teaching but are not given the intellectual equipment with which to evaluate and adapt it to their lives, then they may become frustrated. A dimension of critical thinking about the Church that is legitimated by a philosophically informed pedagogical theory is required, otherwise Catholic schools risk limiting critical thought to a re-visitation or recapitulation of doctrine, or simply leaving it to students' unaided devices that are exercised only during selected token airings within the confines of the classroom or in limited ways at home or in other private settings.

Catholic schools (and education) could gain much from acknowledging that dissent exists and can be the foundation for pedagogical gains. Engaging dissent might have instrumental value in opening discussions with the expression of student interests and leading them to consider the prevailing view, but its pedagogical import is greater than this. Engaging with dissent in a way that develops a student's agency as a dissident within the Church is a way of reaching out to a fellow Catholic with the intent of helping them to re-imagine their place in the Church. Rather than viewing dissent as a deficiency or relativistic immaturity, dissent from certain Church teachings can be thought of from a faithful perspective as being done for the good of the Church, without diluting knowledge of it, in a "thick" way that is distinct from misinformed contrarian grumbling. To put academic rigour behind this aim requires that students take their dissident interest as an opportunity to begin learning the relevant historical, philosophical, and theological knowledge that would support their views. This knowledge must include a generous appreciation of the prevailing view, including its place within the differentiated hierarchy of truths,[15] the context(s) within which it has been expressed, and the positive and negative criticisms it has received. No less important is that students move from their particular dissent to receive a wide view of dissent in the Church. They should learn about all kinds of dissent, including those called "pre-conciliar," "post-conciliar," "liberal," "conservative," and so forth. This exposure should be constructed around learning activities that allow students to see the role dissent has played in the Church (and still plays), as well as the effects of dissent that is expressed and organized publicly versus that which is disorganized and/or privatized. They should also be put into positions where they can appreciate the value of proper treatment of dissenters, and be given the opportunity to predict the effects for themselves and the Church if their practice drops off. As the School finds itself working with students who are leaving the Church because of teachings that cannot be changed or are not being changed, the question becomes one of how can they be taught to frame these "unchangeables" in terms of what is really important – including the relationship with God, the Communion of Saints, the Sacraments, Community, Family, Justice, continuing the work of God on Earth, and so forth. Imagining the school's role in terms of nurturing a mature, learned response to the ambiguity present in a community that does not unanimously agree on everything will go far in this regard.

7

Pedagogy of Dissent

An approach to religious education that is based upon the concept of dissent is sometimes the optimal way to meet students' learning and justice needs in schools and other teaching-learning relationships. The preceding chapters on dissent from the perspectives of history, theology, philosophy, and professional practice could inform discrete pedagogical decisions in this respect, and might definitely be used to describe, interpret, and make valid prescriptions about all aspects of Catholic Education and Schooling. Taken together, however, they do not yet provide a cohesive pedagogical theory to inform practice. This chapter takes that next theoretical step of using their conclusions to inform a theory about the practice of nurturing dissent in teaching and learning relationships. It presents the grounds upon which disaffected students can be given an academic handhold as a way of communicating their dissent and so to continue participating in the Church. In spite of the best efforts of teachers to reinforce Church teachings, disagreement is not going away. This strategy of acknowledging dissent as a Catholic act is, I believe, the best way to help students who are looking for ways to be Catholic and think religiously but who find the current pedagogical models frustrating. No matter what name is given to a dissenter – pre-conciliar, post-conciliar, liberal, or conservative – this theory provides the grounds upon which the school can help them work through their current interest in the Church.

What is the scope of this *Pedagogy of Dissent*? First, it does not outline a curriculum. It is not a practical intervention that directly plans lessons. Translating this proposal into a course offering or using it to orient the overall curricular and administrative aims for the whole school is the job of another work. Instead, this chapter outlines a way of thinking that curriculum designers, teachers, administrators, parents, clergy and religious, and other partners in the relationships of Catholic Education could use to imagine a practical reform of the whole curriculum – including the formal lessons and informal socialization into the institutions – of Catholic Education. It is proposed as an ideal toward which practice might strive, and although it might never be attained, it remains the point upon which the good pedagogical efforts and steady growth of intellectual and cultural structures within the institution might be focused and legitimated.

There is therefore no expectation that individual educators or institutions will be able to implement this theory "perfectly" and without trouble, should they so desire. This expectation represents the error of attempting to directly apply theory to practice without considering the contextual factors of how learners and institutions respond to changes. The school is a political union of multivariate intentions and expectations; thus, reforms to practice take time and the patience of persuasion and collaboration. Dissent is a controversial topic, and so are any ideas that would reform Catholic Education – ranging through various models based on pre- and post-conciliar ideologies. This book is limited to expressing the proposals and justification for a pedagogical theory of dissent.

Importantly, therefore, this theory is not limited in its application to influencing administrative practices and the design and delivery of courses in schools, but is also a touchstone for informing decisions and practices at all times and places – including (but not limited to) the role parents often play in receiving and responding to their children's dissent. While this theory is not limited to teachers in its application, because of their public visibility and responsibility they deserve this encouragement: Teachers should not be asked to take an individual leap of faith and abandon fully their currently successful practice. My invitation to them asks that they consider this proposal as a new direction and territory into which their practice could expand. I hope they consider it a means of responding to concerns and situations with which conventional theory and practice struggle, and sometimes even fail, to meet well. This theory begins from the place where teachers already have high degrees of practical success within the current framework, and suggests ways in which a more pedagogically adequate framework for serving students could be developed.

Pedagogy of Dissent provides a more philosophically and theologically solid approach toward engaging with controversial religious issues than does conventional theory and practice, because it more fairly and comprehensively integrates the needs of students within the web of expectations placed upon the School to teach about the Catholic Church. It differs from the conventional religious pedagogy and expectations because its approach to religious education is based upon first balancing students' own dissent against the fact of normative Catholicism, and then using that interest as the procedural catalyst through which Catholic students learn and achieve competence with prevailing Catholic teachings and subordinated Catholic thought. Teaching and learning in this way should not be limited to learning only about one's own dissent. Students should also learn about the many kinds and qualities of dissent that exist within Catholicism, including those which conflict with their own. Through exposure to the prevailing view and its dissidents, students will acquire an understanding of what the concept of dissent is and means to the Church, and use it as a means to adjudicate moral problems and even contribute to knowledge within the Church. This approach is therefore unique in its use of student interest as both the starting place from which to begin learning about the Church, and, more importantly, the means with which to proceed on a curricular course that develops that interest. The conventional pedagogy, by contrast, can only entertain students' interest for the convenience of accommodating student self-expression[1] or as an entry point into lessons before ultimately discarding it and leaping to the lessons' real, primary intent: to clarify and reinforce the established Church teaching. Students who learn through a pedagogy of dissent should achieve the same (or better) informed fluency with the prevailing view that the conventional pedagogy expects, but should then use that knowledge as a means of entertaining the variety of theological issues surrounding it in theory and practice. In this important way, *Pedagogy of Dissent* surpasses the conventional pedagogy's ability to deal with controversial issues, and represents a philosophically superior means of promoting learning, justice, and a general appreciation of the fact and value of intra-Church plurality for those whose concerns are marginalized.

Proposing dissent as a pedagogical model raises questions as to what place assent maintains. Strictly speaking, *assent* sits outside the scope of this theory; that topic already receives much attention as the primary aim of catechesis, and is already well established. At the same time, the question of assent is nonetheless relevant because dissenters maintain least some kind of assent to the whole. This proposal, therefore, maintains that a commitment to good pedagogy comes first, and so offering pedagogical opportunities for high-quality dissent must sit next to those which enable an equally high-quality assent. This commitment ensures that non-dissenters remain well served, but no less that those who do dissent on certain points also have the opportunity to discern how they assent. At bottom, Catholic schools and their religion classes need not be structured exclusively on dissent or in any way that overshadows assent, but, whether they admit this pedagogy or not, they should provide students with the means to choose critically an authentic response to Catholicism. Ultimately, this theory is proposed so that it is available when necessary and helpful.

This theory balances curricular emphases on the *content* of Catholic thought and the *process* of Catholic thinking and being. It maintains that the official institutional views are important to the Church, but that Catholic life is irreducible to these views and also requires an ability to challenge their appropriateness in certain situations, and occasionally even their general validity. The process of Catholic thinking proposed here is a kind of critical thinking *with* the Church that may or may not agree with the official view, but that is able to differentiate itself from the Magisterium with a rationale that remains grounded in Catholic tradition. "Sitting apart" from the Magisterial view thus does not require that one reject, or separate one's self from, the entire Church, because dissent is thereby expressed *for* and *as part of* the Church. Content and process are thus both considered to be irreducible to but interdependent with official teaching. This theory thus relies upon a claim that institutions and groups work best when they encourage good dissent, which means that they must encourage their members to consider the widest possible range of information and ethical perspectives.[2]

Pedagogy of Dissent is based upon seven theoretical pillars that circumscribe its union of content and process. (1) The concept of dissent provides philosophical support for an illumination of the complex act in a liminal space where one thinks *with* and *for* a group without following its prevailing view or abandoning the association. This model adopts moral dilemmas analogous to the three offered in the general introduction as representative of (2) students' interests in

exploring the intellectual territory that exists outside complete agreement or disagreement with the prevailing view. The model most firmly
establishes its emphasis on the process of Catholic thinking by
(3) imagining students in the place of the amateur theologian who
might, given the problems and data at hand, arguably represent the
institutional ideal of one who might dissent. Although not all theologians dissent, and many theologians are members of the Magisterium or produce work that significantly informs Church teaching, the
office of the theologian encompasses a skill set that actively employs
(4) critical thinking about Catholicism and its relationship with the
world and (5) a critique of the problems of ideology in the Church
and the rest of the world. It is from this institutional perspective, then,
that this model proposes a means for (6) intellectually addressing the
problems that a rigid adherence to binary thinking can pose to the
Church and Catholic Education. (7) The role of Catholic Education-
Schooling can thus be reconsidered as helping students engage with
the Church in a manner that legitimates the liminality of their relationship with it on certain issues. A consideration of the criticisms
that *Pedagogy of Dissent* might face follows the presentation of
this model.

I firmly refrain from suggesting that non-Catholic students would
not benefit from this proposal; but since genuinely Catholic dissent
must emerge from enfranchised Catholics, the value of experiencing
this approach to Catholic Education should, for the non-Catholic,
provide as good a means as the current method to learn about Church
teaching and its accompanying debate. The most important additional
benefit will be the student's increased opportunity to appreciate the
value of dissent and to identify with dissenters in general. For enfranchised and non-franchised alike, this pedagogy should in the abstract
improve the adequacy of students' knowledge about the Church and
the value of any views they have that dissent from the group, and
should foster a more comprehensive understanding and balanced
evaluation of Church teaching and any criticisms that they either pose
or encounter.

Finally, along the continuum between "traditional" and "progressive" approaches to education, this theory can only be considered
"progressive." Those who hold to the epistemologies and politics of
traditionalist schooling would maintain that the suggestion I make
to follow student interests as the basis for engaging dissent as a topic

is flawed because students need to learn "the basics," grounded in an epistemology where knowledge is objective and external to the self, before personal interests can be entertained. This view broadly follows a Platonic epistemology and politics, and one of the most comprehensive current treatments and well-subscribed theories on this subject is found in John Miller and Wayne Seller's book *Curriculum: Perspectives and Practice*, which terms such traditionalist approaches to education and schooling the "transmission" model. Interestingly, however, traditionalist or transmission models do not in themselves necessarily preclude the teaching of dissent. In many militaries, for instance, in addition to learning an authoritarian command structure and culture of conformity, soldiers are also taught to disobey orders that will lead unnecessarily to harm and destruction – especially when the judgment of the person issuing those orders is compromised. Dissent as such is therefore not completely outside the scope of traditionalist approaches, and as the historical, theological, philosophical, and professional chapters which build this theory demonstrate, neither is it necessarily outside of the Catholic tradition.

I CONCEPTUAL GROUNDING

Dissent's seven conceptual criteria (see chapter 5) are crucial philosophical informants of this pedagogical model because they describe the kind and quality of internal criticism that promotes the good of the Church and does not leap immediately to the antithetical stance of abandoning Catholicism. The criterion of *enfranchisement* frames the pedagogy's critical work within the purpose of ameliorating one's membership within the group, enhancing one's contribution to it, and, ultimately, improving the group itself. The concept's two *epistemic* criteria constitute the philosophical basis for some of the curricular content within the pedagogical reform. A view of tradition which retains the past while also being quite malleable is conceived as an essential contributor to individual learning and group development. Theological, historical, and philosophical data from within the Church provide both the past instances and present interpretations of those events to which justifications for dissent attach themselves. Framing dissent from within the Catholic intellectual history and aiming it toward the betterment of the Church legitimates an expanded range of contra-hegemonic choices.

The *ethical* criterion functions as the standard against which the content, relevance, and expression of dissent are measured against the principles of justice and care. In the Catholic school, Catholic perspectives on Christian ethics must also inform this standard. The ethics in this case are partially independent of historical precedent because they do not require appeals to past dissent as the warrant for dissent in the present. The ethical criterion is also the place where the Catholic conception of conscience comes to bear. The triple tension between individual interest, social interest, and the requirements of an abstract moral ideal like justice or care is a major contributor to many secular ethical dilemmas, and in the Catholic context the Christian conscience weighs the same tensions while also including a relationship with God and divine law in the act of moral reasoning. The ethical criterion therefore informs this pedagogy's consideration of the discrepancies between *is* and *ought* within Catholicism's socio-moral, theological, and ecclesial structures.

The final two criteria, of publicity and persuasiveness, most especially bear upon the pedagogical proposal in terms of the technical means and manner through which dissent is to be expressed. Publicity is important because without a climate of circulating dissent, there is a less readily available reasonable check upon the prevailing view. Without publicly known challenges to the prevailing view that aim to promote the good of all, the chances for error increase simply due to the absence and ignorance of legitimately viable alternatives. Encouraging (or at least not suppressing) dissent within Catholicism's public realm is therefore crucial so that all Catholics – including, but not limited to Catholic students – are given opportunities to witness, evaluate, and, where applicable, practice it. Dissent should not be an occasionally used technique whose application is limited to satisfying the discrete moral, epistemic, and political concerns of individuals, because its optimal social value is realized when persons and groups appreciate its general usefulness in disclosing correct information, making valid interpretations of that information, and promoting justice for the good of all. Appreciating the imperative for right treatment of dissenters is no less important. If dissent is confined to the individual level, its socio-political value is mitigated because the whole group or society is denied, at the least, the chance to examine itself and determine what epistemic and moral gains it might obtain from making a genuine intellectual and social engagement with dissidents, and with how it treats dissenters in general. The criterion of publicity places the enfranchised dissenter in a position where he or she is responsible and accountable for the accuracy and adequacy of that view, and so a pedagogy based on dissent should provide the support (materials, techniques, and so forth) to encourage and enhance it.

The persuasive criterion is the point where this proposal differentiates itself from the kinds of reform that would propose the complete overthrow and abandonment of a tradition to replace it with another. This criterion justifies both this pedagogy's philosophical foundation *vis-à-vis* the conventional curriculum and the curricular aims it maintains for students in the development of their own dissent. The changes proposed here mirror Freire's call for the kind of pedagogical reform that replaces relationships based on dominance and dependence with intersubjective interdependence, to the extent that they are designed to promote Catholic franchise and power of ecclesial action in all Catholics without either undermining Catholicism – suggesting that a small group of triumphalist dissenters should usurp control of the prevailing view from the current hierarchy – or proposing that the ecclesial structure of the Church should be dismantled into a state of anarchy. The persuasive criterion thus requires that this pedagogical reform must rely exclusively upon well-reasoned arguments to justify its existence and convince rationally those who subscribe to the prevailing view that change is needed. Persuasion aims to make the pedagogical model for, and learning about, particular dissents an attractive option for all.

2 A GROUNDING IN STUDENTS' INTERESTS

This proposal is grounded in John Dewey's theory that educational systems focused exclusively or primarily upon conforming individual students to the will of the institution and its curriculum are flawed because they do not take advantage of the student's own enterprise and initiative as essential factors that contribute to his or her learning. Dewey maintains that when curriculum is abstracted from students' real lives and experiences, they become alienated from the process of their own development and also from their community. The social contribution of personal enterprise is an essential aspect of education for Dewey because it enables and encourages a maximization of personal growth, and such growth, in turn, maximizes the potential contribution and interest that a person can bring to their community.

On this point, Dewey's philosophical views obtain a high level of congruence with Catholic anthropology. If students in the Catholic school are alienated from the curriculum and social experience of the Church, then a pedagogical approach which remediates this alienation by legitimizing the academic and moral concerns at the root of their disaffection should prove helpful.

Dewey describes very well a way in which students' individual interests should inform the purposes of education. Far from espousing either atomistic individualism or the subordination of one's purposes to the community, Dewey's philosophy of education postulates that individual and community exist in dialectical relationship. Optimizing and coordinating the capabilities of individual selves within society is necessary (although not sufficient) for maximizing the collective interests in any social arrangement. From this position Dewey understands that "self and interest are two names for the same fact; the kind and amount of interest actively taken in a thing reveals and measures the quality of selfhood which exists ... [and] interest means the active or moving *identity* of the self with a certain object."[3] This expression of the self is threefold: a person's occupation or business; the activities that engage a person; and the absorption in that activity or subject that the person expresses as a result of care for it.[4] A complete development of human interest happens when one is able to devote the self completely to the tasks that are important to his or her contribution to society. "Absorption, engrossment, full concern with subject matter for its own sake, nurture it," Dewey continues; "Divided interest and evasion destroy it."[5] Dewey notices that, within the school environment, the student's appropriately balanced devotion to their interests is often disrupted when the curriculum imposes an alien interest upon him or her. These officially imposed interests do not convert the student's aims, says Dewey, but only suppress his or her desire to proceed according to a self-inherent concern. The student's "own desires are not abolished," he writes, because "[t]he mind wanders from the nominal subject and devotes itself to what is intrinsically more desirable. A systematized divided attention expressing the duplicity of the state of desire is the result."[6]

Dividing attention between the intrinsic interest of a self's vocation and the imposed institutional curriculum injures the self's wholeness. According to Dewey, even if the student is able to coordinate these two interests in a socially desirable fashion, the residual philosophical effect of that social desirability is duplicity along the public-private divide: "A double standard of reality, one for our own private and more or less concealed interests, and another for public and acknowledged concerns, hampers, in most of us, integrity and completeness of mental action. Equally serious is the fact that a split is set up between conscious thought and attention and impulsive blind affection and desire."[7]

Dewey does not situate his concerns about this duplicity between private and public selves as a lament that a doctrine of selfish individualism has not been accorded its fair share of space within educational institutions. Rather, his remarks are focused upon the inconsideration of certain teaching and learning environments and institutions toward accommodating authentic selves within their view of society, hence leaving these institutions with a difficult or futile route (or both) toward wholesale conversion of the student's interests, and a certain misapplication of his or her possible contribution to society: "What is native, spontaneous, and vital in mental reaction goes unused and untested," he writes, "and the habits formed are such that these qualities become less and less available for public and avowed ends."[8] A healthy coordination of individuals' interests with the larger institution and society is therefore a requirement of all educative endeavours. At its worst manifestation in Catholic Education, this double standard entails paying sufficiently nominal public respect to the official prevailing view, while privately adhering to another, possibly very different set of beliefs or justifications. On controversial issues it can amount to a kind of socio-moral atmosphere where "don't ask/don't tell" is the dominant practice.

As Dewey attempts to cut through the divisions between intrinsic and imposed interests, and public and private presentations of the self, he also prescribes that educative relationships should not be abstracted from their intended ends: "The only adequate training *for* occupations is training *through* occupations," he writes. "The principle ... that the educative process is its own end, and that the only sufficient preparation for later responsibilities comes by making the most of immediately present life, applies in full force to the vocational phases of education." This notion of occupational vocation should not be limited to one aspect of the agent's life, either, but should be extended to the full range of his or her political and social experiences: "The dominant vocation of all human beings at all times is living – intellectual and moral growth."[9] For students in a traditional Catholic school, if Dewey is correct, the experiences and opinions they bring to class are not philosophically or theologically invalid. These experiences and interests therefore have to be acknowledged and structured into further learning experiences that can count as legitimately Catholic learning outcomes.

Dewey's educational philosophy has had a monumental (even if sometimes tacit) influence upon all kinds of education, including parenting, secular and religious schools, the training for teachers in these schools, and the ways in which all persons interpret the formal and informal relationships in society. In the context of Catholic Education, its application is felt at the foundations of how teachers and parents conceive of the learner and imagine their ideals of instructional design. In the context of Catholic Education it makes sense to assert that structuring the educative relationships in the Catholic School from the perspective of students' moral interests rather than from the perspective of clarifying Catholic Church teaching should have a positive effect upon their perceptions of belonging to the Church community, if belongingness can be considered as something that extends beyond conformity to the dominant power structure and into the domain of an individual's creative and learned ecclesial contribution. A study of the prevailing view absolutely has a significant role within any Catholic educative relationship, whether based on dissent or not; but to draw upon students' dissenting interests as merely the gravitational means to focus on the prevailing view is to trivialize their concerns. Students should certainly study the prevailing view, in part for its merit and significance within the wider view of life and debate within the Catholic Church, but also so that they learn where the Church needs improvement. In this way, educators can help students to achieve an intellectually, morally, politically, and epistemologically enhanced ecclesial citizenship, by teaching them about their relationship to the Church from the perspective of leading them through an intellectual examination of how to refine and trouble the dissent that may define their interests, and to consider the importance of their dissent to the local community. In theory, at least, beginning with students' interests is a means of providing them with an increased range of choices beyond outright conformity to or rejection of prevailing Church teaching as an apparent "complete package."

It is impractical, undesirable, and beyond this theory's scope to suggest that the school should or even could take direct or indirect responsibility for changing Catholic Church teaching, or that it might allow students or teachers to claim authority in parallel with the official Magisterium. However, it is certainly the theory's intent to prescribe that the school should provide students with the informational, critical intellectual, and environmental means to support decisions of conscience and ecclesial choices outside the school that do not reduce to a binary between strict conformity to or rejection of the official prevailing view. It is within the school's mission to provide students with an education that is appropriate to their needs as members of the Church, but as the school is responsible to provide education to the bearers of all majority and minority views within the Church, it is beyond that mission's scope to usurp the laity's agency and religious freedom by assuming responsibility for the political work that students might or must perform in their ecclesial life outside the school.

3 ADOPTING THE PLACE OF AMATEUR THEOLOGIANS

The third pillar of *Pedagogy of Dissent* is to put students in the imagined place of the theologian. Insofar as some professional theologians are among those in the Church who are most capable and best able to exemplify dissent in its most adequate intellectual means, their position within the Church can be used for heuristic purposes to inform a model where students can encounter and engage in legitimate scholarly dissent. Not all theologians are dissenters,[10] but from the imaginative position of one who does dissent, a student can approach the data of Catholic experience in a way that emulates the learned profession which coordinates individual moral authority with Magisterial teaching authority. As theological questions are inherently relevant to everyday Catholic life, it is reasonable to suggest that the emulation and imaginative positioning that students should assume is the legitimately amateur engagement with theology for the decidedly non-amateurish matter of reflecting upon one's ecclesial life.[11]

Adopting the imagined perspective of the theologian is an ideal model of religious reasoning within one's conscience. The person imagined as the exemplar of this perspective is skilled in both the possession and application of spiritual and intellectual knowledge of the Church, including the adjudicative powers of coordinating competing sources of data. This theologian, for example, would integrate doctrinal and pastoral concerns with a conception of divine law and relationship with the Divine presence Itself. This view of theological work derives from Schillebeeckx's view of the theological vocation: "Theologians have a complex role that is ensconced with freedom of inquiry. They work at the intersection of several dialectical relationships: church community as a whole, within academic disciplines, and Magisterium of the church."[12] As Catholic life and thought is identifiable by its doctrine but irreducible to it, Thompson observes that Schillebeeckx does not limit the significance of theology to its abstract or legalistic dimensions, but understands it as an integration of various life experiences: "The theologian's dissent should address the whole received church life, not just its doctrinal statements."[13] In this same sense, the pedagogical heuristic of the dissenting theologian should embrace data that emerges from a variety of ecclesial contexts.

The student-as-amateur-theologian should by no means be considered a trained or licensed theologian, but should rather be thought of as placed for heuristic purposes in a position where he or she interacts with, contests, and creates opinions based upon his or her learned experience with biblical and theological scholarship, moral philosophy, church history, ecclesiology, science, and cultural studies, along with his or her experience of prayer and Church community. This imagined station represents a place of knowledgeable authority in the Church that is currently accessible to ordained, vowed, or lay persons. The office of the theologian bridges the abstract academic and spiritual territory of Catholic knowledge on the one hand, and the institutional territory of the parish, diocese, and whole administrative Church on the other. As a theologian can support either the prevailing view or a variety of dissenting views, the emulation of his or her office is well suited as a pedagogical model of reform from which to grasp the intellectual activity for which some Catholic people are searching. The theologian is a handy construct because that role is distinct from the liturgical, administrative, juridical, and other offices that priests and bishops occupy. Placing the student in this position helps them appreciate the responsibilities and emulate the work of those who are at the learned frontier of coordinating competing points of view. The learned framework within which to discover and adjudicate competing views is important because it calls for an examination of the evidence in support of both prevailing and dissenting views.

It is certainly recognized, though, that not even all professional theologians would themselves embody this ideal, or be interested in embodying it. Some might focus strictly on their work for its independent interest and have no concern with the application of theology to life outside the university. Some others might be skilled thinkers within the abstracted bounds of their discipline, but woefully poor moral reasoners in the rest of their lives. Still others author or subscribe to the prevailing view and would not support any dissent. In any of these respects, the possibility must remain open that any person as an amateur theologian might be more adept than some professional theologians at coordinating the competing concerns of real life in the Church. A scientist, a garbage collector, an athlete, an actor, a person who has devoted their life to child-rearing, a commercial entrepreneur, or any other Christian person may possess this capability better than the scholar whose life's work is the dispassionate study of theology.

"Theologian" in this prescriptive pedagogical sense is thus used loosely enough to describe a person whose amateur emulation of an idealized professional is made with the intent of using the knowledge and perspectives it provides to enhance the adequacy of his or her actions within the Church rather than as a contribution to scholarship. Such an attitude toward theology is not limited to those who wish to dissent, and a similar emulation could be adopted by those wishing to fortify their understanding of orthodoxy.

"Amateur" is used here to mean a person who is following a serious interest without being paid for his or her efforts. "Amateur" in this sense means the *accomplished amateur* without the connotations of "amateurish" which suggest an inferior quality of work. In this sense, "amateur theologian" defines one's relationship with the Church but not one's formal occupation. Media theorist Marshall McLuhan proposes that any value distinction which champions the professional over the amateur reflects a myopic modernist bias: "Professionalism is environmental," he writes. "Amateurism is anti-environmental. Professionalism merges the individual into patterns of total environment. Amateurism seeks the development of the total awareness of the individual and the critical awareness of the ground rules of society. The amateur can afford to lose."[14] McLuhan's comments suggest that the amateur's serious pursuit of an interest reflects a critical approach to living that is preferable to pursuing an interest that is divorced from the rest of reality. The fragmented, modernist professional world, by contrast, discourages risk-taking and hence stifles innovation because it is too heavily invested in the status quo. An uncredentialled but serious person emulating the amateur theologian might in this sense have an advantage over one whose livelihood depends upon their continued contribution and subscription to the prevailing hegemony.

Situating students in the perspective of amateur theologians does not, however, grant them unrestrained permission or license to reshape Catholicism as they please or to act with a contrariness that is care-free of religion and morality. Similarly, it should not replace the current prevailing pedagogical model with a less rigorous requirement for teachers. Instead it should present students with an enhanced duty to achieve a more academically responsible dissent – should they choose it – which would require that the school provide the material, human, and social support that dissenting students require in order to meet these responsibilities.[15] This would include, among other things, providing students with the appropriate access to Church teaching and the scholarly commentary upon it. The teacher should not be obliged to teach the student to dissent or how to dissent, but at the same time should work with the student on how to pose the problem of their dissent in academic terms, how to find and adjudicate sources to support and critique it, and then how to "think religiously" – including informal logic and rhetorical skill – in posing their arguments. As the past chapters show, there is plenty to be studied in terms of the history of Church authority and the context within which certain teachings arose.

4 CRITICAL THINKING ABOUT CATHOLICISM

Critical thinking about Catholicism is a complex notion that involves the same broad range of intellectual and social consideration that inheres in the amateur theologian's discipline. It involves not only intellectual exposition and non-academic spiritual experiences, but also an examination of conscience. Arguably, much Catholic critical thinking is also socio-moral critical thinking, insofar as it bears upon interpersonal relations. The notion of critical thinking is, even in the non-religious sense, a tricky subject because of the potentially multi-variate understandings of what "critical" and "thinking" might mean as independent terms before they are even considered as a compound term. When considered in religious terms, Catholic critical thinking should be considered as a generally broad rubric of religiously informed attitudes for assessing all aspects of life, and it should not therefore be mistaken for an approach that means to condemn the

Church. I submit that the three cases shown in the introduction undoubtedly count in this regard. Catholic critical thinking is also not limited to dissident thinking, and certainly exists within the prevailing view as a critical perspective on the rest of the world. Where the Church perceives the world to be in a state of spiritual crisis, for instance, its critical perspective analyzes this crisis and offers a solution that is based upon a restatement or enhancement of Church teaching.

Aside from the kinds of critical thought that stem from an ostensibly unified Catholic critique upon the world, there is also the kind of Catholic critical thought that turns its critique inward upon the institution of the Church itself. This sort of critical thought relies upon a view of the Church as a representation of the will of God that acts with the best intentions but that nonetheless is also a fallible human social institution. While Church law is a reflection of divine law, it is nonetheless also mediated through human language and cultural and institutional interests, and therefore does not always perfectly reflect a divine ideal. Following this.logic, the laws and practices of the Church can be criticized and refurbished when better expressions of those laws are found or when the existing laws are found to be inadequate to the ideal of Christian life.

Psychologist Lawrence Kohlberg's model of moral reasoning is helpful here as a descriptive secular foil which compares the relative prescriptive adequacy of moral reasoning and decision-making that appeals to institutional authority (Stage Four) against reasoning in accord with principled authority (Stage Six).[16] This description can be transposed into the institutional life of the Catholic Church and applied to the moral decisions that emerge as a natural consequence of its internal functions and interactions with the secular world. From there it becomes apparent that a kind of principled Catholic critical thinking that is in *structural* parallel with Kohlberg's ethical ideal is possible.[17] Divine law or principle does not discriminate by one's station in the Church; all members of the Church have equal access to it through their conscience and are equally subject to its rigour. In this sense, critical thinking and moral reasoning within the institutional Church might become a process by which the entire Church can potentially participate in the learning function (*ekklesia discens*) of moral reasoning and critique. This learning function eventually gives rise to the possibility that the entire Church might be positioned to choose between prescriptive statements that either support or

dissent from the prevailing view. These statements represent one function of the Church's teaching process (*ekklesia docens*), although they
do not necessarily represent the views of the Magisterium.

Critical thinking about Catholicism in the Catholic school is thus
drawn from a discipline-based approach to critical thinking in education in general, and in Catholicism in particular. Four aspects of a
discipline-based approach are the historical, the theological, the
anthropological, and the philosophical. The critical-historical view
regards the Church as a human-formed institution of divine worship
that changes over time and that has political aspects which have also
shaped that history and which continue to shape its posture within
the present world. Catholic historicity is thus the combination of the
evolution of Church teaching within its attendant institutional structures. The critical-theological view of the Church takes the perspective of critical thinking from the integration of Church teaching with
all of Catholic life, and uses that teaching as a means of asking critical questions of the world and of the Church. Theology therefore
provides both the form and content of the means of dissent. The
anthropological understanding of persons-in-communal-relationship
bridges the historical and theological with the philosophical dimension. The philosophical pillar provides a normative ethical, political,
and epistemological ground upon which to critique the Church, which
enables a dispassionate look at how moral problems can be perceived
and addressed from the several sources of data and perspectives that
constitute an understanding of life in the Church.

A major part of the critical approach should be to remain sensitive
to the limitations of binary thinking, to which intra-Church dialogue
is susceptible. An inability to see beyond the deadlock of binary constructions is a major source of frustration within the Catholic school
and the broader Church in which the school is situated. Such dichotomies as public-private, political-personal, restrictive-permissive,
masculine-feminine, and ordained-lay should be blurred when they
prove to be the source of limitations that truncate dialogue and maintain injustice. At the same time, it should be recognized that other
significant means of Catholic critical thinking and dissent are based
upon views that polarize and ossify these distinctions, and that these
perspectives must also be respected and included for their independent interest. Some pre-conciliar dissenting views might contend that
the secular world has intruded into Catholic teachings on religious
liberty and customs on discipline and obedience, thus threatening the

legitimacy of the whole Church. According to these views, such influence threatens the Church's integrity from within and from the hands of external secular forces. It should, these views maintain, therefore be the concern of all Catholics to reclaim the "true" pre-conciliar Catholicism. This model therefore maintains that an appropriate balance between encouraging dissent for its own utility and encouraging the evaluation of dissenting viewpoints is required.

The critical question remains as to the purpose of accommodating dissent within the school. As this pedagogy is grounded in a Deweyan conceptual framework that champions the use of student interest as a means and aim of their education, the utilitarian view argues that it makes sense for students to have opportunities to learn about both their own and others' points of dissent. The result is that a classroom may be a mixture of the prevailing views and several competing dissenting views. Exposure to competing views from any perspective is of utility to critical thinking because it affords pedagogical opportunities for one to refine his or her own views, to possibly change them, and, finally, to appreciate the value that a political framework that admits dissent has for societies in general. A part of that utilitarian value is also ethical because it extends opportunities for real-life justice concerns to be examined in a public place. While it is not the place of the school to become a bastion for dissent of any particular kind, or to publicly moderate religious debates with the intent of favouring and adopting one kind of Catholicism over another, it should be the school's responsibility to accommodate that dissent for the pedagogical purposes of nurturing the critical thinking experiences of the dissenter and his or her contemporaries alike so that they might incorporate it into their broader life experiences. It is the responsibility of the student and groups outside the School to translate lessons on dissent into the structures of the Church.

5 ADDRESSING IDEOLOGY

Catholic critical thinking should be directed at examining the influences of ideology upon society, and, in particular, the ecclesial society of the Catholic Church. The pedagogical aims of critical thinking that are directed at the utilitarian and ethical value of dissent are, in themselves, both a critique of ideology and an ideological perspective. According to Louis Althusser, ideology is expressed in unconsciously enacted social customs and assumptions that reproduce submission to the established order. In his conception, ideology is the total environment that constitutes subjects and their actions, and so is maintained through the institutional instruments of socialization that govern persons' ideas of their competence and social role.[18] In the school, for instance, in addition to learning the content for which they are responsible, students also learn to submit and conform to the social forces that determine success and failure in the total ideological sphere. Students do not learn to critique these rules, but are unconsciously socialized into them. It is through this means that ideology and its supporting institutional apparatus ensure their own reproduction.[19] Although John Stuart Mill's work exists within a different era and theoretical framework than Althusser's, his contention that a difference exists between the (repressive) tyranny of the magistrate and the tyranny of the prevailing feeling or custom within a group[20] suggests a similar awareness that the political and institutional zone of social control is shaped by both formal decree and the momentum of cultural construction.

Althusser states that ideology is inevitable, total, and probably cannot be overcome.[21] Beyond any cynical resignation to social determinism, however, his critique may also be interpreted in an uplifting manner for its potential to identify, challenge, and possibly reduce the limiting effects of ideology and ideological apparatuses. The importance of considering critiques of ideology is therefore to be found along a distinction between *is* and *ought*: If ideology constructs and reproduces the conditions of conventional social structures, for instance, do these conditions properly reflect principled religious and secular notions of what society ought to be? And what ideology underwrites these principles? This pedagogy of dissent therefore critiques ideology by asking what sort of Catholic ideology is represented in the prevailing view, what sorts of Catholic ideologies persist elsewhere within the Church, and what is to be gained by juxtaposing and critiquing them.

According to Daniel Speed Thompson's observations on Edward Schillebeeckx's theology, ideology functions within Catholicism along the lines of authority and obedience. The Church is surely the human embodiment of God's work on Earth, but its work is ultimately mediated by fallible humans whose own experiences are shaped by conscious and unconscious cultural assumptions. These experiences and assumptions are expressed in language – another human creation – which adds a further layer of ideological influence into the Church.

Although human beings might be fundamentally good and the Church proceeds with a mission to do good works and continue the work of Jesus on Earth, it must struggle with these concerns as natural obstacles to its attempts at grace. According to Thompson, "Schillebeeckx understands that human beings are co-constituted by their place in time and culture. Language and history are the framework that make knowledge possible."[22] Moreover, "Schillebeeckx understands all experience as interpreted experience, because the linguistic medium of encounter with the world signifies that human beings understand themselves and the world around them by participating in the creation of meaning."[23] The limitations of experience and language thus affect the Church's unconscious desires regarding human subjectivity and ecclesiology.

The effects of holding explicitly encoded teachings alongside unconsciously enacted ideological practices are thus sometimes a source of tension within the Church. Those who criticize the prevailing view are ideologically shaped, but so is the Magisterium. The role of the critically thinking theologian, or the person acting in emulation of him or her, is to question the ideological basis of the Church and oneself and, when appropriate, to dissent: "The critical aspect of theology implies the obligation to unmask ideological language and praxis in the Church's life ... [including the] manipulation, monopolization, and distortion of language by those in power to maintain that power over others."[24] As Catholic history shows, such a function is important in considering issues like slavery and religious freedom: "The Holy Spirit can be distorted by the manipulation of those in office or their negligence. The Magisterium can produce poorly formulated or one-sided doctrines that need correction in the context of wider Christian tradition."[25]

Issues of ideology are not only relevant to a discussion of the curricular content and perspectives that students bring to the religion course and to the Catholic school; they are also inherent in the methods and approaches to teaching and learning religion that teachers and students bring to the school, and in the expectations that other stakeholders in Catholic Education project upon it. If all persons are constituted by ideology and their social location,[26] then any subject's efforts to teach from a "neutral" perspective are themselves bound by the subject's own conscious and unconscious ideological conceptions of what neutrality and neutral values are, if they even exist at all. A Catholic teacher cannot make a neutral presentation of Catholicism, for example, without suppressing his or her own social location within that religion and making judgments about biases in other forms of Catholic thought, attitude, and practice. Neutrality is therefore a non-starter because it elides its own ideological grounding.

It is beyond the scope and expectation of this theory to resolve the theoretical and practical problems with neutrality, but two important prescriptions regarding neutrality can be made that are philosophically adequate insofar as they do not fall into the trap of believing neutrality is real or possible. The first prescription is that the teacher should not pretend that his or her personal attempt at a neutral pedagogical posture, or a professed belief in the neutrality of the school and its curriculum, can support a claim that he or she is not upholding the prevailing view and cover any bias the school has toward it. The prevailing view is, after all, a prevailing *biased* view that stands in relation with several similarly biased dissenting views.

The second prescription is therefore made to protect the personal religious freedom of the teacher and students in the situation of addressing and confronting ideology. The teacher who follows this theory should have some practically imaginative means of staying dispassionately detached from the issue of his or her own personal ideological grounding, in order to show a pedagogical openness to students that will not stifle their dissent for fear of contradicting the teacher. Students, after all, are placed in a situation of asymmetrical power relations within the school, but their opportunities to enhance their personal interests should not be suppressed by structured ideological intimidation from the office of the teacher. Similarly, teachers should be allowed to retain the appearance of detachment or at best a "committed impartiality" for the sake of being in control of their own personal professional safety and religious freedom *vis-à-vis* other stakeholders in the school, Church, and community.[27] For now, it suffices to assert that taking the steps toward troubling current claims to supposed neutrality with the aim of accommodating more dissent, and hence more utilitarian and ethical value in the presentation of religion, is required at this point in the history of Catholic Education.

6 RECASTING DICHOTOMIES AS HEALTHY TENSIONS

One of the most damaging outcomes of ideologically dependent thinking is that it can lead to perspectives on moral and political issues that depend upon strict adherence to value-laden binary thinking. The tensions listed above – public-private, political-personal, restrictive-permissive, masculine-feminine, and ordained-lay – are good examples of where dichotomies can become harmful when they reinforce distinctions according to the value of one side and the diminution of the other. Harm emerges when attempts are made to translate that evaluation into hierarchical social arrangements that maintain and reinforce structures of oppression. For example, if one were to evaluate the dichotomies listed above by ascribing preference to the first partner in each pair and subordinating the second, it could be seen that there is a greater value placed on the public political lives of "masculine" men who maintain regulatory control over the standards of morality and who might be ordained in the Church.

Other tensions in this field are no less susceptible to the same polarization: sacred-secular, Catholic Education–Catholic Schooling, doctrinal-pastoral,[28] and abstract-concrete can all be viewed in terms of the first partner in each pair being granted or representing the ideal of Catholic service and identity, and the second partner its less emphasized or less valued aspect.[29] Thus, in the rhetoric about Catholic identity in schools, one might find a bias toward a kind of school that eschews secular influence, aims primarily at the formation of students rather than simply "educating" them as a Christian social service, struggles to adapt to certain "secular" and non-Catholic influences without slipping into the language of "contamination" or "corruption," and chooses its curriculum in a manner that emphasizes formal, abstract lessons over the informal, concrete lessons of real life.

A rigid adherence to the current value distinctions in these and other dichotomies, in one way or another, maintains the prevailing structures that inspire pre- and post-conciliar dissent. Some perspectives suggest that since the prevailing view marginalizes women and non-heterosexual persons, the dichotomous tensions listed above should be blurred in the interests of justice; others suggest that the Church is too sympathetic with the mores of the modern world and should return to a greater emphasis on doctrinal rigour, devotion, and obedience to the hierarchy: views that would in fact harden and tighten these dichotomous distinctions. This theory therefore recognizes that dissent encompasses a wide spectrum of political views, and is not restricted to relatively "liberal" or democratizing post-conciliar elements. Dissent might be good for democracy and democracy might be good for education, but not even all the views that inform secular democratic societies agree with those assertions.

An educational atmosphere which hardens distinctions like those above will suffer for lack of social intercourse between competing

views. To promote the greatest variety of Catholic views, any pedagogical model should instead regard these distinctions as representative of the tensions that are inherent in the Catholic educational
institution and in Catholic life. The competing perspectives listed
above might only begin to describe what constitutes Catholicism,
Catholic thought, and Catholic practice in the world; but for the
heuristic purpose of considering how Catholicism translates into
an institution of public educational service, they illustrate a range of
competing views that compose the institution. A disposition to
(a) recognize these tensions as inherent within the institution, and
(b) recognize and predict the undesirable outcome should they fall
out of balance, is an essential part of maintaining any educative interpersonal relationship within Catholic schools.

In order to provide an educational service that is fairly inclusive of
all points of Catholic view, this theory proposes four imperatives for
optimizing their educative benefit. First, educators should recognize
the tensions listed above, among others, as inherently constituting the
institutional structure of Catholic educational service. Second, educators should examine the pedagogical utility and intrinsic moral implications of maintaining a balance between these tensions as central
aims of the formal objectives of their courses, in addition to the learning that results from students' exposure to the comprehensive experience of curriculum, administrative practices, social atmosphere, and
other experiences in the school. Third, the school should aim to max-
imize the amount of social interpenetration between the competing
views present within it, with the understanding that it is these views
which constitute Catholic community. If the community becomes
fragmented, the school risks the undesirable outcomes of group
polarization, misrepresentations of the Other, and the lost opportunities for bearers of divergent views within the same institution to learn
from each other by refining their currently held views in response to
challenges presented through communicative exposure to persuasive
argument, and possibly changing their minds as a result. The promotion of these experiences leads to the final aim, which is to promote
dissent's value for all persons, and not exclusively for the (albeit
sometimes warranted) vindication of self-interest; hence this theory
promotes the social accommodation of dissent in accord with an aim
to encourage an affective disposition to identify with dissenters in
general. It is with fidelity to the above four aims that this theory
considers dissent to be constitutive of the comprehensive school

atmosphere. Accordingly, those who would base their practice on this theory are bound to accommodate a high tolerance for reasonable intellectual ambiguity and a low need for administrative, curricular, and ecclesial closure regarding the tensions inherent in the school.

The need to identify with dissenters in general is more than simply a curricular aim for individual students to take away from the classroom. It is in fact central to applying dissent in the cultural reform of the school. Certain dissenting constituencies within the school, however, might not be interested in accommodating the dissent of others. A pre-conciliar dissenting perspective might wish to restore practices in the school to those of an era that would suppress or not even admit feminism and queer theory;[30] just the same, post-conciliar dissent might regard its views as following the natural evolution of the Church, and would thus censor pre-conciliar views as harmfully retrograde. In theory, each of these views could present reasons that the other should remain silent in the school – reasons that on the surface do not suggest an appreciation for the value of dissent *in general*. Any application of this theory will face the practical challenge of accommodating various dissenting stances that are mutually incommensurable and would suppress each other.

The proposal to allow such an apparently high degree of possibly incommensurable theological and philosophical latitude within the school might seem analogous to a proposal that disputing oligarchs and democrats resolve their problems democratically. From the perspective of a dissenting constituency that wishes to constrict the dissent of its competitors, attempts at accommodation and resolution beg the question and are non-starters. Similar criticisms might be made that this pedagogy undermines any illiberal dissenters who wish that they could supplant the prevailing liberally influenced institutional view and then abruptly begin to consolidate their hegemony by suppressing further dissent.

Such criticisms might be inescapable, as they ultimately descend from a standing critique of the liberal theoretical framework within which this pedagogy resides; but there are some counterarguments that can stand against them. The chief retort descends from utilitarian and ethical arguments that suggest allowances for a climate that includes more dissent in fact protects the whole society from errors brought on by epistemic narrowness. Should a restrictive party usurp control, it might succumb to internally propagated error and corruption and therefore require correction. If the usurping view restricts dissent, it leaves itself more vulnerable to rebellion as the only option for correcting error. Likewise, "group exit" would be the only option for those within the system who wish to avoid any error in the prevailing view.[31] Encouraging dissent generally preserves more available options, which in turn benefit students by affording a greater range of spiritual, psychological, and intellectual choice than do the current pedagogy and relatively more restrictive views. In addition, there is the possible benefit that follows from the explicit coordination of the formal academic curriculum with the informal socioecclesial curriculum/atmosphere in the school.

It is imperative that the application of this theory provide spiritual, theological, philosophical, psychological, institutional, and other sorts of intellectual breadth so as to overcome the frustration that the conventional technique of "deliberately suspending questions" perpetuates. As an attempt to ameliorate and perhaps preclude frustration, this pedagogy begins where "suspension" ends, and shows students a means of adjudication according to a variety of Catholic intellectual traditions. It should explicitly place them in a position where they can alleviate frustration by articulating their position within the range of institutional and local practice and scholarship within the Church. Rather than leaving the question of "what to believe" so ambiguously open that the student can only perceive the limited, binary choice of either defaulting back to the prevailing view or rejecting the Church entirely, this pedagogy enables students to identify their place amid the range of ideological assumptions they recognize within the universal and local Church.

7 RETHINKING CATHOLIC EDUCATIONAL SERVICE

Strong visions of Catholic Educational Service as Catholic *formation* show the mission of the School to be the provision of experiences in curriculum and school environment that develop students as Catholic persons who belong to the Church and express that membership through some conventional degree of devotion. In practice, what Catholic Educational Service provides is broader than that. The institution of Catholic Schooling is also known for providing educational experiences to students in places where no other service is available, to students of all religious backgrounds who deliberately choose the Catholic school over other options, and, inclusively, as a Christian service to all, regardless of their religious affiliation. As one example among many, in Canada and elsewhere there are many Muslim students who choose to attend Catholic schools for their perceived prestige, their occasional single-sex institutional housing, or their proximity to home. It might also be conjectured reasonably that the presence of a religious faith within the school, an explicitly stated respect for religious freedom, sympathy with religious belief, acknowledgment of the Abrahamic God, and understanding and acceptance of religious expression are also important for these students and their families.

The term "Catholic Education-Schooling," in addition to its rhetorical convenience for recognizing the occasional tension between formation and Christian social service, is perhaps most helpful for suggesting that the institutions of Catholic Educational Service appropriately represent and serve a diversity of aims within the many permutations of Catholic Education and Catholic Schooling. The mixture of these two general categories of aims and service in a single institution means that although a school, Catholic curriculum, or any Catholic teaching-learning relationship has a responsibility to present the prevailing view of the Church as part of its epistemic grounding, its responsibility for the spiritual formation of students in that view is limited to its role in partnership with the intentions of the student, the community, the family or home, and the Church. However, dissent should not be misinterpreted as a corrupter of or impediment to Catholic formation, or even as incompatible with it. To the contrary, dissent would imply a kind of Christian formation that respects but does not defer to the prevailing view. If dissent is imagined appropriately – congruent with Socratic citizenship and John Paul II's conception of solidarity – then it should aim toward an enhanced ecclesial citizenship that is no more or less "formed" than the prevailing kind: especially given that the question of formation according to *what* ideal remains contestable, and that the influence and responsibilities of the home and (parish and worldwide) Church must be remembered with respect to any decline in the faith.

With Catholic Education-Schooling in the position of coordinating distinct but interdependent aims within one institution, articulating a single role for the School becomes impractical beyond a certain point. For those students who attend the Catholic school intending to advance their formation in the prevailing view of the faith, it must be recognized that the school can only properly serve this aspect of their development to the extent that its mission will allow. Its share in this process cannot include or compensate for the work of the home and the Church, even if some students and their families may have dysfunctional relationships with the Church and their school may function as the closest experience that some students have to Catholic life. The school's existence depends on the Church, to be sure, but it also depends on the people it serves; and as it serves people in a much different manner than does the parish, it cannot repair any dysfunction within the hierarchical Church any more than a Catholic hospital, shelter for the homeless, or Third-World Mission could. Consequentially the school should not be handed the responsibility of rehabilitating students and their families to a declining Church. So since the intellectual concerns this theory supports represent issues already festering elsewhere within the same community that constitutes the school, it cannot be fairly asserted that the school's approach to dissent is the cause of any corruption within the Church, or is undermining its work. To the contrary, assuming such corruption or decline does exist or is perceived to exist, this theory aims to reach out intellectually to those who would otherwise leave the Church over a perceived lack of options.

In the context of an environment that embodies mixed intellectual aims, this theory assists the Church and home by providing the intellectual service that enhances the contribution that students can make in these spheres, and should also supplement the efforts of those parents and other persons who are trying to support concerned students. Where the home or parish possibly encounter intellectual limits when dealing with moral concerns, this theory provides the public intellectual criteria to continue that conversation without reducing its terms to a binary choice between outright acceptance and refusal of the Church.

Where the Church is experiencing a lapse in membership due to perceptions among its youth that its teaching is irrelevant to modern life, this pedagogy provides aid by giving students the intellectual means of discovering both the breadth of content in Catholic thinking and the skills by which to adjudicate that content. If Catholic society is struggling to overcome the problems that binary thinking poses, this approach offers an intellectual process through which students might ameliorate their relationship with the Church without feeling forced to abandon their concerns in order to accomplish that task. An educative experience based upon an intellectually, morally, and spiritually sound approach to dissent should enable individuals and the Church to achieve a much more comprehensive understanding of solidarity, and so not dismiss all dissent as a threat to the Church's unity and goodness.

Pedagogy of Dissent shifts the pedagogical focus from relaying the content of Catholic thought to emphasizing the process of Catholic thinking. To an outsider this shift might innocently resemble the seemingly trivial debates between traditionalists and progressivists who are inflexibly entrenched in habitual commitments to certain modes of teaching. Making this shift in the school and the religion classroom, however, can potentially have a profound impact upon the way in which Catholic identity is perceived. The school should recognize a variety of Catholic expressions and so expose students to the range of intellectual and practical experiences that constitute the processes of thinking and acting as a Catholic in the world; and across that range of available practices, students might be exposed to many kinds of dissent. Teaching methods should follow a Catholic theological (including ecclesiological, philosophical, and historical) norm for dissent, but should not prescribe its content – although the school should most certainly uphold a high academic standard and also proscribe any expressions of hate, disparagement, and so forth. The school's Catholic identity should then cease to rest exclusively upon a defence of the Magisterium and should become much less connected to and concerned about the content of *what* its students believe. It should rather be concerned with the intellectual manner in which students might choose to comport themselves as Catholics. From here it makes logical sense that an emphasis on *how* one is Catholic would be less likely to result in the kind of internally divided personal Catholicism that publicly defers to the Magisterium and keeps dissent a private matter. Certainly there are kinds of Catholicism that are known for their rigorous doctrinal discipline and allegiance to the papacy as the procedural hallmarks of faith, but these kinds only exist in addition to those which display a cautious respect for the pope and the Magisterium, ascribe more weight to a pastoral than legalistic interpretation and application of doctrine, and make dissent a publicly known affair so that all Catholics might learn from it.

8   POSSIBLE CRITICISMS OF THE MODEL

A model for the reform of Catholic Education cannot be without its detractors. The following are some issues which critics might have with this proposal as a legitimate approach to reforming Catholic Education. Some question the proposed pedagogy's conceptual foundation; others are based upon a view that perceives dissent as a legitimately erudite theological interest in the abstract, but certainly not something that should be applied to a program of education, where it would threaten to fracture the solidarity of an institutional Church and Catholic culture that is already perceived to be under siege by a world ignorant of and even hostile to religion. These criticisms are raised as a means of philosophical self-reflection so that this pedagogical theory can reinforce its legitimacy by responding to its detractors.

The first criticism is that dissent as a concept emphasizes cognitive criteria to a fault, because its ethical and utilitarian adequacy relies too heavily upon advanced knowledge that is beyond the capacity of many students and even some adults. In short, in order to dissent properly, one must have access to a complex and comprehensive body of knowledge and advanced reasoning skills that are characteristic of only an elite intellectual cohort. This problem potentially makes dissent an inappropriate means of responding to the injustices that a wide variety of persons experience, irrespective of cognitive ability. A young adolescent female student who believes herself discriminated against by the restriction of the Catholic priesthood to celibate men might not be able to match the cognitive level of the prevailing Magisterial arguments and meet their argumentative complexity point for point. Nor might that student be able to understand a comprehensive and nuanced concept like dissent. She might still be convinced of her position and its ethical validity; but to insist upon her argument being formulated according to the rules of dissent in its most precise form would be to distract the focus of her complaint and hinder it with formal concerns about a concept that is intimately related to it, but is at the moment only a secondary concern to the justice needs of its bearer.

A moral concern descends from this challenge. The dissent students bring to class should not be prematurely dismissed on the formal grounds that it is immature grumbling, not knowledgeable enough of the situation from which it dissents, and hence inadequate because it does not match dissent's formal ideal. The moral response to this issue is that fairness is something that should extend to all people, regardless of their ability to understand the ideals that govern it or even to function according to them. Civil and ecclesial laws no less govern and protect all persons in the same manner. Students' relative state of immaturity to an adult standard for dissent should not be misperceived as a permanent deficiency and should instead be understood as a normal, developmental part of their personhood.[32] Students who might be unable to grasp immediately the full intellectual significance of dissent's ideal state should have a more productive experience if they are exposed to it as both content to be learned in its own right and a concept or attitude that underlies a pedagogical approach to the entire curriculum. This moral argument leads to the pedagogical issue of nurturing student learning at a level that is appropriate to their cognitive and moral development. The lessons students learn from engagement with socio-moral problems in the Church should be ongoing, and it is well within the mission of the school to introduce the sort of moral and epistemic variety that encourages this intellectual growth. The requirements for dissent and accommodations of dissenting perspectives should therefore be scaled according to the cognitive abilities of the students processing these problems.

A second major criticism of this model is that it places too much responsibility for dissent upon the individual, and hence does not overcome the problem of privatization that dissenters within the prevailing view currently face. While it might be desirable to teach individuals the most adequate means of dissent, such lessons and the accommodating environment within the School do not overcome the political fragmentation that keeps dissenters' voices disorganized and unheard within the Church. As the prevailing view is already a well-established spiritual and administrative presence within the Church, dissenting views in the current ecclesial structure have difficulty making their presence felt in any formal manner because they are not encouraged. It therefore becomes the responsibility of individuals to bear the load of pushing forth dissent from the margins and, as such, to situate themselves both within and against a very large and powerful institution. This criticism holds that *Pedagogy of Dissent* might make individuals more articulate, thorough, and morally powerful dissenters, but it does nothing to overcome the institutional climate within the Church that resists any change brought upon by dissent, and that actively works to suppress and silence dissent. Where the Church successfully neutralizes dissent by isolating it into individual portions that it can easily conquer through privatizing and dismissing them as selfish or relativistic concerns, this criticism holds that *Pedagogy of Dissent* stops far too short of overcoming these practices and only makes the quality of what will inevitably be enfeebled more philosophically rigorous.

This criticism has some valid aspects that compel any pedagogical reform project to mark out its own scope within the school's mission and, in addition, to face the consequences that this demarcation brings. In its most limited way, this pedagogy is offered so that individuals might become aware of dissent's conceptual existence, the possibility of dissent, and the idea that the best dissent is expressed with the intent of improving the Church and everyone's place in it. The fear that dissent would be narrowed, individualized, and privatized is of course mitigated by the concurrent aim of having students appreciate the value of dissent for the good of all and for the good of the institutions in which they are situated; at their best, however, these aims only indirectly challenge the prevailing view within the Church, because they do not explicitly extend into any structured institutional embodiment beyond the mission of the school. The school might do a very good job of educating students who are able to dissent according to the conceptual criteria established in chapter 5, but as its mission is not to appropriate responsibility for problems that the parish, diocesan, or universal Church must address, there is only a limited role that the school can take in organizing any dissent.

However, this same observation also applies outside the Church to any school that is qualitatively distinct from its surroundings. A participatory democratic secular school, for example, might leave its graduating students bewildered if it does not pass them on to a similarly participatory organization and leaves them without any guidance for what next steps they ought to take in a society that is at best only a representational democracy. As the school is only one part of a student's total experience, no matter how important, it follows that an important consequence of enacting reform in one area of that experience is to consider its impact upon other contributors to that experience: For instance, might it be extended into these areas or resisted by them? These are important questions that ultimately require more examination in separate works.

A third criticism is that any reform of Catholic Education toward a consideration of dissent is impractical, given the current political nature of the Church. As the Magisterial Church already has a history and established practice of not favouring any dissent from theologians, clergy, religious, or lay persons, it seems highly unlikely that there would be a favourable response to adopting a practice of teaching and learning that publicly institutionalizes it. Perhaps the current obstacles toward its reception are the normal consequence of an ecclesial climate that has a history of underestimating and under-appreciating the value that dissent brings to an organization. Those who see Catholic schools as instruments of the "new evangelization" directed at places where Catholic practice is perceived to have deteriorated would likely see this theory as incompatible with John Paul II's call to "re-evangelize ... entire groups of the baptized [who] have lost a living sense of the faith, or even no longer consider themselves members of the Church, and live a life far removed from Christ and his Gospel."[33] These persons, according to this view, do not need more dissenting knowledge; they instead need to be rehabilitated to the Church's freeing message. Also, if John Allen's predictions are correct, in the Catholicism of the next fifty years internal theological questions regarding birth control, decentralizing the Church's distribution of power, female ordination, and recognizing the right to dissent "will largely be a dead letter, at least in terms of the potential to shape official Church teaching and practice. Under the impress of evangelical Catholicism," he continues, "the debate has been closed."[34] If these circumstances do not change regarding dissent's practicality in its own right, then options for a theory and practice of dissent in education look very bleak indeed.

I contend that this objection is based on misunderstandings about dissent's value as a contributor to life in the Church, coupled with an inability to distinguish between faithful dissent and outright rebellion. Ironically, attempts to re-invigorate the Church with confident evangelization seem to have the opposite effect – in some places, anyway. Church teachings on controversial issues are failing to persuade many young people who otherwise believe in the Trinitarian God, the Eucharist, and other core teachings. The net result is their disaffection and sometimes abandonment of the Church because of the way it speaks about women, non-heterosexuals, sexuality, and so forth. Moreover, there is also much misunderstanding about other controversial groups within the Church, including the Society of St Pius X, sedevacantists like the Society of St Pius V, and other preconciliar dissidents. Dissent is widespread but officially ignored. Differences of this sort need to be explored publicly to prevent an informal culture of misunderstanding and caricatures from prevailing. Since suppressing, ignoring, or making polite but insubstantial acknowledgments of dissent so as not to fracture "Church unity" seems to exacerbate extant internal differences to the point where Church members cannot communicate with each other, the challenge to preserve Church unity appears to rest on finding a new way of thinking about it. To address that challenge, this pedagogy attempts not to smooth over intra-ecclesial differences, but to learn to appreciate them. From the pragmatic view of teaching and learning, appreciation and knowledge of difference should be promoted as an important step toward ameliorating the conditions in which persons understand their Catholic heritage and the way in which they and others are Catholic.[35] To wit, following Rossiter, arguments between various vested interests will inevitably take second place to what students know they need: "No matter what view religious authorities might take on trying to limit the scope of a critical approach in religious education," he states, "nothing will stop the students from questioning; not to acknowledge their questions or trying to fob them off would be counterproductive."[36] It seems that following a method where the widest reasonable plurality within the Catholic conversation can be nurtured best serves the institutional good of Catholic Education and the whole Church.

A fourth objection is that dissent destroys the character of Catholic schools. It is the job of Catholic schools, this view suggests, to present a normative picture of Catholicism and to promote that picture as the acme of Catholic identity in contrast to the secular world. To challenge Catholic teachings on ordination and marriage, among other matters, would be to contaminate the foundational norms of those schools with worldly ideas that would corrupt their Catholicity and anticipate their decay into secular institutions.

There are two responses to this objection. The first is that it uses "Catholic identity" as a narrowly unproblematized end to justify the means of current practice. In that sense it places one view of Catholicism's distinctiveness from the secular world above the moral concerns of the faith's own members. Strangely, it suppresses the needs of those who participate in Catholic distinctiveness in order to emphasize an image of Catholicism's unsullied unity and permanence. The indignity of shutting off any means for publicly legitimating and expressing their concerns is added to the moral difficulties that dissenting persons and groups already experience. Given that on average approximately half the Catholic population of a (mixed-gender) school is female and a certain percentage non-heterosexual, it baffles one to understand exactly what sort of morally just Catholic identity is shared in common among all in the Catholic school. A Catholic means of genuinely and adequately addressing these moral concerns is certainly called for, and given these counter-objections it seems that "Catholic identity" also requires a major reform influenced by scholarship on dissent.

The second response to the objection that dissent destroys the character of the Catholic school stems from another side of the issue concerning what, precisely, constitutes Catholic identity. Quite the opposite of introducing secular ideas into the Catholic school, some dissent is in fact aimed at restoring a pre-conciliar picture of Catholic identity to the School – dissent that is representative of a view that the prevailing Catholicism and identity of the present-day Catholic School is already corrupted by the modern, secular world. If one believes that the Second Vatican Council compromised Catholicism, and that the Church is currently following a wayward path that is in too cozy a relationship with the modern world, has lost its focus on salvation, and has seen the quality of its sacraments decline, it follows from this dissenting perspective that the current Catholic identity of Catholic schools is already severely crippled and in need of repair. Given the validity of this restorative view as a dissenting position, it is therefore impossible to argue that *all* dissent erodes the Catholic identity of Catholic schools, when dissent of this variety suggests that Catholic identity in these schools has already been eroded and must be salvaged by a return to some version of pre-conciliar rigour.

The objection that dissent undermines Catholic identity is also mitigated (and possibly refuted) by an observation that there are multiple Catholic identities, some of which are also seemingly contending claimants for dominance as the prevailing view. The question that emerges from this observation is therefore what role, if any, the school has in representing this fact and serving the various constituencies that themselves embody these identities. This issue is also perhaps best attended to in a different study, but it seems from the course of this discussion that the notion of a single, universal, universalizable, and stable notion of Catholic identity is highly problematic at best. "Coexisting Catholic *identities*"[37] is probably a more accurate description of the socio-religious terrain in the Catholic Church and the Catholic population in Catholic Schools. It seems highly unlikely that a conceptually supported pedagogy of dissent can corrupt the Church simply by acknowledging this diversity, affording opportunities for improved expression by diverse groups, and articulating their importance to the religious and political institution of the whole Church.

CONCLUSION

Proposals for reform in Catholic Education are complex because they involve coordinating many of the same complexities that are part of secular educational institutions with the religious requirements of the Catholic Church and the culture of local Catholic communities. This theory maintains that rigorous thinking about the experiences of educational practice can greatly assist in the improvement of this interdependent relationship. Its historical, philosophical, and theological grounding provide sufficient evidence of its concern for the value of minority rights in general and of rigour as a faithful approach to the reform of Catholic Education. This proposal is advanced with the primary intent of providing the theoretical beginning from which one might improve the aims of Catholic Education; the secondary intent of improving individuals' notions of ecclesial agency in the Catholic Church; and, possibly, the tertiary intent of reconsidering the role of the School and the aims of Catholic Education within the ecclesial structure of the Church itself.

This pedagogical theory is not the final word on either dissent or the reform of Catholic Education. The issues of what constitutes Catholic critical thinking, and how Catholic Education should intersect with ecclesial citizenship, need further philosophical and theological work to imagine the possibilities in these areas and their consequences. The issue of what students' spiritual interests are and how they interact with their other, more secular interests might also merit a further empirical study of Catholic students' interactions with Catholicism. If this model is to influence the implementation of a new style of teaching and learning and a new curriculum that would reflect the approaches within that style, other theoretical and practical issues that are unimaginable at this time should arise and require studies of their own. I hope that this pedagogical model will influence theory and practice of Catholic Education everywhere, and that whatever its benefits and deficiencies are, they provide enough fodder for the continued conversation about the important practical and symbolic contributions that Catholic Education makes to the development of persons in society and to the development of a society that recognizes the importance of religion and dissent to the public good. I also hope that this model may serve as a case study or template for other concerns that might find dissent an attractive concept, whether they be religious, secular, educational, or non-educational interests.

Notes

1 The designation of a term for persons who are not exclusively
   heterosexual is problematic, and this act of naming is even more difficult
   when the author, like me, is exclusively heterosexual. Terms like homosexual, gay, lesbian, bisexual, transgendered, and queer (among others) have
   different denotations in general, and different connotations depending on
   the speaker and listener. A term like "homosexual" is too narrow, and
   some readers might question my substitution of the term "queer" in its
   place, given the politics of my own sexual standpoint. Hence I acknowledge the difficulties herein and have chosen "non-heterosexual" in an
   effort to be as inclusive as possible. Where other personal or corporate
   authors use particular terms such as "gay," "homosexual," or "queer"
   I will quote and follow their usage as it reflects their standpoint.
2 The prevailing usage in Catholic Church documents is "homosexual," as
   exemplified in the title of the Congregation for the Doctrine of the Faith's
   (CDF) 1986 *Letter to the Bishops of the Catholic Church on the Pastoral
   Care of Homosexual Persons.*
3 *Hall (Litigation Guardian of) v. Powers* [2002] O.J. 1803 (Ontario
   Superior Court of Justice).
4 There is currently controversy surrounding Pope Benedict XVI's reported
   belief in the infallibility of John Paul II's 1994 teaching that confirms the
   restriction of ordination to men. See Allen 2011 and McBrien 2011. Also
   see discussion on infallibility and dissent at note 133 in chapter 2.
5 For accounts of how Canadian Catholic Schools suffer from a lack of
   doctrinal rigour, see Collins 2003 and Kennedy 2002. Also see Cuneo's

1997 comprehensive scholarly account of what he terms "conservative" dissent in the contemporary North American Catholic Church.

6 Bibby 2009, 56.

7 Ibid., 57.

8 Bibby 2004, 18, 20.

9 Bibby 2002, 77.

10 Ibid., 77.

11 Pew Forum 2008, 18, 90, 92.

12 Pew Forum 2010.

13 Public Religion Research Institute 2011.

14 Ibid.

15 Jones and Dreweke 2011, 4.

16 Collins 2003.

17 SSPX 2011.

18 SSPV 2011, nos. 2 and 5–10.

19 Ibid., no. 19.

20 Ibid., no. 12.

21 The question of whether teachers dissent is irrelevant to this book, because its purpose is to propose and justify a theory that serves students and not teachers in Catholic Education. This theory is designed to help teachers, parents, administrators, clergy and religious, and so forth respond when students dissent. It is an abuse of their station for teachers to use it to promote *their* dissent.

22 Canadian education is a provincial and territorial responsibility, and so educational offerings depend on the conditions of each jurisdiction's entry into the national Confederation as well as its current politics. Catholic schools currently receive full government funding in Alberta, Ontario, and Saskatchewan, and in the Northwest, Nunavut, and Yukon Territories. Nunavut is unique among these jurisdictions because although the Nunavut Act (23.1.m.ii) allows for separate Roman Catholic and Protestant Schools, none are currently established there. The CCSTA (2011) obscures this fact when it notes that Nunavut's Catholic schools "receive no government funding," which in spite of itself is a true statement considering that in the current absence of *separate* Catholic schools no public funds are available there for any parochial, diocesan, or other Catholic schools. Catholic Schools receive partial funding (up to 50%) in British Columbia and Manitoba.

23 Feinberg 2006, xi, xiv.

24 Not all Canadian separate schools are Catholic schools. Section 93 of the Canadian Constitution allows for Catholic and Protestant dissenting

schools, depending on what the majority in a school district is. While they are relatively rare entities today, Protestant separate schools exist in some places where Catholics are the majority: for instance, St Albert Protestant Schools in Alberta, the Penetanguishene Protestant Separate School Board in Ontario, and Englefeld Protestant Separate School Division No. 132 in Saskatchewan.

25 Catholic Church 1983, nos. 804(§2), 805.
26 Firestone 1993, 17.

CHAPTER ONE

1 Moran 1968, 15.
2 Rossiter 2003 argues that Catholic Schools are subjected to a standard for transmission of values that other Catholic social agencies are not.
3 McCluskey 1968, 29, emphasis original.
4 Olson 2003; Congregation for Catholic Education (hereafter CCE) 1998, no. 6; CCE 1988, no. 67.
5 Issues can range from legal questions on the inclusion of non-Catholic students in Catholic schools (Donlevy 2008), to varying degree of enthusiasm on demands that Catholic schools help restore faith, Mass attendance, and a more stringent sexual morality and "pro-life"/"anti-abortion" attitude among the laity in response to a declining Church.
6 This caricature relies on a straw-person premise that indoctrination is compatible with Catholicism, which it is not. See "Declaration on Religious Liberty / Dignitatis Humanae" (DH), nos. 1, 10.
7 John Paul II 1993, no. 101.
8 See Bailin 2001.
9 The possibilities in this list are multiple given religion's synoptic scope. See Phenix 1964, chapter 19.
10 McDonough 2011 responds to this question.
11 Andrew Wright 2008, chapter 10, similarly prescribes the learning of how to rationally discuss and evaluate the competing truth claims that religions make as the object of study for a secular study of religions.
12 Wright 2008, 234.
13 Ibid., 237.
14 Catholic Church 1983, no. 1398.
15 Apostolicam Actuositatem (AA), no. 24.
16 "Declaration on Christian Education / Gravissimum Educationis" (GE), no. 3; cf. "Dogmatic Constitution on the Church / Lumen Gentium" (LG), no. 11.

17 Following Scheffler's distinction between teaching students: (a) *the fact* of religion, (b) *to be religious*, and (c) *how to be religious* (1960, 100–1).
18 O'Gara 1998, 105.
19 Moran 1968, 98–9.
20 Ibid., 100–1.
21 Ibid., 1968, 106.
22 Ibid., 107.
23 Ibid.

CHAPTER TWO

1 Miller 2007, 449.
2 John Paul II 1988, no. 1.
3 Ibid., no. 115.
4 Ibid., no. 94.
5 Congregation for the Clergy (hereafter CC) 1997, no. 120, citing the introduction to its 1971 edition.
6 Miller 2007, 450; cf. John Paul II 1988, no. 94.
7 CCE 2009, no. 17.
8 Catholic Church 1997, no. 5.
9 CC 1997, no. 67. The CC refers to "slow stages" in the process of evangelization, the first of which is "bearing witness" and "proclaiming the Gospel" (no. 48) to non-believers or to those nominal Christians who are indifferent to their faith (no. 49). This exposure precedes any acts of affective and spiritual conversion and initiation into faith.
10 CC 1997, no. 73; cf. no. 260.
11 Ibid., no. 73.
12 I intentionally use the word "learner" instead of Groome's word "student" to mean a person who is not necessarily institutionalized in school for his or her education. "Learner" is congruent with Catholic Education's aim to include schooling only within the broader context of a lifetime of Christian formation.
13 Groome 1996, 118.
14 Ibid., 116.
15 Ibid., 115.
16 CCE 1988, no. 67.
17 CC 1997, nos. 51, 73–6.
18 Adapted from Scheffler 1960, 100–1; cf. chapter 1 at note 17.
19 CC 1997, no. 184.
20 See Rymarz 2011.

21 D'Souza (2003) remarks that in the first half of the twentieth century there was much intellectual activity directed at a Catholic philosophy of education, but that in the period following the Second Vatican Council, activity in the field has dropped off substantially and has not experienced "anything close to a rejuvenation" (373). Groome 1998 is a very important recent exception to this claim; unfortunately, it has few contemporaries.

22 Catholic Church 1997, nos. 223, 362.

23 Ibid., no. 363.

24 Ibid., no. 1738.

25 Saskatoon Catholic Schools 2005, 1.

26 Groome 1996, 114.

27 Boyd 1980, 204; cf. Boyd 1989.

28 Groome 1996, 115. The Canadian Catholic School Trustees Association (hereafter CCSTA) 2002 describes how Catholic Schools "yearn for community" (29), and also states the imperative of Catholic Education to encourage in children "the constant will to make our money and power serve the purpose of Christ, [lest] money and power enslave us" (35).

29 CCE 1988, no. 1.

30 Ibid., no. 25.

31 CCE 1998, no. 7.

32 Ibid., no. 17.

33 Ibid., no. 11; 1988, no. 34; 1977, nos. 38–52. See also Miller 1997, 460.

34 CCE 1977, no. 35; Miller 2007, 462.

35 Jesus of Nazareth, the Christ and Son of God.

36 Pilarczyk 1998, 407; cf. CCE 1998, no. 9.

37 CCE 1988, no. 54.

38 CCE 1998, no. 1; cf. CC 1997, no. 20.

39 CCE 1988, no. 10.

40 Ibid., no. 13.

41 Ibid., no. 45.

42 Ibid., no. 45; cf. Miller 2007, 467.

43 CCE 1998, no. 6.

44 CCE 1988, no. 100.

45 Ontario Conference of Catholic Bishops 2002, 5–6.

46 Chapter 3 relates that story.

47 Miller 2007, 460. Cf. GE, no. 8, and CCE 1977, no. 29.

48 Catholic Church 1997, no. 1939.

49 Miller 2007, 467; cf. Benedict XVI 2005, no. 20.

50 Murphy 1992, 78.

51 Ibid., 77.

52 John Paul II 1987, nos. 20–3.

53 John Paul II 1993, no. 101; cf. John Paul II 1991, no. 46.

54 There have been numerous elected and non-elected Catholic leaders throughout history. For an example in recent Canadian history see McGowan 2008, 89–90.

55 John Paul II 1993, no. 84.

56 Ibid., no. 106.

57 Adapted from Miller 2007, 453ff.

58 Sullivan 1983, 24.

59 Pius XII 1950.

60 The Catholic usage of *ordinary* in the Magisterial and administrative sense refers to the office of a bishop, archbishop, or other prelate or prefect, including the pope as bishop of Rome and head of the Catholic Church in the world.

61 Papal encyclicals are "circulating" letters that the pope addresses to the Catholic people (usually through the episcopacy) on the subject of Catholic doctrine.

62 The Synod of Bishops is an advisory body to the pope. It was created during the Second Vatican Council, and is composed of representative bishops who meet only at the discretion of the pope, its president, to advise him on matters within the Church.

63 McBrien 1981, 68.

64 Pilarczyk 1986, 175.

65 Ibid., 175.

66 See Boyle 2000.

67 McBrien 1981. McBrien maintains a more stringent definition of doctrine, maintaining that it is any official pronouncement the Church makes. Teachings gain the status of doctrine when they are expressed by and with the official approval of "the pope, or a body of bishops in union with the pope" (75). McBrien then contrasts this first level of official Church teaching with the more solemn dogma. For McBrien, then, there is a progression of formal truthfulness from the wide variety of teachings to the more stringent set of doctrine and finally to dogma.

68 cf. 1 Cor. 11:23 and 15:3–5.

69 McBrien 1981, 68.

70 Sullivan 1996, 38.

71 Cf. LG.

72 McBrien 1981, 68. McBrien points to Rom. 12:6–8 and 1 Cor. 12:28–31 as early evidence for a dual Magisterium.

73 Ibid., 69.

74 Ibid.

75 There are too many early Christian heresies to provide an exhaustive list or description here. For reference, though, notable heresies include Arianism, Gnosticism, Docetism, Donatism, Manichaeism, Monophysitism, Nestorianism, and Pelagianism.

76 McBrien 1981, 69.

77 Aquinas 1956, 47 (*Quodlibet* III, Question 4, Article 1, Reply 3); also see Congar 1982.

78 Sullivan 1983, 24–5.

79 Dulles 1988, 102.

80 McBrien 1981, 69.

81 Catholic Church 1917, no. 107.

82 Pius X 1906, no. 8.

83 Nilson 2000, 401.

84 "Decree on the Apostolate of Lay People / *Apostolicam Actuositatem*" (AA), no. 2.

85 Nilson 2000, 401; cf. LG, no. 32, and AA, no. 25.

86 LG, no. 30.

87 Nilson 2000, 405; cf. Coriden 1998, 10.

88 O'Gara 1998, 119; cf. Crowe 1989, 371.

89 Crowe 1989, 373–4.

90 McCormick 1970, 676.

91 O'Gara 1998, 120.

92 Sullivan 1983, 25–6; cf. Sullivan 1996, 1.

93 McBrien 1981, 72.

94 Sullivan 1983, 29. Sullivan's position on the impracticality of a dual Magisterium echoes that of several other prominent theologians, and his notes point to several excellent articles that offer further discussion on this topic. See Brown 1978, 291, and McCormick 1979, 95. See also CDF 1990, 34, and Örsy 1987a, 481–5.

95 Örsy 1987a, 481–5.

96 Ibid., 483; cf. Schillebeeckx 1982, 15.

97 McBrien 1981, 68.

98 Schillebeeckx 1982, 16.

99 McBrien 1981, 72; cf. "Pastoral Constitution / *Gaudium et Spes*" (GS), nos. 4–10.

100 The roots of conflict are diverse and include differences in (disciplinary) styles of discourse; perspectives (pastoral, speculative, administrative); cultural context; epistemic issues like empiricism, idealism, realism; moral issues; and others.

101 McBrien 1981, 73.

102 See note 153 below regarding Aquinas.

   Marie-Joseph Lagrange's (1855–1938) advances in the use of the historical-critical method in biblical study aroused reservations and even rejections of his work by his Dominican superiors and Roman authorities. His commentary on *Genesis* has still not been published. His work nonetheless influenced several documents before, during, and after the Second Vatican Council, which affirmed the primacy of this method (Montagnes 2006, esp. vii–ix, 95–104, and 191).

   Henri de Lubac (1896–1991) saw the publication of his work on the relationship between nature and grace blocked in the 1950s by his Jesuit superiors, as it did not conform to the prevailing neo-scholastic paradigm of the day, and he was removed from his teaching duties at the theological faculty in Lyons. He was vindicated, however, when Pope John XXIII appointed him as *peritus* (advising theological expert) to Vatican II – his work influenced DV and GS – and John Paul II made him a cardinal in 1983 (Mettepeningen 2010, 95–8).

   Karl Rahner (1904–1984) might be considered one of Catholicism's most influential theologians of the twentieth century. His work, however, has attracted varied reception. His pre-conciliar writings on Mariology and concelebration were subjected to intense scrutiny and censorship, and sometimes blocked. His difficulties with Rome ended when John XXIII appointed him as *peritus* to Vatican II, and one finds Rahner's influence in its documents on biblical inspiration, the sacraments, the Church in the modern world, and salvation outside the Church (Dych 2000, 13).

   Yves Congar (1904–1995) faced censorship from 1947 for his writings on ecclesiology and ecumenism, and from 1954 was forbidden to teach. His difficulties ended in 1960 when John XXIII appointed him as a *peritus* at Vatican II, and his influence crosses many of its documents. John Paul II made him a cardinal in 1994 (Groppe 2004, 22–4, 26).

   John Courtney Murray (1904–1967) faced opposition in the preconciliar era for his writings justifying the separation of Church and State, and for his views on religious freedom. The Vatican censored his works throughout the 1950s; throughout this period Murray continued the practice of submitting his work to the Holy Office for review. He was invited to the second session of Vatican II, and is regarded as very influential in authoring DH (Alvis 2005).

103 GS, no. 16.

104 Ibid., no. 16.

105 DH, no. 3.

106 Ibid., no. 3.
107 Ibid., no. 14.
108 Ibid.
109 AA, no. 5.
110 LG, no. 36.
111 Curran 2004, 4.
112 Ibid., 5.
113 Hogan 2004, 82.
114 Fuchs 1987, 490, cited in Hogan 2004, 83; cf. DH, no. 3.
115 GS, no. 50.
116 Hogan 2004, 83; cf. Fuchs 1987, 490.
117 Hogan 2004, 83.
118 Ibid., 84.
119 Fuchs 1987, 439, in Hogan 2004, 84.
120 Ibid., 85.
121 Hogan 2004, 85.
122 Pius XI 1931, no. 79, in Pontifical Council for Justice and Peace 2005, no. 186.
123 DH, 5.
124 GE, 3.
125 Pontifical Council for Justice and Peace 2005, no. 187.
126 cf. LG, no. 36, and AA, no. 5.
127 Kaufman 1989, 6.
128 Ibid., 10, emphasis original.
129 Örsy 1987a, 490.
130 Coriden et al. 1985, 548, at no. 752.
131 O'Gara 1998, 112.
132 Tensions on how dissent is to be expressed are not limited to the (institutional) religious domain, and exist in fields such as politics and ethics. Medical ethics, for instance, must balance the rights of individuals (free investigation and expression – libertarian approaches), public policy (calculus of social costs and risks – utilitarian approaches), and matters of value (meanings that inform human living – deontological approaches).
133 So for example, regardless of whether Benedict XVI's reported beliefs on the infallibility of John Paul II's "*Ordinatio Sacerdotalis*" are correct, ordination continues to be restricted to males. Notice that there is a distinction between dissenting from accounts of Benedict's belief and dissent from the official pronouncements of John Paul's teaching. To date, Benedict has not issued any papal confirmation of this belief, which, according to McBrien's account (2011), has raised serious doubts within Catholic theological

circles. Should Benedict or a future pope explicitly confirm the infallibility
of John Paul's teaching, the educative response for dissident students
would thus expand to include a critique of the institution of papal
infallibility.

134 Dulles 1988, 100.

135 Ibid., 102.

136 Novak 1988, 120.

137 In secular philosophy the conceptions of "freedom" used here are
consonant with Isaiah Berlin's (1969) thought.

138 CDF 1990, no. 38.

139 National Catholic Conference 1968, 10.

140 Pastoral letter of 22 September 1967: in Dulles 1988, 108.

141 Levada 1986, 199.

142 Novak 1988, 113.

143 Dulles 1988, 109.

144 McCormick 1986, 267.

145 Principe 1987, 71.

146 Kaufman 1995, 23.

147 In 1866 the Holy Office, successor to the Inquisition and antecedent of the
CDF, affirmed: "Slavery itself, considered as such in its essential nature, is
not at all contrary to the natural and divine law, and there can be several
just titles of slavery" (in Kaufman 1995, 48).

148 Kaufman 1989, 48.

149 LG, nos. 27, 29.

150 Kaufman 1989, 24.

151 cf. Kinkead 1891, 126.

152 Principe 1987, 71.

153 Ibid., 72.

154 Kaufman 1989, 59.

155 Ibid., 60.

156 Örsy 1987a, 476.

157 Principe 1987, 70; cf. Pottmeyer 1998.

158 Principe 1987, 73.

159 Curran 1986, 375.

160 Ibid., 376; cf. this chapter note 102.

161 Örsy 1987a, 478.

162 Ibid., 478.

163 Schillebeeckx 1982, 10.

164 Curran 1986, 376.

165 Ibid., 376; CCCB 1968, no. 17.

166 Curran 1986, 376.
167 Ibid., 376; cf. chapter 3, note 65.
168 Curran 2006, 93.
169 Bibby 2009, 56–7. This finding contravenes HV's norm of reserving sexual intercourse for a married heterosexual couple (Paul VI 1968, no. 8).
170 Greeley 2004, 92.
171 Pius XI 1930, no. 56.
172 Ibid., no. 59.
173 Pius XII 1951.
174 Horgan 1972, 238; cf. Kaufman 1995, 45.
175 Kaufman 1995, 8; cf. *Council Daybook Vatican II, Session 3*, 203ff.
176 GS, nos. 50–1. The instruction in §51 directly cites *Casti Connubii.*
177 HV, no. 6.
178 Kaufman 1995, 102; Wills 2000, 74.
179 Greeley 2004, 34–5.
180 CCCB 1968, nos. 2–3.
181 Ibid., no. 17.
182 Ibid., no. 26.
183 Foy 1988, 7–8.
184 CCCB 2008, no. 19.
185 CC 1997, no. 185.

CHAPTER THREE

1 Walker 1955, 36.
2 Ibid., 17, 18.
3 Ibid., 22, 23.
4 Murphy 2001, 2.
5 Macdonell's influence came as a result of his military service, his "keeping Catholic settlers loyal," and his "stimulating the Scots to defend Canada during the War of 1812" (Walker 1964, 24). From 1830 he served in Upper Canada's Legislative Council.
6 Walker 1955, 27.
7 Ibid., 36–7.
8 Ibid., 37; Duncombe 1836, 50–1.
9 Sissons 1959, 14.
10 Ibid., 14.
11 Ibid., 18.
12 Walker 1955, 80.
13 Ibid., 82–3.

14 Walker 1964, 2.
15 Walker emphasizes the diversity among Protestants as well, most notably that "free Presbyterians, Methodists, and Baptists resented any supposed monopoly by the Church of England" (Walker 1955, 78).
16 Walker 1955, 78.
17 Nicolson 1984, 293–4.
18 Ibid., 294.
19 Walker 1955, 152.
20 Ibid., 163.
21 *Globe*, 8 June 1855, cited in Walker 1955, 167.
22 Walker 1955, 251.
23 Ibid., 250.
24 Ibid., 267.
25 Nicolson 1984, 296–7.
26 McGowan 1999, 119.
27 Ibid., 132.
28 Ibid., 137.
29 Ibid., 132.
30 Ibid., 134.
31 Saskatoon Catholic Schools 1994 articulates a means of integrating a Catholic approach to curriculum with the Saskatchewan government's cross-curricular "Common Essential Learnings": "Mathematics is an expression of the natural order; understanding and respecting the meaning of this order is part of students' learning intended to serve morality" (10). This orientation, however, does not presume distinctively Catholic subject matter or teaching methods.
32 See McGowan 1999, 134.
33 Ultramontane means "over the mountains," which in European Catholicism means looking "over the Alps" to the pope in Rome as one's principal authority. "In the nineteenth century," writes McGowan (2008), "ultra-montane Catholics looked to Rome for stability, order, sensibility, and moral authority in a quickly changing world of competing 'isms'" (93).
34 Ibid., 64–5.
35 Pius IX 1864.
36 Catholic Church 1870. Vatican I was also influential in bringing forth important dogmatic constitutions like the refutations of modern panthe-ism, materialism, and atheism. It also replied to assertions that faith and reason are in conflict, stating instead they are mutually supportive (*Oxford Dictionary of the Christian Church*).

37 McCarthy 1998, 49–55; cf. Bokenkotter 1977, 387–90. Also see chapter 2
    note 102 for the biographies of several influential thinkers in this era.
38 McCarthy 1998, 54–5.
39 Ibid., 52–3.
40 See Flannery 1996 for a compendium of Vatican II's core documents.
41 DH, nos. 3, 4.
42 DH, no. 6.
43 LG, no. 8.
44 Kinkead 1891, 126.
45 Council of Trent 1568, Session 7, canon 3.
46 Kinkead 1891, 126.
47 AA, nos. 5, 7, 9, 10.
48 DV, no. 22.
49 Ibid., nos. 8, 9.
50 Ibid., no. 12.
51 See *Sacrosanctum Concilium* nos. 21–45 for a comprehensive treatment of
    the changes made in Catholic liturgy.
52 Graham Haydon 1995 defines the difference between "thick" and "thin"
    in terms of the depth of particularistic cultural content. In terms of the
    moral differences that separate cultures, "thickness" is defined as being
    so "rooted in a particular cultural tradition" that it "could [not] properly
    be transmitted to all in a plural society" (54). "Thin" values are minimal
    expressions upon which all, regardless of cultural or religious
    commitments, might agree (153).
53 Sullivan 2002, esp. 83–4, provides an incisive summary of some of the
    more common controversies.
54 Baum 2005, 26–9.
55 Ibid., 18ff; see also 30, 105, 108.
56 Ibid., 25.
57 Ibid., 29.
58 Ibid., 31.
59 GS, no. 44, cited in Baum 2005, 30.
60 Baum 2005, 30.
61 Ibid., 31.
62 Ibid.
63 Ibid., 147–8. The overwhelmingly inadequate response to sexual abuse by
    clergy represents problems in the Church's culture of administrative
    practice, and so does not fit under the heading of doctrinal credibility
    problems that Baum uses here.

64 Allen 2009, 435.
65 Ibid., 243. This is a classic problem posed famously in Plato's *Euthyphro*: "Is the pious loved by the gods because it is pious, or is it pious because it is loved by the gods?" (1981, 10a)
66 Allen 2009, 81.
67 Ibid., 432–4.
68 Ibid., 433.
69 Ibid., 434.
70 Ibid., 450.
71 CCSTA 2002, 44.
72 See McDonough 2011 for an articulation of this problem in terms of what "ecclesial agency" it is assumed and expected Catholic students are to acquire.
73 Institute for Catholic Education 1998. The second edition of these expectations was released in 2011. The Institute's website states that "[a]fter extensive consultation with the Catholic community the seven overall and fifty-two specific expectations have been validated and remain unchanged." (Institute for Catholic Education 2011)
74 CCSTA 2002, 20.
75 Rymarz 2011 offers a detailed critique of this problem.
76 Murphy 2001, 3.
77 McLaughlin 1996, 147.
78 Ibid., 138.
79 Mulligan 2005, 12–23.
80 Ibid., 223–30.
81 The Magisterial Church has proposed more rigorous scholarly arguments against relativism. See John Paul II 1993, no. 101, and 1995, nos. 19–20. Also see Ratzinger's warnings about "the dictatorship of relativism" in his capacity as Dean of the College of Cardinals (2005), and as pope in his address to Canadian bishops regarding Catholic schools (Benedict XVI 2006, no. 4).
82 Mulligan 2005, 85.
83 Ibid., 71.
84 Lyotard 1984 is an influential philosophical text that uses the term "postmodern" to mean incredulity toward and deconstruction of the metanarratives of modernity.
85 Saul 1997, 129.
86 Ibid., 102.
87 Ibid., 131.
88 Mulligan 1999, 47.

89 Consider Said's 1978 postcolonial critique of racism, Butler's 1990 feminist and queer theory critiques of masculinist social structures, and Baudrillard's 1970 critiques of consumerism as some examples within the corpus of postmodernism that are directed at social justice issues.

90 Murphy 2001, 16.

91 Smith 2005, 210.

92 Ibid., 215.

93 Ibid., 212.

94 Olson 2003.

95 GE, no. 3.

96 See Mulligan's open letter to parents (2005, 330 and 1999, 103) in which he exhorts them to improve the state of "Catholic socialization" that today's youth experience.

97 Bibby 2002, 12, 18–20, 80–1; 1993, 4–6; and 1987, 16–21.

98 Murphy 1992, 86.

99 Carr et al. 1995, 162–3.

100 Sullivan 2002, 73–8; cf. McCarthy 1994, 76.

101 Joseph 2001, 12; cf. Elias 1999; Carr et al. 1995; and Langan 1978.

102 Halstead and McLaughlin 2005, 66; McLaughlin 1996, 138.

103 McLaughlin 1996, 138. Interestingly, Mulligan also refers to the indiscriminate use of terms like "gospel values" and "catholicity" that are used to justify the curriculum, administrative actions, and existence of Catholic schools as philosophically vacuous. See Mulligan 1999, 135–6.

104 McLaughlin 1996, 149–50.

105 See Wills 2000, chapter 12.

106 Saul 1997, 3.

107 Kymlicka 1995, 35.

CHAPTER FOUR

1 See Portelli 1996, 9–21.

2 DH, no. 4; cf. CCE 1988, no. 6, and Catholic Church 1983, no. 748(§2).

3 See CC 1997, no. 108, for example.

4 Boys 1989, 209; see also Boys 1984, 267.

5 Cox 1983, 135–6.

6 Moran 1968, 52, cf. 61. Moran's book bears the *Imprimatur* of Robert F. Joyce, Bishop of Burlington, Vermont, 13 February 1968.

7 CC 1997, nos. 157, 158, 167, 183.

8 Moran 1968, 44, cf. 140.

9 Groome 1998, 107–8.

10 Ibid., 438.

11 Rossiter 1988, 265.

12 Ibid., 273.

13 Ibid., 270.

14 Carson 2002, 558; LG, 40; cf. Warren 1988, 118ff, for a discussion of modern re-interpretations and recoveries of the term "spirituality."

15 Groome 1998, 325.

16 Carson 2002, 555.

17 Ibid., 560.

18 Ibid., 558.

19 Cox 1983, 53; cf. Warren 1988, 132.

20 Phenix 1964, 244.

21 Warren 1988, 118ff.

22 Ibid., 129.

23 Ibid., 132.

24 Ibid., 123; later (1988, 119) he discusses how it was Adolf Eichmann's indifference to human dignity and the suffering he oversaw which stands as one of history's greatest evils. See also the discussion of Eichmann in Brown 2005, 28, and Cohen 1964 in chapter 5 at note 26.

25 Rossiter 2003, 105.

26 Ibid., 106.

27 Ibid., 111.

28 Ibid., 108.

29 Ibid.

30 Moran 1968, 51.

31 CC 1997, no. 109.

32 Paul VI 1975, no. 63c, cited in CC 1997, no. 112. The CC follows a different version from the official English translation of *Evangelii Nuntiandi* on the Vatican website.

33 Adapted from a close reading of Cox 1983, 56. Cox's original model is of the problems faced by an individual teacher who has religious commitments, and it is ostensibly presented in the more generic terms of a secular school. Nonetheless, it still obtains within a religious school, especially since religious schools house students of many faiths besides the prevailing one, and even within any faith there are varying degrees of commitment through which a teacher must negotiate.

34 Crawford and Rossiter 1996, 139.

35 Ibid., 140.

36 Ibid., 139–40.

37 Boys 1984, 253.

38 Nuthall 2004, 275.
39 Boys 1984, 255; cf. Lee 1973, 17.
40 Little 1978, 18, cited in Boys 1984, 256.
41 CC 1997, no. 29; cf. no. 149.
42 McLuhan 1964, 23ff.
43 McDonough 2011 examines the impact that foundational assumptions about a Catholic school student's ecclesial agency have upon conceptions of that person as a current and future participant in the Church.
44 Boys 1984, 265.
45 Groome 1998, 202–3.
46 Groome 1980, 148–9.
47 Rossiter 2011, 66–7.
48 See also Moran 1979.
49 Moran 1968, 79.
50 Boys 1979, 196.
51 Neuner 1973, 364.
52 See McDonough 2011, 383.
53 Rossiter 1988, 265.
54 Crawford and Rossiter 1996.
55 Rossiter 2003, 128.
56 The GDC acknowledges that students are "participants and active subjects too of the educational process," and that their education takes place in cooperation with family and community (CC 1997, no. 259) as well as with the Church.
57 Rossiter 1988, 266.
58 Crawford and Rossiter 1996, 139.
59 Rossiter 2003, 11.

CHAPTER FIVE

1 A version of this chapter is published in the *Journal of Moral Education* (McDonough 2010).
2 O'Gara 1998, 113; cf. Örsy 1987b, 90–3.
3 Sarat 2005, 7.
4 Brown 2005, 24.
5 In Ober 1998, 48–9; cf. Walzer 1988 and 1987.
6 Sarat 2005, 2.
7 Wills 2002, 290.
8 Brown 2005, 27.
9 John Paul II [Wojtyla] 1979, 284–5.

10 Ibid., 286.

11 Ibid.

12 Ibid., 286–7, emphasis original.

13 Thompson 2003, 12.

14 Thiessen 1993, 130.

15 Ibid., 154.

16 O'Gara 1998, 162.

17 Ibid., 162.

18 Ibid., 166; cf. CDF 1973, 667–70.

19 Thompson 2003, 138.

20 Mill 1978, 4.

21 Carter 1998, 31.

22 Ober 1998, 4.

23 Ibid., 5.

24 Sarat 2005, 9.

25 Brown 2005, 27.

26 Ibid., 28. See Leonard Cohen's 1964 poem "All There Is to Know about Adolph Eichmann," which considers Eichmann's thoughtless acquiescence to the status quo and mechanical disregard for the dignity of human life. For Cohen, the shock of Eichmann's monstrosity is found in the stunning realization that an evil presence could reside behind such a banal and unremarkably benign appearance.

27 Platt 1971, 41.

28 Sunstein 2003, 7.

29 Sabine 1961, 714.

30 Ibid., 715.

31 Shiffrin 1999, xii, 77.

32 Ibid., xii.

33 Ibid., 77.

34 Saul 1997, 447.

35 Callan 1997, 28. The OED defines *heresy* as an "opinion profoundly at odds with what is generally accepted: the heresy of being uncommitted to the right political dogma." *Heresy's* etymology is interesting in the context of discussing epistemological diversity, as the origin of the modern term lies in the Greek word *haireomai*, meaning "to choose."

36 Callan 1997, 27.

37 Sunstein 2003, 24.

38 Ibid., 20.

39 Thompson 2003, 27.

40 Chesterton 1932, 257–8.

41 See Morris's (1966, 69–73) treatment of Jean-Paul Sartre's, Martin
   Buber's, and Gabriel Marcel's descriptions of subject-to-subject encounters
   which do not annihilate one's existential integrity. Morris's earlier sections
   on "Hell is Other People" and "Man and Society" (60–6) describe the
   annihilation of subjectivity, and so provide a helpful foil for intersubjective
   existentialism.
42 Sunstein 2003, 29.
43 Ibid., 86.
44 cf. Mill 1859, 7.
45 Sunstein 2003, 31.
46 Rawls 1993, xvi.
47 Curran 2006, 68.
48 Ibid., 81, 243.

CHAPTER SIX

1 See introduction for a description of participants.
2 DH, no. 5.
3 In *Republic* (1945, 508e), Plato maintains that knowing the good means
  that one will do good.
4 Dewey 1916, 41–2.
5 In McCormick 1995, ix.
6 Some Catholic school districts do not require that their teachers be
  Catholic but maintain a preferential hiring policy for those who profess
  the Catholic faith. "Faith-as-condition-of-employment" is therefore not
  absolute, and some non-Catholics teach in Catholic schools. Religion
  teachers are, with extremely rare exceptions, always Catholic, however.
7 In this case *curriculum* is used to mean the limits of programmed course
  content and methods in the Catholic school. Of course, given the theorized
  "seamless garment" of Catholicism, any course in Catholic religious study
  properly concerns the whole of ecclesial life; hence, what is *extracurricular*
  to the limits of the course nonetheless remains within the scope of
  Catholic Education.
8 Bennett and Rolheiser 2001, 98.
9 Catholic Church 1997, no. 2357; cited in CDF 2003, no. 4.
10 In November 2010 the Halton (Ontario) Catholic School Board voted to
   ban Gay-Straight Alliances in its schools on the grounds that these groups
   conflict with Catholic teachings on sexuality (*National Post*, 10 January
   2011). This policy was lifted shortly thereafter, following much-publicized
   criticism. According to the *Toronto Star* (16 February 2011) the Board

approved a replacement plan to allow "safety, inclusivity, diversity and equity" groups, "a policy that neither approves of nor bans gay-straight student groups" and omits any reference to sexual orientation in its title. There is no indication given that the GSAs were being organized for a direct challenge to Church teachings or to promote actions of which the Church would disapprove.

11 In some cases the allocation of resources even includes transportation and curricular time for the purposes of promoting Catholic teachings in public rallies (*Globe and Mail,* 13 May 2010).

12 See Jung and Coray 2001, for example.

13 McDonough 2011, 288–9.

14 Murphy 2001, 16; Rossiter 2011, 57. Rossiter argues that "a greater emphasis on critical, interpretive, and evaluative inquiry" is needed because "it is no longer adequate to aim exclusively at reproducing a traditional Catholic spirituality" (58). Rossiter observes that controversial matters like "women priests, new Christian interpretations of sexuality and contemporary interpretations of doctrines like original sin, atonement, salvation, the virgin birth, the immaculate conception, etc." would likely be excluded from formal inclusion on the grounds that they "would be likely to prove unacceptable to a number of clergy and bishops." At the same time, however, he remarks that dismissing these issues if students raise them is "counterproductive" (66).

15 Hunter and Potterton 2010, 6–8.

CHAPTER SEVEN

1 Educational psychologist Carl Bereiter warns that reduction of teaching and learning experiences to student self-expression subordinates cognitive objectives and renders teaching and learning ambiguous (2003, 286).

2 This utilitarian view of how to conduct organizational or interpersonal relationships is distinct from the question of whether one should evaluate Catholic moral questions according to deontological or consequentialist modes of thought. See the final paragraphs of section 4 in chapter 5.

3 Dewey 1916, 352.

4 Ibid., 126.

5 Ibid., 176.

6 Ibid., 176–7.

7 Ibid., 177.

8 Ibid., 178.

9 Ibid., 310, emphasis original.

10 Even those whom the Magisterium licenses to teach theology are ostensibly constrained from full-blown public dissent, although formal licensure is neither a necessary nor sufficient condition to ensure that one is validly doing academic theology or "thinking theologically."

11 Catholics cannot be differentiated along amateur-professional lines. Some have professional roles within the Church by way of vocation, but that fact does not qualify them as superlative "professional Catholics" relative to an inferior class of "amateur Catholics" in the realm of faith and sacramental relationship that all Catholics share. To maintain this distinction is as mistaken as considering oneself a "professional citizen" in secular life.

12 Thompson 2003, 135.

13 Ibid., 152.

14 McLuhan and Fiore 1967, 93.

15 McDonough 2008 articulates a parallel space for teachers to teach from the position of the theologian. The difference between the view in that article and what is proposed here is that the former is more specific in its scope and therefore its attestation to allow the teacher to follow the student's interests. That article argues for the legitimacy of freeing teachers from perceived stances of "indoctrinator" or "equivocator" in order to sit in the place of an imagined dispassionate theologian who can follow student interests more freely.

16 Kohlberg 1984, 174–6.

17 This claim is based solely on an observation of the *structural* parallels between Kohlberg's stages 4 and 6 on the one hand, and a construction of human institutional law and divine law on the other. Very importantly, this claim is limited to this description of parallels in terms of the formal aspects of justice reasoning. Namely, to appeal to the institution of Catholic law for its own sake has formal similarity with appealing to civil law for the same reason. Kohlberg describes the reasoning patterns which makes these appeals (i.e. "for their own sake") as stage 4. A similar formal similarity exists between appeal to divine law and stage 6's appeal to principles of justice. Past these formal similarities, this claim does not assert further similarity between Kohlberg's stage 6 and divine law, nor does it deny criticisms of Kohlberg's body of work.

18 Althusser 1971, 168.

19 Ibid., 132–3, 155.

20 Mill 1978, 4.

21 Althusser 1971, 170, 175.

22 Thompson 2003, 27.

23 Ibid., 28–9.

24 Ibid., 138.

25 Ibid., 129.

26 Boyd 1998.

27 See Kelly 1986 for an argument that "committed impartiality" is a legitimate and preferable role for teachers to adopt in discussing controversial issues.

28 "Doctrinal" here refers to the legalistic emphasis and priority on following written Church teaching, while "pastoral" refers to placing emphasis on the care of persons' spiritual, psychological, and physiological well-being. The limitation of polarizing these terms is evident in the fact that all pastoral action is based on good doctrine (and good interpretations of doctrine), and likewise pastoral experience informs the creation and revision of doctrine. In thought and practice, polarization occurs when this interdependent distinction breaks apart because one side is being privileged at the other's expense.

29 Baum 2005 observes the pre-conciliar Church's tendency to emphasize salvation-grace over social justice teachings: a dichotomy which depended on a mirroring value distinction that attached the former exclusively to the Church, and the latter to the whole World (35–7).

30 This use of *queer* is established in social science theory. See Walter 2004.

31 Sunstein's 2003 discussion of cascades and group polarization significantly informs this response (113, 131).

32 Following the line of thought in Dewey 1916, 42.

33 John Paul II 1990, no. 33; cf. CC 1997, no. 58c.

34 Allen 2009, 439.

35 Rossiter 2011 maintains that "good access to one's historical religious tradition is not only a birthright, but a spiritual resource that serves as a starting point in a lifelong search for meaning, purpose, and value in life" (58; cf. 61).

36 Rossiter 2011, 66.

37 See Jordan 2003, 110, note 1.

Works Cited

Allen, John L. 2009. *The Future Church: How Ten Trends Are Revolutionizing The Catholic Church.* Toronto, ON: Doubleday.
– 9 May 2011. "A Long Simmering Tension over 'Creeping Infallibility.'" *National Catholic Reporter.* http://ncronline.org/news/vatican/long-simmering-tension-over-creeping-infallibility. Accessed 27 March 2012.
Althusser, Louis. 1971. *Lenin and Philosophy, and Other Essays.* Translated by Ben Brewster. New York, NY: Monthly Review Press.
Alvis, Robert E. 2005. "Murray, John Courtney." *The Dictionary of Modern American Philosophers.* Thoemmes Continuum 9 March 2012. http://www.oxfordreference.com/views/ENTRY.html?subview=Main& entry=t308.e712. Accessed 27 March 2012.
Aquinas, St Thomas. 1956. *Quaestiones Quodlibetales.* Edited by Raymundi Spiazzi. Torino, Italy: Marietti.
Bailin, Sharon. 2001. "Critical and Creative Thinking." In *Philosophy of Education: Introductory Readings, Third Edition,* edited by William Hare and John P. Portelli, 167–76. Calgary, AB: Detselig Press.
Baudrillard, Jean. (1970) 1998. *The Consumer Society: Myths and Structures.* London, England: Sage.
Baum, Gregory. 2005. *Amazing Church: A Catholic Theologian Remembers a Half-Century of Change.* Maryknoll, NY: Orbis.
Benedict XVI. 2005. "*Deus Caritas Est* / God Is Love." http://www. vatican.va/holy_father/benedict_xvi/encyclicals/documents/ hf_ben-xvi_enc_20051225_deus-caritas-est_en.html. Accessed 27 March 2012.
– 2006. "Address of His Holiness Benedict XVI to the Bishops of the Episcopal Conference of Canada-Ontario on Their 'Ad Limina' Visit." http://www.vatican.va/holy_father/benedict_xvi/speeches/2006/

september/documents/hf_ben-xvi_spe_20060908_canada-ontario_
en.html. Accessed 27 March 2012.

Bennett, Barrie B., and Carol Rolheiser. 2001. *Beyond Monet: The Artful Science of Instructional Integration*. Toronto, ON: Bookation.

Bereiter, Carl. 2002. *Education and Mind in the Knowledge Age*. Mahwah, NJ: Lawrence Erlbaum Associates.

Berlin, Isaiah. 1969. *Four Essays on Liberty*. New York, NY: Oxford University Press.

Bibby, Reginald W. 1987. *Fragmented Gods: The Poverty and Potential of Religion in Canada*. Toronto, ON: Irwin Publishing.

– 1993. *Unknown Gods: The Ongoing Story of Religion in Canada*. Toronto, ON: Stoddart Publishing.

– 2002. *Restless Gods: The Renaissance of Religion in Canada*. Toronto, ON: Stoddart Publishing.

– 2004. *Restless Churches: How Canada's Churches Can Contribute to the Emerging Religious Renaissance*. Toronto, ON: Novalis.

– 2009. *The Emerging Millennials: How Canada's Newest Generation is Responding to Change and Choice*. Lethbridge, AB: Project Canada Books.

Bokenkotter, Thomas S. 1977. *A Concise History of the Catholic Church*. Garden City, NY: Doubleday & Company, Inc.

Boyd, Dwight R. 1980. "The Rawls Connection." In *Moral Development, Moral Education, and Kohlberg: Basic Issues in Philosophy, Psychology, Religion, and Education*, edited by Brenda Munsey, 185–213. Birmingham, AL: Religious Education Press.

– 1989. "The Character of Moral Development." In *Moral Development and Character Education: A Dialogue*, edited by Larry Nucci, 95–123. Berkeley, CA: McCutchan Publishing Corporation.

– 1998. "The Place of Locating Oneself(ves)/Myself(ves) in Doing Philosophy of Education." In *Philosophy of Education 1997*, edited by Susan Laird, 1–19. Urbana, IL: Philosophy of Education Society.

Boyle, John P. 2000. "The Teaching Office of the Church." In *The Gift of the Church: A Textbook on Ecclesiology*, edited by Peter C. Phan, 355–71. Collegeville, MN: Liturgical Press.

Boys, Mary C. 1979. "Religious Education and Contemporary Biblical Scholarship." *Religious Education* 74 (2): 182–97.

– 1984. "Teaching: The Heart of Religious Education." *Religious Education* 79 (2): 252–72.

– 1989. *Educating in Faith: Maps and Visions*. San Francisco, CA: Harper and Row.

Brown, Raymond E. 1978. "The Dilemma of the Magisterium vs. the Theologians: Debunking Some Fictions." *Chicago Studies* 17 (2): 282–99.

Brown, Wendy. 2005. "Political Idealization and Its Discontents." In *Dissent in Dangerous Times*, edited by Austin Sarat, 23–45. Ann Arbor, MI: The University of Michigan Press.

Butler, Judith. 2006. *Gender Trouble: Feminism and the Subversion of Identity*. New York, NY: Routledge.

Callan, Eamonn. 1997. Creating *Citizens: Political Education and Liberal Democracy*. New York, NY: Clarendon Press.

Canadian Catholic School Trustees Association. 2002. *Build Bethlehem Everywhere*. Nepean, ON.

– 2011. "Toonies for Tuition." http://ccsta.ca/content.php?doc=4. Accessed 1 May 2012.

Canadian Conference of Catholic Bishops. 1991. "Statement on the Encyclical *Humanae vitae* ['The Winnipeg Statement']." In *Love Kindness: The Social Teaching of the Canadian Catholic Bishops (1958–1989) – A Second Collection*, edited by Edward F. Sheridan, 142–9. Sherbrooke, QC: Editions Paulines.

– 2008. "Liberating potential." http://www.cccb.ca/site/images/stories/pdf/humanae_vitae_en.pdf. Accessed 27 March 2012.

Carr, David, John Haldane, Terence McLaughlin, and Richard Pring. 1995. "Return to the Crossroads: Maritain Fifty Years On." *British Journal of Educational Studies* 43 (2): 162–78.

Carson, D.A. 2002. *The Gagging of God: Christianity Confronts Pluralism*. Grand Rapids, MI: Zondervan.

Carter, Stephen L. 1998. *The Dissent of the Governed: A Meditation on Law, Religion, and Loyalty*. Cambridge, MA: Harvard University Press.

Catholic Church. 1983. *The Code of Canon Law in English Translation*. London, England: Collins Liturgical Publications.

– 1997. *Catechism of the Catholic Church*. http://www.vatican.va/archive/ENG0015/_index.htm. Accessed 27 March 2012.

– 2001. *The 1917 or Pio-Benedictine Code of Canon Law: In English Translation with Extensive Scholarly Apparatus*. Translated and edited by Edward N. Peters. San Francisco, CA: Ignatius Press.

– 2005. "*Pastor Aeternus* / Dogmatic Constitution of the Church of Christ." In *Primary Source Readings in Catholic Church History*, edited by Robert Feduccia and Nick Wagner, 144–9. Winona, MN: Saint Mary's Press.

Chesterton, Gilbert K. 1932. *Chaucer*. New York, NY: Farrar & Rinehart.

Cohen, Leonard. 1993. "All There is to Know about Adolph Eichmann."
    In *Stranger Music*, 53. Toronto, ON: McLelland & Stewart Ltd.
Collins, Lorene. 2003. *Salvation Redefined: Catholic Parents and Religious
    Education in Post–Vatican II Canada.* Toronto, ON: Life Ethics
    Information Centre.
Congar, Yves. 1982. "A Semantic History of the Term *Magisterium.*" In
    The Magisterium and Morality, edited by Charles Curran and Richard
    McCormick, 297–313. New York, NY: Paulist Press.
Congregation for Catholic Education. 1977. "The Catholic School."
    http://www.vatican.va/roman_curia/congregations/ccatheduc/
    documents/rc_con_ccatheduc_doc_19770319_catholic-school_en.html.
    Accessed 28 March 2012.
– 1988. "The Religious Dimension of Education in a Catholic School."
    Origins 18: 213–28.
– 1998. "The Catholic School on the Threshold of the Third Millennium."
    Origins 28: 409–12.
– 2009. "Circular Letter to the Presidents of Bishops' Conferences on
    Religious Education in Schools." http://www.vatican.va/roman_curia/
    congregations/ccatheduc/documents/rc_con_ccatheduc_doc_20090505_
    circ-insegn-relig_en.html. Accessed 28 March 2012.
Congregation for the Clergy. 1971. General Catechetical Directory.
    http://www.vatican.va/roman_curia/congregations/cclergy/documents/
    rc_con_cclergy_doc_11041971_gcat_en.html. Accessed 28 March 2012.
– 1997. "General Directory for Catechesis." http://www.vatican.va/
    roman_curia/congregations/cclergy/documents/rc_con_ccatheduc_doc_
    17041998_directory-for-catechesis_en.html. Accessed 28 March 2012.
Congregation for the Doctrine of the Faith. 1973. "*Mysterium Ecclesiae /
    Declaration in Defence of the Catholic Doctrine on the Church Against
    Certain Errors of the Present Day.*" *The Tablet* 227: 667–70.
– 1986. "Letter to the Bishops of the Catholic Church on the Pastoral
    Care of Homosexual Persons." http://www.vatican.va/roman_curia/
    congregations/cfaith/documents/rc_con_cfaith_doc_19861001_
    homosexual-persons_en.html. Accessed 28 March 2012.
– 1990. "Instruction on the Ecclesial Vocation of the Theologian."
    http://www.vatican.va/roman_curia/congregations/cfaith/documents/
    rc_con_cfaith_doc_19900524_theologian-vocation_en.html. Accessed
    28 March 2012.
– 2003. "Considerations Regarding Proposals to Give Legal Recognition
    to Unions Between Homosexual Persons." http://www.vatican.va/
    roman_curia/congregations/cfaith/documents/rc_con_cfaith_

doc_20030731_homosexual-unions_en.html#fnref4. Accessed 28 March 2012.

Coriden, James A. 1998. "Church Authority in American Culture: Cases and Observations." Privately published paper prepared for meeting of the Common Ground Initiative.

Coriden, James A., Thomas J. Green, and Donald Heintschel, eds. 1985. *The Code of Canon Law: A Text and Commentary.* New York, NY: Paulist Press.

Council Daybook Vatican II, Session 3. 1965. Washington, DC: National Catholic Welfare Conference.

Council of Trent. (1568) 1978. *The Canons and Decrees of the Council of Trent,* translated by Henry J. Schroeder. Rockford, IL: Tan Books.

Cox, Edwin. 1983. *Problems and Possibilities for Religious Education.* Toronto, ON: Hodder and Stoughton.

Crawford, Marisa L., and Graham M. Rossiter. 1996. "The Secular Spirituality of Youth: Implications for Religious Education." *British Journal of Religious Education* 18 (3): 133–43.

Crowe, Frederick E. 1989. "The Church as Learner: Two Crises, One Kairos." In *Appropriating the Lonergan Idea,* edited by Michael Vertin, 370–84. Washington, DC: The Catholic University of America Press.

Cuneo, Michael W. 1997. *The Smoke of Satan: Conservative and Traditionalist Dissent in Contemporary American Catholicism.* Toronto, ON: Oxford University Press.

Curran, Charles E. 1986. "Authority and Dissent in the Church." *Origins* 16: 375–6.

– 2004. "Conscience in the Light of Catholic Moral Tradition." In *Conscience,* edited by Charles E. Curran, 3–24. Mahwah, NJ: Paulist Press.

– 2006. *Loyal Dissent: Memoir of a Catholic Theologian.* Washington, DC: Georgetown University Press.

Dewey, John. (1916) 1968. *Democracy and Education.* Toronto, ON: Collier-Macmillan.

Donlevy, J. Kent. 2008. "The Common Good: The Inclusion of Non-Catholic Students in Catholic Schools." *Journal of Beliefs and Values* 29 (2): 161–71.

D'Souza, Mario O. 2003. "Some Reflections on Contemporary Canadian Catholic Education." *Interchange* 34 (4): 363–81.

Dulles, Avery. 1988. "Authority and Conscience." In *Dissent in the Church,* edited by Charles E. Curran and Richard A. McCormick, 97–111. Mahwah, NJ: Paulist Press.

Duncombe, Charles. 1836. "Report on the Subject of Education,"
    submitted to the Upper Canada House of Assembly. Toronto, ON.
Dych, William V. 2000. *Karl Rahner*. London, England: Continuum.
Elias, John L. 1999. "Whatever Happened to Catholic Philosophy of
    Education?" *Religious Education* 94 (1): 92–101.
Feinberg, Walter. 2006. *For Goodness Sake: Religious Schools and
    Education for Democratic Citizenry*. New York, NY: Routledge.
Firestone, William A. 1993. "Alternative Arguments for Generalizing
    from Data as Applied to Qualitative Research." *Educational Researcher*
    22 (4): 16–23.
Flannery, Austin, ed. 1996. *Vatican Council II: The Basic Sixteen
    Documents*. Northport, NY: Costello Publishing Co.
Foy, Vincent. 1988. "Tragedy at Winnipeg." http://www.lifesitenews.com/
    ldn/2004_docs/tragedyatwinnipeg.pdf. Accessed 28 March 2012.
Fuchs, Josef. 1987. "A Harmonization of the Conciliar Statements on
    Christian Moral Theology." In *Vatican II: Assessment and Perspectives:
    Twenty-Five Years After (1962-1987), Volume 2*, edited by René
    Latourelle, 479–500. Mahwah, NJ: Paulist Press.
Freire, Paulo. 1970. *Pedagogy of the Oppressed*. Translated by Myra
    Bergman Ramos. New York, NY: Herder & Herder.
Globe and Mail. 13 May 2010. "Anti-Abortion Activists Praise Harper's
    Maternal-Health Stand." http://www.theglobeandmail.com/news/
    politics/anti-abortion-activists-praise-harpers-maternal-health-stand/
    article1568191/. Accessed 28 March 2012.
Government of Canada. (1993) 2012. Nunavut Act. http://laws-lois.justice.
    gc.ca/PDF/N-28.6.pdf. Accessed 1 May 2012.
Greeley, Andrew M. 2004. *The Catholic Revolution: New Wine, Old
    Wineskins, and the Second Vatican Council*. Los Angeles, CA: University
    of California Press.
Groome, Thomas H. 1980. *Christian Religious Education: Sharing Our
    Story and Vision*. New York: Harper and Row.
– 1996. "What Makes a School Catholic?" In *The Contemporary
    Catholic School: Context, Identity, and Diversity*, edited by Terence H.
    McLaughlin, Joseph O'Keefe, and Bernadette O'Keefe, 107–12.
    London, England: The Falmer Press.
– 1998. *Educating for Life: A Spiritual Vision for Every Teacher and
    Parent*. New York, NY: Crossroad.
Groppe, Elizabeth T. 2004. *Yves Congar's Theology of the Holy Spirit*.
    New York, NY: Oxford University Press.
Haldane, John. 1996. "Catholic Education and Catholic Identity." In *The
    Contemporary Catholic School: Context, Identity, and Diversity*, edited

by Terence H. McLaughlin, Joseph O'Keefe, and Bernadette O'Keefe, 126–35. London, England: The Falmer Press.

Halstead, J. Mark, and Terence H. McLaughlin. 2005. "Are Faith Schools Divisive?" In *Faith Schools: Consensus.or Conflict?* edited by Roy Gardner, Denis Lawton, and Jo Cairns, 61–72. London: Routledge-Falmer.

Haydon, Graham. 1995. "Thick or Thin? The Cognitive Content of Moral Education in a Plural Democracy." *Journal of Moral Education* 24 (1): 53–64.

Hogan, Linda. 2004. "Conscience in the Documents of Vatican II." In *Conscience*, edited by Charles E. Curran, 82–8. Mahwah, NJ: Paulist Press.

Horgan, John, ed. 1972. *"Humanae Vitae" and the Bishops: The Encyclical and the Statements of the National Hierarchies.* Shannon, Ireland: Irish University Press.

Hunter, Peter, and Mark Potterton. 2010. "Church Teaching and the Catholic School Leaver." *International Studies in Catholic Education* 2 (1): 3–18.

Institute for Catholic Education. 1998. *Ontario Catholic School Graduate Expectations.* http://www.occb.on.ca/ice/online_docs/Graduate%20 Expectations.pdf. Accessed 25 April 2007.

– 2011. *Ontario Catholic School Graduate Expectations.* http://www. iceont.ca/page13015019.aspx. Accessed 28 March 2012.

John Paul II [Wojtyla, Karol]. 1979. *The Acting Person.* Translated by Andrzej Potocki. Boston, MA: D. Reidel.

– 1987. *"Sollicitudo Rei Socialis /* On Social Concern." http://www. vatican.va/holy_father/john_paul_ii/encyclicals/documents/hf_ jpii_enc_30121987_sollicitudo-rei-socialis_en.html. Accessed 28 March2012.

– 1988. *"Pastor Bonus /* The Good Shepherd." http://www.vatican.va/ holy_father/john_paul_ii/apost_constitutions/documents/hf_jp-ii_apc_ 19880628_pastor-bonus-index_en.html. Accessed 28 March 2012.

– 1990. *"Redemptoris Missio /* On the Permanent Validity of the Church's Missionary Mandate." http://www.vatican.va/holy_father/john_paul_ii/ encyclicals/documents/hf_jp-ii_enc_07121990_redemptoris-missio_ en.html. Accessed 28 March 2012.

– 1991. *"Centesimus Annus /* On the One Hundredth Anniversary of Pope Leo XIII's 'Rerum Novarum – On Capital and Labor; On Catholic Social Teaching.'" http://www.vatican.va/holy_father/john_paul_ii/ encyclicals/documents/hf_jp-ii_enc_01051991_centesimus-annus_ en.html.

– 1993. "*Veritatis Splendor* / The Splendor of Truth." http://www.vatican.
va/holy_father/john_paul_ii/encyclicals/documents/hf_jp-ii_enc_
06081993_veritatis-splendor_en.html. Accessed 28 March 2012.

Jones, Rachel K., and Joerg Dreweke. 2011. "Countering Conventional
Wisdom: New Evidence on Religion and Contraceptive Use."
New York, NY: Guttmacher Institute. http://www.guttmacher.org/pubs/
Religion-and-Contraceptive-Use.pdf. Accessed 28 March 2012.

Jordan, Mark D. 2003. *Telling Truths in Church: Scandal, Flesh, and
Christian Speech*. Boston, MA: Beacon Press.

Joseph, Ellis A. 2001. "The Philosophy of Catholic Education." In
Handbook of Research on Catholic Education, edited by Thomas C.
Hunt, Ellis A. Joseph, and Ronald Nuzzi, 27–64. Westport, CT:
Greenwood Press.

Jung, Patricia Beattie, and Andrew Coray, eds. 2001. *Sexual Diversity and
Catholicism: Toward the Development of Moral Theology*. Collegeville,
MN: The Liturgical Press.

Kaufman, Philip S. 1989. *Why You Can Disagree and Remain a Faithful
Catholic*. New York, NY: Crossroad Publishing Company.

– 1995. *Why You Can Disagree and Remain a Faithful Catholic: New
Expanded and Revised Edition*. New York, NY: Crossroad Publishing
Company.

Kelly, Thomas E. 1986. "Discussing Controversial Issues: Four Perspectives
on the Teacher's Role." *Theory and Research in Social Education* 14 (2):
113–38.

Kennedy, Leonard A. 2002. *The Catholic School in an Age of Dissent*.
Toronto, ON: Life Ethics Information Centre.

Kinkead, Thomas L. (1891) 1921. *An Explanation of the Baltimore
Catechism of Christian Doctrine*. New York, NY: Benzinger.

Kohlberg, Lawrence. 1984. *Essays on Moral Development: Volume II:
The Psychology of Moral Development*. San Francisco, CA: Harper
and Row.

Kymlicka, Will. 1995. *Multicultural Citizenship: A Liberal Theory of
Minority Rights*. Oxford, England: Oxford University Press.

Langan, Thomas. 1978. "Is a Catholic Philosophy Department Possible?"
Occasional Papers on Catholic Higher Education 4 (1): 12–17.

Lee, James M. 1973. *The Flow of Religious Instruction*. Birmingham, AL:
Religious Education Press.

Leo XIII. 1891. "*Rerum Novarum* / On Capital and Labour." http://www.
vatican.va/holy_father/leo_xiii/encyclicals/documents/hf_l-Xiii_enc_
15051891_rerum-novarum_en.html. Accessed 28 March 2012.

Levada, William. 1986. "Dissent and the Catholic Religion Teacher." *Origins* 16: 195–200.

Little, Sara. 1978. "Ways of Knowing: An Approach to Teaching About Teaching." In *Process and Relationship*, edited by Iris V. Cully and Kendig B. Cully, 15–21. Birmingham, AL: Religious Education Press.

Lyotard, Jean-Francois. 1984. *The Postmodern Condition: A Report on Knowledge*. Minneapolis, MN: University of Minnesota Press.

McBrien, Richard P. 1981. *Catholicism*. Minneapolis, MN: Winston Press.

– 13 June 2011. "Infallibility on Women's Ordination in Question." *National Catholic Reporter*. http://ncronline.org/blogs/essays-theology/infallibility-womens-ordination-question. Accessed 28 March 2012.

McCarthy, Timothy G. 1998. *The Catholic Tradition: The Church in the Twentieth Century*. Chicago, IL: Loyola Press.

McCluskey, Neil G. 1968. *Catholic Education Faces its Future*. Garden City, NY: Doubleday.

McCormick, Richard A. 1970. "Loyalty and Dissent: The Magisterium – A New Model." *America* 122: 674–6.

– 1979. "Notes on Moral Theology: 1978." *Theological Studies* 40 (1): 59–112.

– 1986. "L'Affaire Curran." *America* 154: 261–7.

– 1995. "Foreword." In *Why You Can Disagree and Remain a Faithful Catholic, New Expanded and Revised Edition*, by Philip Kaufman, ix–x. New York, NY: Crossroad Publishing Company.

McDonough, Graham P. 2008. "Contextualizing Authority for the Religion Teacher." *Religious Education* 103 (1): 48–61.

– 2010. "Why Dissent is a Vital Concept in Moral Education." *Journal of Moral Education* 39 (4): 421–36.

– 2011. "What is Assumed About a Catholic Student's Ecclesial Agency, and Why it Matters to Catholic Schooling." *Catholic Education* 14 (3): 272–91.

McGowan, Mark G. 1999. *The Waning of the Green: Catholics, the Irish, and Identity in Toronto, 1887–1922*. Montreal, QC: McGill-Queen's University Press.

– 2008. "Roman Catholics (Anglophone and Allophone)." In *Christianity and Ethnicity in Canada*, edited by Paul Bramadat and David Seljak, 49–100. Toronto, ON: University of Toronto Press.

McLaughlin, Terence H. 1996. "The Distinctiveness of Catholic Education." In *The Contemporary Catholic School: Context, Identity, and Diversity*, edited by Terence H. McLaughlin, Joseph O'Keefe, and Bernadette O'Keefe, 136–54. London, England: The Falmer Press.

McLuhan, Marshall. 1964. *Understanding Media: The Extensions of Man (Second Edition)*. New York, NY: McGraw-Hill.

McLuhan, Marshall, and Quentin Fiore. 1967. *The Medium is the Massage: An Inventory of Effects*. Toronto, ON: Bantam Books.

Mettepeningen, Jürgen. 2010. *Nouvelle Théologie – New Theology: Inheritor of Modernism, Precursor of Vatican II*. New York, NY: T & T Clark.

Mill, John Stuart. (1859) 1978. *On Liberty*. Edited by Elizabeth Rappaport. Indianapolis, IN: Hackett Publishing Company.

Miller, J. Michael. 2007. "Challenges Facing Catholic Schools: A View from Rome." In *International Handbook of Catholic Education: Challenges for School Systems in the 21st Century*, edited by Gerald R. Grace and Joseph O'Keefe, 449–80. Dordrecht, the Netherlands: Springer.

Miller, John P., and Wayne Seller. 1990. *Curriculum: Perspectives and Practice*. Toronto, ON: Copp Clark Pitman.

Montagnes, Bernard. 2006. *The Story of Father Marie-Joseph Lagrange: Founder of Modern Catholic Bible Study*. Translated and Foreword by Benedict Viviano. Mahwah, NJ: Paulist Press.

Moran, Gabriel. 1968. *Vision and Tactics: Toward an Adult Church*. New York, NY: Herder and Herder.

– 1979. *Education Toward Adulthood*. New York, NY: Paulist Press.

Morris, Van Cleve. 1966. *Existentialism in Education*. New York, NY: Harper and Row.

Mulligan, James T. 1999. *Catholic Education: The Future is Now*. Ottawa, ON: Novalis.

– 2005. *Catholic Education: Ensuring a Future*. Ottawa, ON: Novalis.

Murphy, Dennis J. 1992. "Catholic Education: Toward the Third Millennium." *Grail* 8 (2): 68–91.

– 2001. "Catholic Education at the Crossroads." *Catholic Register* 20–27 August.

National Conference of Catholic Bishops. 1986. "Human Life in Our Day." Washington, DC: United States Council of Catholic Bishops.

National Post. 10 January 2011. "Halton Catholic School Board Raises Ire After Ban on Gay-Straight Alliance Groups." http://news.nationalpost.com/2011/01/10/halton-catholic-school-board-raises-ire-after-ban-on-gay-straight-alliance-groups. Accessed 28 March 2012.

Neuner, Josef. 1973. "Directory for the Application of Principles and Norms on Ecumenism." In *The Christian Faith in the Doctrinal Documents of the Catholic Church*, edited by Josef Neuner and Jacques Dupuis, 501. Dublin and Cork, Ireland: The Mercier Press.

Nicolson, Murray W. 1984. "Irish Catholic Education in Victorian
Toronto: An Ethnic Response to Urban Conformity." *Histoire Sociale –
Social History* 17 (34): 287–306.

Nilson, Jon. 2000. "The Laity." In *The Gift of the Church*, edited by Peter
C. Phan, 395–414. Collegeville, MN: The Liturgical Press.

Novak, Michael. 1988. "Dissent in the Church." In *Dissent in the Church*,
edited by Charles E. Curran and Richard A. McCormick, 112–26.
Mahwah, NJ: Paulist Press.

Nuthall, Graham. 2004. "Relating Classroom Teaching to Student Learning: A Critical Analysis of Why Research Has Failed to Bridge the
Theory-Practice Gap." *Harvard Educational Review* 74 (3): 273–306.

Ober, Josiah. 1998. *Political Dissent in Democratic Athens: Intellectual
Critics of Popular Rule*. Princeton, NJ: Princeton University Press.

O'Gara, Margaret. 1998. *The Ecumenical Gift Exchange*. Collegeville,
MN: The Liturgical Press.

Olson, David. 2003. *Psychological Theory and Educational Reform:
How School Remakes Mind and Society*. New York, NY: Cambridge
University Press.

Ontario Conference of Catholic Bishops. 1989. *This Moment of Promise:
A Pastoral Letter on Catholic Education in Ontario*. http://acbo.on.ca/
englishweb/publications/promise.htm. Accessed 28 March 2012.

Örsy, Ladislas. 1987a. "Magisterium: Assent and Dissent." *Theological
Studies* 48 (3): 473–97.

– 1987b. *The Church: Learning and Teaching: Magisterium, Assent,
Dissent, Academic Freedom*. Wilmington, DE: Michael Glazier.

Paul VI. 1968. "*Humanae Vitae* / On Human Life." http://www.vatican.va/
holy_father/paul_vi/encyclicals/documents/hf_p-vi_enc_25071968_
humanae-vitae_en.html. Accessed 28 March 2012.

– 1975. "*Evangelii Nuntiandi* / Evangelization in the Modern World."
http://www.vatican.va/holy_father/paul_vi/apost_exhortations/
documents/hf_p-i_exh_19751208_evangelii-nuntiandi_en.html.
Accessed 28 March 2012.

Pew Forum on Religion and Public Life. 6 October 2010. "Support For
Same-Sex Marriage Edges Upward." http://www.pewforum.org/
Gay-Marriage-and-Homosexuality/Support-For-Same-Sex-Marriage-
Edges-Upward.aspx. Accessed 28 March 2012.

– 2008. *us Religious Landscape Survey: Religious Beliefs and Practices:
Diverse and Politically Relevant*. Washington, DC.

Phenix, Philip H. 1964. *Realms of Meaning*. New York, NY: McGraw-Hill.

Pilarczyk, Daniel. 1986. "Dissent in the Church." *Origins* 16: 175–8.

– 1998. "What Is a Catholic School?" *Origins* 28: 405–8.

Pius IX. 1864. *Syllabus of Errors*. http://www.ewtn.com/library/
PAPALDOC/P9SYLL.HTM. Accessed 28 March 2012.
Pius X. 1906. "*Vehementer Nos* / On the French Law of Separation."
http://www.vatican.va/holy_father/pius_x/encyclicals/documents/
hf_p-x_enc_11021906_vehementer-nos_en.html. Accessed
28 March 2012.
Pius XI. 1930. "*Casti Connubii* / On Christian Marriage." http://www.
vatican.va/holy_father/pius_xi/encyclicals/documents/hf_p-xi_enc_
31121930_casti-connubii_en.html. Accessed 28 March 2012.
– 1931. "*Quadragesimo Anno* / On Reconstruction of the Social Order."
http://benedictumxvi.va/holy_father/pius_xi/encyclicals/documents/
hf_p-xi_enc_19310515_quadragesimo-anno_en.html. Accessed
28 March 2012.
Pius XII. 1950. "*Munificentissimus Deus* / Defining the Dogma of the
Assumption." http://www.vatican.va/holy_father/pius_xii/apost_
constitutions/documents/hf_p-xii_apc_19501101_munificentissimus-
deus_en.html. Accessed 28 March 2012.
– 1951. "Allocution to Italian Midwives on the Nature of Their
Profession." http://www.ewtn.com/library/PAPALDOC/P511029.HTM.
Accessed 28 March 2012.
Plato. 1945. *The Republic of Plato*. Translated by Francis M. Cornford.
New York, NY: Oxford University Press.
– 1981. "Euthyphro." In *Plato: Five Dialogues*, translated by George
M.A. Grube, 5–22. Indianapolis, IN: Hackett.
Platt, Thomas. 1971. "The Concept of Reasonable Dissent." *Social Theory
and Practice* 1 (4): 41–51.
Pontifical Council for Justice and Peace. 2005. *Compendium of the Social
Doctrine of the Church*. Vatican City: Libreria Editrice Vaticana.
Pottmeyer, Hermann J. 1998. *Towards a Papacy in Communion:
Perspectives from Vatican Councils I & II*. New York, NY: Crossroad
Herder.
Portelli, John P. 1996. "Democracy in Education: Beyond the Conservative
and Progressivist Stances." *Inquiry: Critical Thinking Across the
Disciplines* 16 (1): 9–21.
Principe, Walter. 1987. "When 'Authentic' Teachings Change." *The
Ecumenist* 25 (5): 70–3.
Public Religion Research Institute. 22 March 2011. "News Release:
Catholics More Supportive of Gay and Lesbian Rights than General
Public, Other Christians". http://publicreligion.org/newsroom/2011/03/
catholics-more-supportive-of-gay-and-lesbian-rights-than-general-
public-other-christians/. Accessed 28 March 2012.

Ratzinger, Josef. 2005. "Homily *Pro Eligendo Romano Pontifice.*"
http://www.vatican.va/gpII/documents/homily-pro-eligendo-pontifice_
20050418_en.html. Accessed 28 March 2012.

Rawls, John. 1993. *Political Liberalism.* New York, NY: Columbia
University Press.

Rossiter, Graham. 1988. "Perspectives on Change in Catholic Religious
Education Since the Second Vatican Council." *Religious Education*
83 (2): 264–76.

– 2003. "Catholic Education and Values: A Review of the Role of
Catholic Schools in Promoting the Spiritual and Moral Development of
Pupils." *Journal of Religion in Education* 4: 105–36.

– 2011. "Reorienting the Religion Curriculum in Catholic Schools to
Address the Needs of Contemporary Youth Spirituality." *International
Studies in Catholic Education* 3 (1): 57–72.

Rymarz, Richard. 2011. "Catechesis and Religious Education in Canadian
Catholic Schools." *Religious Education* 106 (5): 537–49.

Sabine, George H. 1961. *A History of Political Theory.* Toronto, ON: Holt,
Rinehart, and Winston.

Said, Edward. (1978) 2003. *Orientalism.* New York, NY: Vintage Books.

Sarat, Austin. 2005. "Terrorism, Dissent, and Repression: An Introduction." In *Dissent in Dangerous Times*, edited by Austin Sarat, 1–19.
Ann Arbor, MI: The University of Michigan Press.

Saskatoon Catholic Schools. 1994. *Putting on the Mind of Christ.*
Saskatoon, SK.

– 2005. *Celebrating the Gift of Catholic Education in Saskatchewan:
1905–2005.* Saskatoon, SK.

Saul, John Ralston. 1997. *Reflections of a Siamese Twin: Canada at the
End of the Twentieth Century.* Toronto, ON: Penguin.

Scheffler, Israel. 1960. *The Language of Education.* Springfield, IL: Charles
C. Thomas.

Schillebeeckx, Edward. 1982. "The Magisterium and Ideology." *Journal of
Ecumenical Studies* 19 (1): 5–17.

Sissons, C.B. 1959. *Church and State in Canadian Education.* Toronto,
ON: Ryerson Press.

Shiffrin, Steven H. 1999. *Dissent, Injustice, and the Meanings of America.*
Princeton, NJ: Princeton University Press.

Smith, Christian. 2005. *Soul Searching: The Religious and Spiritual Lives
of American Teenagers.* Oxford: Oxford University Press.

Society of St Pius V. 2011. "Declaration of Principles." http://www.
stpiusvchapel.org/flash_paper/articles/003_declaration_principles.swf.
Accessed 28 March 2012.

Society for St Pius X in Canada. 2011. "What Is the SSPX?" http://www.
sspx.ca/FAQs.htm. Accessed 28 March 2012.

Sullivan, Francis A. 1983. *Magisterium: Teaching Authority in the
Catholic Church*. Ramsey, NJ: Paulist Press.

– 1996. *Creative Fidelity: Weighing and Interpreting Documents of the
Magisterium*. Mahwah, NJ: Paulist Press.

Sullivan, Maureen. 2002. *One Hundred One Questions and Answers on
Vatican II*. Mahwah, NJ: Paulist Press.

Sunstein, Cass R. 2003. *Why Societies Need Dissent*. Cambridge, MA:
Harvard University Press.

Thiessen, Elmer J. 1993. *Teaching for Commitment: Liberal Education,
Indoctrination, and Christian Nurture*. Kingston, ON: McGill-Queen's
University Press.

Thompson, Daniel S. 2003. *The Language of Dissent: Edward Schillebeeckx on the Crisis of Authority in the Catholic Church*. Notre Dame,
IN: Notre Dame University Press.

Toronto Star. 16 Feb 2011. "Halton Catholic Board Backs Gay-Straight
Student Group Policy." http://thestar.com/news/article/939590--halton-
catholic-board-backs-gay-straight-student-group-policy. Accessed
28 March 2012.

Walker, Franklin A. (1955) 1976. *Catholic Education and Politics in
Upper Canada: A Study of the Documentation Relative to the Origin of
Catholic Elementary Schools in the Ontario School System*. Toronto,
ON: J.M. Dent and Sons.

– (1964) 1976. *Catholic Education and Politics in Ontario: A Documentary Study. Volume II*. Toronto, ON: Federation of Catholic Education
Associations of Ontario.

Walter, S.D. 2004. "Queer Theory." In *International Encyclopedia of the
Social and Behavioural Sciences*, edited by Neil J. Smelser and Paul B.
Baltes, 12659–63. Toronto, ON: Elsevier.

Walzer, Michael. 1987. *Interpretation and Social Criticism*. Cambridge,
MA: Harvard University Press.

– 1988. *The Company of Critics: Social Criticism and Political
Commitment in the Twentieth Century*. New York, NY: Basic Books.

Warren, Michael. 1988. "Catechesis and Spirituality." *Religious Education*
83 (1): 116–32.

Wills, Garry. 2000. *Papal Sin: Structures of Deceit*. Toronto, ON:
Doubleday.

– 2002. *Why I Am a Catholic*. Boston, MA: Houghton Mifflin.

Wright, Andrew. 2008. *Critical Religious Education, Multiculturalism and
the Pursuit of Truth*. Cardiff, Wales: University of Wales Press.

Index

abortion, 7–8, 31–2, 188; pedagogical treatment of, 211
academic freedom, 69, 70
administrators, 33
adolescence, 3, 7, 10; *see also* adolescent
adolescent, 113, 189, 197; disaffection, 112; faith, 198
affective response, 18, 128, 130, 131, 142, 144; aim toward, 40, 41, 245; to catechesis, 39; to evangelization, 262n9; excluded, 190
agent. *See* ecclesial agent
Alberta, 84, 260n22, 260–1n24
Allen, John, 100–2, 113, 254
Althusser, Louis, 240–1
Americans. *See* United States of America
anarchy, 230
Andersen, Hans Christian, 167
Anglo-Protestant, 84, 85, 91
anthropology, 231, 239; Catholic identity, 51; personal and communal, 42–7, 215
anti-Catholicism, 27, 123; bigotry, 89, 107, 108; sentiment, 86, 107

Aquinas, St Thomas, 35, 55; reversal of Church views on, 74; *see also* Scholasticism; Thomism
Arendt, Hannah, 159
Aristotle, 74, 148
Assembly of Catholic Bishops of Ontario. *See* Ontario Conference of Catholic Bishops
assent, 76; coerced, 164; and conscience, 60, 73; critically informed, 207, 208; and dissent, 35, 66; *obsequium*, 66–7, 68, 73, 76; and pedagogy of dissent, 225–6; popular, 158, 169; to propositions, 35; and religious freedom, 127; teachers' public, 187; varying degrees of, 37, 64
Athens, 149, 156–8, 169, 170–1
atmosphere, classroom, 181, 190; *see also* climate, school
Augustine, St, 35, 78

Baltimore Catechism, 95
Baum, Gregory, 97–100, 101–2, 280n29; changed Church teaching, 98–9; responsible dissent and, 99

Benedict XVI, Pope, 8, 68, 259n4, 267–8n133; see also Ratzinger, Joseph Cardinal
best practice, 173, 176, 177
Bibby, Reginald, 6–8, 10, 78
Biblical interpretation, 57, 96, 209; see also exegesis; historical-critical method
binary, 243, tendency toward, 3, 120–1, 212, 234, 249; contingent, 34, 149–50; dissolve, 33, 148, 151; limitations of, 212, 214, 227, 239, 247, 249; mapping territory between, 6, 34; occasionally helpful, 6; see also dichotomy; polarization
bin Laden, Osama, 160
birth control. See contraception
bishops, 16, 38; as audience, 24; current trends among, 101; and Magisterium, 52–3, 55, 58, 69; relative to theologians, 235; see also German bishops
Boys, Mary, 127–8, 138, 139
British Columbia, 260n22
British North America Act, 89; see also Confederation, Canadian; separate school legislation
Brown, Wendy, 148, 149–50, 159
Bryk, Anthony, 119

Callan, Eamonn, 164
Canadian Catholic School Trustees Association (CCSTA), 102, 104–5, 260n22
Canadian Conference of Catholic Bishops (CCCB), 78–9; Humanae Vitae and, 80–1; see also Winnipeg Statement

Canon Law, 31–3; 1917 Code of, 56; 1983 Code of, 9, 57
Carr, David, 117
Casti Connubii, 78–9
catechesis, 22, 23, 131, 134, 135; aim of school, 41–2; critical thought and, 81; religious instruction and, 38–9, 51
Catechism of the Catholic Church, 38
Catholic Church; credibility of, 9–10, 72, 100; Global South, 101; uncompromising, 100; see also changed teachings, Catholic
Catholic curriculum, 248; mathematics in, 92; vision of, 51
Catholic Education; authoritarian model of, 126–7, 128–9; definition, 21–2; lacking theoretical grounding, 5–6, 42, 47, 117–20, 122–3, 174, 263n21; multi-dimensional theory of, 124–6; student-centered, 128–31
Catholic Education-Schooling, 13, 104, 106, 176, 216; aims of, 134, 142, 144; Church credibility and, 10; home and, 115; as hyphenated term, 23–4; needing improvement, 47; problems with discussing, 10, 19–20; re-imagining role of, 227, 247–50; Second Vatican Council, 97, 102
Catholic identity; initiatives for change, 101; pedagogy of dissent eroding, 255–6; plural, 256; of school, 5, 22, 51, 103, 115, 250; Second Vatican Council, 96; social recognition of, 89–90
Catholic distinctiveness, 91, 109, 119, 122, 255; decline begun in

home, 115; instability of term,
107–8, 119; rhetorical difficulties
with, 118; of school, 44, 84, 89,
105; in Upper Canada, 88;
school as model for, 121; socially
integrated, 91, 92; socially recognized, 89–90
Catholic school; conflicting values
within, 48–9, 83; confluence of
partners, 25, 40–1, 51, 174, 214;
confluence of values, 90–2, 106;
as dissenting entity, 120–3, 233;
limited mission of, 253; as meeting place, 24, 33, 102, 112, 133–4,
249; perceived as indoctrinatory,
26, 179–81; as public space, 187,
206; rejecting government interference, 92
Catholic Schooling, 174, 182; definition, 22; and mainstream Catholic
values, 90–2; as social service,
40, 117; see also Catholic distinctiveness; Smith, Christian
changed teachings, Catholic, 73–5,
as justification for dissent, 76;
see also Baum, Gregory
Chesterton, Gilbert, 165
citizenship, 17, 90–1, 233
clarification of doctrine; Magisterial
act of, 54, 58, 154; and obsequium,
67; as teaching technique, 195–6,
225, 233; theologians and, 59
clergy, 109; clericalism, 112; and
controversy, 120
climate, school, 176, 186; as
Catholic atmosphere, 40, 43, 47,
48; as school atmosphere, 91,
107, 128, 137, 232, 244–7;
see also atmosphere, classroom
Cohen, Leonard, 276n26

committed impartiality, 243, 280n27
community, Catholic; application in
education, 43, 44, 51; compared
with secular conception, 47–8;
and conscience, 215–16; integration of individual and group, 46
Confederation, Canadian, 89, 92,
260n22
conformity, 143–4, 150, 166, 168–9,
228, 233–4; in Catholic school,
114; and conscience, 63; Dewey,
230; and dissent, 146, 149; ecclesiology of, 68–9; freedom from,
70; to ideology, 241; internal
restrictions, 121; lack of, 100,
117; norms for public expression, 218; opposition to, 150–1;
to peers, 189; public versus private, 115–16; and religious freedom, 181; in secular states, 111;
thoughtless, 159
Congar, Yves, 59, 73, 76, 97,
266n102
Congregation for Catholic Education (CCE), 33, 38, 44, 45, 46
Congregation for the Clergy (CC),
33, 38, 39, 41; methods of religious instruction, 81, 139
Congregation for the Doctrine of
the Faith (CDF), 70, 77
conscience, 13, 186, 229, 234; definition, 60; examination of, 237;
exegetical difficulties, 63–4; and
dissent, 70–1; informed, 189,
213–16; objective and subjective
aspects of, 62–3; Second Vatican
Council on, 60–2
consequentialism, 162–3, 226, 240,
246–7, 267n132, 278n2; as
social utility, 166–7

contraception, 28, 75, 78, 97, 121,
    254; morality of, 79; Winnipeg
    Statement, 76–7; *see also* Pontifi-
    cal Commission on Birth Control
contra-hegemonic, the, 168, 228;
    as criterion for dissent, 155–9
contrarians, 167–8, 189–90, 193,
    221; and critical thinking, 208
Coriden, James, 57
Cox, Edwin, 128, 132, 140,
    274n33
Crawford, Marisa, 137–8, 144
critical thinking, 17, 27–9, 32, 130,
    138, 142, 257; and affective aims,
    128; in Catholic educational con-
    text, 20, 138; and contrarianism,
    208; discipline-based approach,
    239; engaging controversial
    issues through, 207–13; evaluat-
    ing questions, 207–13; informed,
    191; limitation of, 12; and peda-
    gogy of dissent, 17, 227, 237–40;
    public legitimacy of, 220; as reli-
    gious thinking, 17, 32, 141, 142,
    206, 210, 226, 237; as social
    action, 212, 219; teachers' mis-
    understandings of, 210–11, 214;
    as thinking with the Church, 34,
    141
Crowe, Frederick, 57
Cuneo, Michael, 9, 259–60n5
Curran, Charles; and conscience,
    62–3; as controversial figure, 77;
    as dissenter, 171–2; justifications
    for dissent, 76–7
curriculum, 30

Dalhousie, Lord, 85
deficit, intellectual, 183, 186, 194–5,
    221

democracy, 122, 158–9, 169, 170–1,
    172, 244; Catholic schools
    within, 46; change in Church,
    101; and Pope John Paul II, 49;
    and Pope Pius IX, 49; representa-
    tive, 253; weakness of, 157–8; *see
    also* Athens; *hoi oligoi/hoi polloi*
deontology, 162–3, 267n132, 278n2
Dewey, John, 110, 165, 230–3, 240
dichotomy; depolarizing, 150–1;
    false choice implied, 6, 186, 212,
    249; needing mollification, 217–8;
    pedagogical problems with, 227,
    247; recasting as healthy tensions,
    243–7; reinforcing, 212–13; and
    spirituality, 132; *see also* binary;
    polarization
disabilities, persons with, 161
disclosers, 167–8, 189–90, 193
dissent; and assent, 67–8; definition,
    146–7; faithful, 34, 35, 171;
    expression of, 160, 177–81; for
    and with the Church, 226; for the
    good of all; 245–6; grounds for,
    160, 178; ignored, 254–5; loyal,
    35, 149–51, 171; non-antithetical
    dialectical relationship, 152; obli-
    gation to, 73; pedagogical scope
    of, 221–2, 225, 227, 233; peda-
    gogy of, 227, 228–30; proscribed
    by Church, 68–72; relative to pre-
    vailing view, 52; utility of, 159,
    161, 229, 240; *see also* conse-
    quentialism; Kymlicka, Will
dissenters, 149, 220, 221; existen-
    tial status of, 166; marginaliza-
    tion of, 101; utility of favouring
    all, 31, 89, 169; *see also* Athens;
    Curran, Charles
dissident. *See* dissenters

divorce, 188
doctrinal legalism, 25, 280n28;
Second Vatican Council and, 95;
tension with pastoral care, 95,
211, 244; *see also* pastoral care;
psychological well-being
doctrine, 54, 234–5; assent-
obsequium to, 67; and conscience, 214; as curriculum, 25,
32, 179, 182, 190, 196, 250; and
dissent, 59, 68, 76; school disseminating, 205–6; *see also* dogma
Drewke, Joerg, 9
Dulles, Avery Cardinal, 55; and
academic freedom, 69; and
authority, 69; and free speech,
69; and obligation to dissent, 73
Duncombe, Charles, 85
duty. *See* deontology

ecclesial agent, 140, 219, 220, 257,
275n43; assenting, 219
ecclesial citizenship, 28, 29, 233,
248, 257
ecclesial subject. *See* ecclesial agent
ecclesiology, 140, 141; as justification for dissent, 77
educational reform, 24–5
Eichmann, Adolf, 159, 274n24,
276n26
ekklesia docens/ekklesia discens,
32, 56–7, 238–9; and assent-
obsequium, 67, 68–9; and
school-home relationship, 206;
see also O'Gara, Margaret
Emperor's New Clothes, The, 167
enfranchisement, 170, 196, 227,
228; as criterion for dissent,
148–52; and publicity, 230
English monarchy, 153

epistemological; adequacy of home,
203–6; breadth, 202; conscience,
70–1; criterion for dissent, 13, 34,
147–8, 152–5, 163–6; disparity,
68–9, 140–1, 186, 194, 200, 215–
16; justification for dissent, 76, 190,
193, 196; *see also* epistemology
epistemology, 166, 168, 170, 193,
214; Catholic primacy of in
school, 184, 190, 194, 203, 206–
7, 212, 215; and educational
reform, 228–9; existential, 166;
and hierarchy of truth, 53–4;
Platonic, 72, 228; and traditionalist education, 227–8; *see also*
epistemological
ethical, 171; criterion for dissent,
160–3, 229
evangelization, 22, 23, 116, 262n9;
applied to teaching, 182, 183;
critique of, 134–5; "New," 254;
overly earnest, 179; parish, 117;
Pope Paul VI and, 136; qualified,
42; Second Vatican Council and,
98–9; student interests and, 131
exegesis, 71; *see also* Biblical interpretation; historical-critical
method
existential; authentic response, 226;
dissent, 36, 166, 196; freedom,
196, 216; reading of Second
Vatican Council documents, 94;
student readiness, 128, 130, 131,
133; subject-to-subject encounters, 277n41
external protections, 89, 107; *see
also* Kymlicka, Will

false dichotomy. *See* binary; dichotomy; polarization

family life, 198
families, 21, 24, 25, 104, 217;
assertion by, 115–16; diversity
among, 31; as partners in Catholic education, 51, 65, 96, 248–9;
pedagogical reliance upon, 200–7;
primacy of in Catholic education,
65, 115; and religious experiences, 183; and subsidiarity, 65,
115
Feinberg, Walter, 25
female ordination, 97, 184, 212,
251, 278n14; possible future of,
254; as sex equity, 100, 198;
support for, 7–8, 78
feminism, 25, 246, 273n89
First Vatican Council, 54, 93, 94
Fleischacker, Samuel, 156
Foley, H.M., 88
formation, 23, 136; among multiple
aims, 20, 40, 220, 247–9; biblical,
105; mediating, 182–3; problems
with as exclusive aim, 41, 131,
137; of teachers, 103, 109
Foy, Vincent (Monsignor), 80
France, 111
freedom; of conscience, 186; existential, 196, 216; negative and
positive, 70, 182, 202; potential
for pedagogical misuse of, 206–7;
religious, 242, 248; student,
135–6, 178–9, 180, 182, 183;
and subsidiarity, 202; teachers',
187, 243
free speech, 69, 70
Freire, Paulo, 29, 230
Fuchs, Josef, 64

Galilei, Galileo, 160
gay-straight alliance, 218, 277–8n10

General Directory for Catechesis,
38, 136, 275n56
German bishops, 71, 76
Glengarry County (Upper Canada/
Ontario), 84–5
Greeley, Andrew, 7–8, 78
Gregory XVI, Pope; compared with
Pope John XXIII, 98; on slavery,
73
Groome, Thomas; on catechesis,
39–40; on school community, 40;
on spirituality, 131; on teaching
and learning, 129–30, 132

Halton Catholic School Board,
277–8n10
hegemony, 156, 164, 237; of
Catholic education, 175–6; and
restrictions, 11, 246; see also
contra-hegemonic
heresy, 123, 165, 171; definition,
54, 276n35; in early Church, 55,
265n75; reasonable, 163–5, 166
hermeneutics, 97, 165; see also
Biblical interpretation; exegesis;
historical-critical method
hidden curriculum, 139–40, 141; as
informal socialization, 224, 247
historical-critical method; 93,
266n102; see also Biblical interpretation; exegesis; hermeneutic
Hitler, Adolph, 160
Hogan, Linda, 63–4
hoi oligoi/hoi polloi, 157–8; see
also oligarchy
Holy Spirit; and changed teachings,
75; distortion of, 242; as guide
for Church, 53, 77
home, 5, 117, 143, 190, 249;
incongruity with school, 220;

marginalized, 24; participants' illustrations of, 178, 203; as partner in Catholic education, 32, 114–17, 187, 248; as source of pre-critical opinions, 178; supplementing classroom discussion, 23, 34, 200–7, 221; *see also* public-private distinction

homosexuals, 6–8, 259n1; same-sex marriage and, 218

homosexuality, 7, 28, 31, 184, 192, 198; and dissent from Church teaching, 192; sensitivity regarding, 188

hope, 35–6

Humanae Vitae, 171, 186, 212; adherence to, 78, 79–80, 81; non-reception of, 75; promulgation of, 77

ideology, 164, 167, 240–3; critique of, 17, 25, 227; dissent and, 155; prevailing, 83, 152; support for, 52; *see also* Athens

impartiality, 180, 181, 186

indoctrination, 183, 202, 212; and religious freedom, 39, 206; students' presumptions about, 179–81

infallibility, 53; as absolute truth, 197–8; infallible teaching, 76, 186–7; *see also* truths, hierarchy of

Institute for Catholic Education (Ontario), 103–5

intentions; Catholic Education-Schooling, 13; parent, 20; student, 11, 20, 104, 128, 143, 248

internal restrictions. *See* Kymlicka, Will

Jefferson, Thomas, 160

Jews; Nazi persecution of, 161; and salvation, 98

John XXIII, Pope; on birth control, 79; compared with Pope Gregory XVI, 98; on signs of the times, 98–9

John Paul II, Pope; 15, 248; and dissenting theologians, 68; on ordination, 100, 267–8n133; on relativism, 49–50, 272n81; on social justice, 49; on theology of the body, 80; *see also* Wojtyla, Karol Cardinal

Jones, Rachel, 9

Joseph, Ellis, 118

justice, 4, 34, 161–2, 193, 229, 240; Catholic school aims and, 45, 51, 104; heresy and, 164; Kohlberg on, 279n17; as pedagogical aim, 225; prevailing view and, 155; promoting, 223, 225, 244, 251; student concern for, 194, subsidiarity and, 65; as principle, 158; Socratic, 159; *see also* ethical; social justice

Kant, Immanuel, 161

Kaufman, Philip; on assent and *obsequium*, 66–7; on changed teachings, 73–5; and Pope Paul VI, 79

King, Martin Luther, 160, 161

knowledge falsification, 164

Kohlberg, Lawrence, 238, 279n17

Ku Klux Klan, 161–2, 164

Kymlicka, Will, 121, 122

Lagrange, Marie-Joseph, 59, 97, 266n102

laity, 109, 112, 114, 207; as audience, 33; and clericalism, 112; and contraception, 75; and cooperation with réligious persons, 33, 51; distinct from Magisterium, 56; franchise of, 207, 219; governance by, 97; Magisterium of, 54–5; response to controversy, 10, 31–2; Second Vatican Council on, 61–2, 95, 96; as teachers, 103, 109; as theologians, 69–70, 235

Lee, James, 139

Lenin, Vladimir, 160

Leo XIII, Pope, 49; on slavery, 73

Levada, William Cardinal, 71, 72

liberal, 43, 110, 112; Catholic, 9, 101, 171, 221, 223; pedagogy of dissent, 224; revolution, 49; society, 43, 86, 98, 106, 112; state, 70, 111; subject, 111; theorists, 110; see also Kymlicka, Will; liberalism

liberalism, 109–10, 111, 112; accommodating illiberal views, 158, 172, 246; emphasis on individual liberty, 170; plurality within, 170; reaction against, 93, 98; see also liberal

liberation, 25, 133

liberation theology, 25

Little, Sara, 139

Lower Canada; 1841 Act of Union, 85; support for Upper Canadian Catholics, 88

de Lubac, Henri, 59, 76, 97, 266n102

Luther, Martin, 149, 152

McBrien, Richard, 54–5, 58, 59

McCarthy, Timothy, 93

McCluskey, Neil, 23

McCormick, Richard, 57, 73

Macdonald, John A., 88

Macdonnell, Alexander (Bishop), 84–5

McGowan, Mark; on curriculum, 90–2; on Catholic civil leaders, 264n54; on nineteenth-century Catholicism, 93

McLaughlin, Terence, 118

McLuhan, Marshall, 139, 236

Magisterium, 7, 13, 28, 52–60, 81–2, 187; critical appreciation of, 27, 28, 99–100; curriculum to support, 215; etymology, 52; home and, 205; as learning Church, 67; as partner in Catholic education, 26; plural, 54–6, 58, 265n94; relationship with individuals, 28, 46–7, 142, 219; school as organ of, 25, 26, 114, 126, 250; and theologians, 235; see also doctrine; ekklesia docens/ekklesia discens; truth, hierarchy of

Manitoba, 260n22

married priests, 7–8; see also ordination

media, 45, 133, 178, 184, 191; in school, 218

Mill, John Stuart, 156, 161, 164, 169, 241

Miller, J. Michael (Archbishop), 47, 50–1

Miller, John, 228

modernism. See postmodernism

Moran, Gabriel, 132; and Catholic Education-Schooling, 21–2, 23; on education for adult experience

of Church, 141; on hope, 35; on
revelation, 128–9, 140; on salesmanship, 135–6, 137; on theology and religious education, 141
Mulligan, James, 108–13, 114–15;
on erosion of Catholic school
identity, 108–9; on liberalism and
relativism, 109–10; on modernism and postmodernism, 110–12
Murphy, Dennis, 48, 106, 111,
113–15, 220
Murray, John Courtney, 59, 73, 76,
97, 266n102
Muslim students, 42, 248

National Conference of Catholic
Bishops (United States); on dissent, 71, 76
natural law, 100–1, 217
Nazis, 161, 164
neutrality, ideology of, 164; school,
88, 92; teacher, 30, 181–2, 184–7,
242–3; see also committed
impartiality
Newfoundland and Labrador, 105,
108
Nicene Creed, 186; assent to, 66–7
nihilism, 45, 162
Nilson, Jon, 56
non-Catholic students, 22, 40, 42,
44, 104, 109, 220, 261n5; benefit
from pedagogy of dissent, 227;
Muslims, 247–8; respect for
beliefs of, 39, 41
non-heterosexual, 4, 97, 161, 188,
218, 244, 254; marriage, 192;
persons constituting Catholic
school, 255–6
non-infallible ordinary teaching,
53, 186–7, 212; dissent from, 57,

71, 76; obsequium to, 67; see
also truth, hierarchy of
Northwest Territories, 260n22
Novak, Michael; on dissenting
theologians, 71–2
Nunavut, 260n22

Ober, Josiah, 156–8, 169
obsequium, 66–7, 68, 73, 76, 187,
212
O'Gara, Margaret, 15, 148; on
assent-obsequium distinction, 68;
on recovery and transposition,
153–4; on teaching process in
Church, 57
oligarchy, 169–71; see also hoi
oligoi/hoi polloi
Ontario, 14, 89, 105, 106; Catholic
schools, 11, 15; government
funding for Catholic schools, 11,
12; see also Upper Canada
Ontario Conference of Catholic
Bishops, 46, 116
open-mindedness, 180
opposition; and solidarity, 150–1
Orange Order, 88–9
ordinary universal teaching, 53, 54;
see also non-infallible ordinary
teaching
ordination, 28; see also female
ordination
Örsy, Ladislas; on Magisterium, 58;
on changed teachings, 75, 76

parents, 18, 211, 224; as audience,
33–4, 177; pedagogical reliance
upon, 200–7; see also families
parish, 23, 31, 104, 115, 117,
200; housing teachers, 109;
nineteenth-century, 89; as

partner in Catholic education,
18, 202; as public space, 206;
school adopting function of, 116,
117, 138, 143, 249, 253; school
distinct from, 40; theologian and,
235; withdrawal from, 116
pastoral care, 32, 38, 95, 211, 244,
250, 280n28; concern for in
school, 41, 188, 211; and *Humanae Vitae*, 80; tension with
doctrinal legalism, 244, 250,
280n28; theologians and, 234;
see also doctrinal legalism; psychological welfare of students;
Second Vatican Council
Paul VI, Pope; on contraception,
75–8, 79; on evangelization, 136;
and *Humanae Vitae*, 80;
response to Pontifical Commission on Birth Control, 79; *see
also Humanae Vitae*
pedagogical stance, 181–7; defined,
181; mediator, 182–4; facilitator
and informer, 184–7
pedagogy; definition, 29
pedagogy of dissent; burdensome
on individual, 252–3; criticisms
of, 250–6; erodes Catholic character of school, 255–6; impractical, 253–5; over-emphasis on
cognition, 251–2
personhood, Catholic conception
of, 42–5
persuasive criterion for dissent,
169–72; and pedagogy of dissent, 229, 230
Pilarczyk, Daniel (Archbishop), 44;
on hierarchy of truths, 53
Pius IX, Pope, 49, 93
Pius X, Pope, 56

Pius XI, Pope, 64, 78; *see also Casti
Connubii*
Pius XII, Pope, 9, 53, 76; on dissenting theologians, 93; on natural family planning, 78; on
religious liberty, 74
Plato, 182; epistemology, 72, 227–8;
Euthyphro, 272n65; *Republic*, 171
Platt, Thomas, 160
polarization, 6, 214, 244, 245;
abolishing, 148, 150–2; of
Church, 9–10; doctrinal-pastoral
distinction, 280n28; of groups,
219, 280n31; risk of, 120–1,
214, 244
Pontifical Commission on Birth
Control, 78, 79, 186, 212
Pontifical Council for Justice and
Peace, 65
pope, 3, 5, 77, 264n60; authority of
office, 69; and Catholic education, 38; as Magisterium, 32,
52–3, 58, 59, 66, 187; Protestant
resistance against, 87; relations
with pre-conciliar groups; 9;
Roman, 76; support for, 7–8;
post-conciliar, 3–5, 31, 221, 223,
224, 246; sedevacantists, 9;
spirituality, 131; *see also* pre-
conciliar; Second Vatican Council
postmodernism, 110–12, 120
pre-conciliar, 4–5, 9, 31, 239–40,
246, 254; Catholic identity, 256;
belief in decline, 109; images of
Church, 103, 256; idea of salvation, 280n29; see also post-
conciliar; Second Vatican Council
Principe, Walter, 73–5
privatization, 73, 144, 195, 200,
215, 221; disutility of, 169; as

marginalization, 101, 214–15, 252; and pedagogy of dissent, 252; and public sphere, 203, 205, 218; ramifications of, 218

progressive education, 227–8, 250

protest, 149

Protestant; -Catholic relations, 94; -Catholic tensions, 90; diversity, 270n15; Luther as, 149; Reformation, 56, 94, 149; salvation, 98; schools, 85–6, 88–9, 260n22, 260–1n24, suspicion of Catholics, 86–8; see also Anglo-Protestant; Orange Order

psychological welfare of students, 188, 280n28; see also pastoral care

publicity criterion for dissent, 166–9; and pedagogy of dissent, 229–30

public-private distinction, 114–16, 119; and conscience, 215; Dewey on, 231–2; in expression of belief, 72–3, 116–17, 186–7, 250; and home, 205; see also home

Quebec, 6–7, 89, 105, 108; see also Lower Canada

queer, 259n1; see also queer theory

queer theory, 246, 273n89

Rahner, Karl, 59, 76, 97, 266n102

rapport, classroom, 179

Ratzinger, Joseph Cardinal; on dissent, 68; on relativism, 272n81; see also Benedict XVI, Pope

Rawls, John, 110, 170

relativism, 27, 109–10, 120, 137, 162, 272n81; and student dissent, 178, 195, 221

reform. See educational reform

Republic, Plato's, 171, 277n3

Rerum Novarum, 49, 73

Roma, 161

Rossiter, Graham; on curriculum, 130–1, 220, 255, 278n14, 280n35; on educational outcomes, 133–5, 136, 137–8, 143, 144, 261n2

Ryerson, Egerton, 87

sacred-secular, 132; integration, 120; tension, 4, 92, 119, 214, 244

salvation, 9, 28, 190, 212, 278n14; as avoiding damnation, 5; and social justice, 280n29

same-sex marriage, 6, 78, 210, 218

Sarat, Austin, 149, 159

Saskatchewan, 84, 260n22

Saskatoon Catholic Schools, 42

Saul, John Ralston, 111, 120, 162

scandal; dissent as, 68, 71, 216–17; in school, 48; sexual abuse, 9

Schillebeeckx, Edward, 152, 155, 165, 235, 241–2

scholasticism, 93, 96, 97–8; see also Aquinas, St Thomas; Thomism

school. See Catholic school

Scott, Richard, 88–9

Second Vatican Council, 4, 9, 102, 109, 114–15, 117; on assent and obsequium, 66–7; on conscience, 60–1, 63–4; context prior to, 93–4; on contraception, 79; damaging the Church, 9, 96–7, 256; on education, 65, 96, 117–18; on laity, 56, 95–6; meaning and impact of, 96–102; on pastoral care for persons, 95; on religious liberty, 74, 127; on revelation, 95–6; on salvation,

95; on slavery, 74; on subsidiarity and education, 65, 114–15; survey of changes enacted, 94–6; vindicating censured theologians, 76, 93

secularism, 49, 105–6, 108, 112, 143, 144, 251; and critical thinking, 209

sedevacantists, 9, 254

self-expression, 193, 225, 278n1

Seller, Wayne, 228

separate school legislation, 85–9; 1841 Common School Act, 85–6; 1843 Act for Establishment of Common Schools, 86; 1855 Taché Act, 88; 1863 Scott Act, 88–9; 1867 British North America Act, 89

separate school opposition, 86–8

sex; premarital, 6–8, 78; and sexuality, 100, 201, 254

sex education, 201

sex equity, 4, 100, 101, 121, 122

sexual abuse, 9, 271n63

Shiffrin, Steven, 161

Sinti, 161

slavery, 57, 73–4, 160, 242, 268n147

Smith, Christian, 113, 114

social justice, 47–9, 51, 98, 161–2, 190; in Canadian social contract, 122; in Catholic schools, 51, 131, 212; critical thinking and, 209; in future Church, 101; and hegemony, 156, 158–9; postmodernism and, 273n89; in Rerum Novarum, 49; and salvation, 97–8, 280n29; an student dissent, 190; within Church, 97

Society for St Pius V, 9, 254

Society for St Pius X, 9, 254

Socrates; on dissent, 149–50, 151, 159, 248; on questioning, 147, 165

solidarity, 162, 251; and opposition, 150–1

South Africa, 156

Spence, Robert, 88

spirituality, 131–3, 137; Catholic, 133; as spiritual growth, 198, 202

state, 106, 143; separate schools, 11–12, 23–5

student-centred, 196; see also student interests

student interests, 193, 227, 233, 240; and engaging dissent, 221; recognition of, 17; and transmission pedagogy, 227–8; see also student-centered

subsidiarity, 51, 64–6, 100; and family autonomy, 115, 201; and student moral formation, 200

Sullivan, Francis, 52, 58, 265n94; see also Magisterium

Sunstein, Cass, 160, 164, 168–9, 280n31

teacher education, 138–9

teachers; as audience, 33; Catholic beliefs of, 180, 181, 185, 260n21; and dissent, 260n21; impartiality of, 180; interpreting curriculum, 192; loyalty to Church of, 183; as research participants, 16, 174–6; responsible for reform, 176, 224; vocation and witness of, 51

techniques of teaching, 187–216; definition, 187; holding questions

open, 207–13; informed conscience, 213–16; leaving to students and families, 200–7; omitting offensive material, 188–9; questioning, 197–200; understanding before criticizing, 189–97
theologians, 55–6; and dissent, 68, 69, 71–2; duty to examine doctrine, 58; franchise of, 58–9, 69; students-as-amateur-, 227, 234–7
theory and practice; of community, 47; gap between, 16, 135, 219; movement between, 72; relationship between, 30–1
Thiessen, John Elmer, 153
Thomism, 74, 77, 272n65
Thompson, Daniel Speed, 155, 235, 241–2
tradition, 230; living, 153, 154, 228
traditionalist education, 227–8, 250
transmission pedagogy, 126–7, 128, 137, 140, 228, 261n2
Trent, Council of, 93, 94, 95
Tridentine, 90, 93, 117; Mass, 96; see also Trent, Council of
triumphalists, 171, 230
truths, hierarchy of, 53–4; as levels of teaching authority, 187; see also infallibility; non-infallible ordinary teaching; ordinary universal teaching

ultramontane, 93, 270n33
United States of America, 7–9, 111

Upper Canada, 106; Catholic minority in, 84; Catholic school distinctiveness in, 89; religious public schooling model in, 85; union with Lower Canada, 84; see also separate school legislation
utilitarianism. See consequentialism

Vatican I. See First Vatican Council
Vatican II. See Second Vatican Council
vocation, 104, 279n11; decline in, 96; Dewey on, 231–2; teachers', 51; theologians', 234–5; women's, 5, 100

Walzer, Michael, 148, 152–3
Warren, Michael, 133
Wills, Garry, 149; on Pope Paul VI, 79
Winnipeg Statement, 186, 212; Canadian bishops distanced from, 80–1; as justification for dissent, 76–7; on faithful non-adherence to Humanae Vitae, 78, 79–80; issued, 79
Wojtyla, Karol Cardinal; solidarity, 150–1; see also John Paul II, Pope
women, 4, 102, 121, 122, 198, 244, 254; see also female ordination; feminism; sex equity; vocation
womens' rights. See feminism; sex equity
Wright, Andrew, 29

Yukon, 260n22